Tartans for the Irish!

Suggested Tartans for Irish and Ulster Scots Names

Philip D. Smith, Jr.

Ph.D., FSTS, GTS, FSA Scot
Director of Tartan Studies
The International Association for Tartan Studies

HERITAGE BOOKS
2009

HERITAGE BOOKS
AN IMPRINT OF HERITAGE BOOKS, INC.

Books, CDs, and more—Worldwide

For our listing of thousands of titles see our website
at
www.HeritageBooks.com

Published 2009 by
HERITAGE BOOKS, INC.
Publishing Division
100 Railroad Ave. #104
Westminster, Maryland 21157

International Standard Book Numbers
Paperbound: 978-0-7884-3590-4
Clothbound: 978-0-7884-8075-1

FOR

Jim McGuire,
James McAslan,
Alistair Buchan,
Blair Macnaughton,
and
Blair A.C. Macnaughton

2005

FOREWORD

I began the study of tartans and the names associated with them over fifty years ago. For many years these were limited to Scottish names. In 1981 I published my first edition of *Tartan For Me!* In compiling that name list with a tartan associated with each one, I first became aware that there were names associated with certain tartans that were clearly Irish in origin.

This should not have come as a surprise. From Fair Head to the Mull of Kintryre, Ireland and Scotland are only twelve miles apart. It was on Rathlin Island that Robert the Bruce sought refuge. There is also a story that the McCurdy's tell that their ancestors rowed from Bute to Ireland overnight.

For many years I included Irish names with suggested tartans in *Tartan For Me!* as it grew from a simple list of 6,000 names to the present eighth edition of nearly 30,000. However, the time has finally come for a separate list devoted solely to Irish names.

The Scots came from Ireland in the fifth century and for a millennium the two nations shared a mutual culture and a mutual language. What they did *not* share was the development of tartan. While many cultures weave in bands of crossing colours in the same twill style, only in Scotland did this become identified as a national symbol. This is partially due to preserve a "Scottish identity" when Scotland became "North Britain" (1707) and perhaps as a reaction to English and Lowland Scottish intrusion after the battle of Culloden (1746) and the repression of Highland Gaeldom.

The nineteenth century costume of a self-proclaimed Druid in the Welsh Folk Museum near Cardiff displays the "Royal Stuart" tartan. Perhaps the same reaction of idealized Pan-Celticism caused the Irish to develop a desire for tartan and kilts for it was during this same time that the first Irish families began to develop tartans. In the past decades many more tartans have become available for the Irish -- both "District" and "Name" tartans.

It is in this spirit that I have developed this list of names and one or more tartans suggested for each surname.

Philip D. Smith, Jr., PhD
Member, The Guild of Tartan Scholars

TABLE OF CONTENTS

IRISH TARTANS

Irish historians and especially Irish clothing specialists agree on one thing – that **historically the Irish did not wear tartans**. But, again, neither did the Scots in early times. It was not until 1594 that Lughaidh O' Clery could observe that Scottish mercenaries in Ireland, "…were recognized among the Irish Soldiers by the distinction of their arms and clothing, their habits and their language, for their exterior dress was mottled cloaks of many colours…" (McClintock, p. 93). At nearly the same time Scottish and Continental artists and writers began to portray the Scots dressed in tartan.

The mainland of Scotland is farther north than Ireland with a harsher climate. Much of Ireland is arable and well sited to catch the benefits of the warm waters of the American Gulf Stream. The fertile fields with loughs and streams filled with fish made Ireland very desirable to outsiders – Vikings, Normans and English. There were even a few Welsh enclaves. Most modern Irish cities were earlier Viking or English trading posts. In example, Dublin was first a Viking trading post on the River Liffey.

The milder Irish climate made the cultivation of flax profitable. The fibers of flax, pounded from the stalks in the open air, were woven into linen. This became the staple from which the majority of Irish clothing was made. This is not to say that the Scots did not produce linen. Indeed, flax was grown in historic times as far north as the Orkneys. But in the British Isles it was only in Ireland that linen production flourished – and continues to this day.

England, in the meantime, turned to the production of wool for export to the continent, especially Flanders. The flocks of sheep slowly moved north into Scotland or were introduced by the Vikings from Scandinavia. These began to displace the native Soay sheep with dark, short wool that had to be plucked and was more difficult to make into thread than flax fibers. Wool also had the advantage of being able to be sheared, spun and woven indoors, a plus in the harsher Scottish climate.

As late as 1592 Scots raiding each other were seen in yellow "warr coats". A yellow linen coat was sometimes the mark of a leader while ordinary Highlanders wore darker clothing (McClintock, p. 116).

An individual has posted on the Internet that he has discovered that the ancient Irish *did* wear kilts. Little evidence is given. He also states that "Irish clans" wore kilts of the same solid colour hues. He writes that widely separated branches of the same "clan" wore slightly different shades of the same colour. This is manifestly unsound.

First, there are not enough hues in the Irish colour system to accommodate this claim as there are more "clans" than hues. Second, the very nature of the process using natural dyes precluded the production of evenly coloured hues from dye lot to dye lot. Thirdly, all of the early descriptions of Irish dress speak of "saffron" (q.v.) as the predominant colour. Even today it is very difficult to dye wool threads evenly even within the dye lot with modern aniline dyes. H. F. McClintock in his valuable resource *Old Irish and Highland Dress* shows rather convincingly that there is no evidence that Irish dress included such things as the kilt, shoulder plaid, sporran or flat bonnet in the sixteenth century (McClintock, p. 105). These were peculiar to Highland and Island Scottish costume.

In the nineteenth century the British government equipped Irish regimental pipe bands with plain kilts of a light brown hue which they labeled "saffron". Clearly, there was not enough true saffron to dye this much material cost effectively. The colour would need to be a far brighter yellow than the artificially brown modern "saffron kilt." However, for many years this was and still is the traditional kilt worn by Irish pipe bands. Occasionally one sees a plain dark blue or rose kilt, especially among male Irish dancers.

"Saffron" is obtained from the crocus flower and gives a bright yellow color. In the existing dye recipes from the fifteenth century for "saffron dyes" the major ingredient is poplar.

The earliest known "Irish tartan" is the "Ulster" (see history below) dated *circa* 1600). The next oldest "Irish tartan" group is late nineteenth century, perhaps two hundred years later. The latest group of "Irish tartans" is less than thirty years old, dating from the 1980's to the date of this publication.

THE IRISH AND THE SCOTS

The Scots came from Ireland in the fifth century. The two nations are only twelve miles apart at their closest point and clearly visible one from another. The word from which "Scots" or "Scotch" is derived is the Latin, *Scotus*, meaning "Irishman." In 1980, Mícheál Ó Siadhail wrote:

> **Two hundred years ago, a good speaker of Irish, traveling slowly from Kerry to Antrim (and on to the north of Scotland), could have spoken the language all the way and noticed only minute dialectal changes as**

2

he passed from place to place. One dialect shaded into another in the most gradual fashion. (O' Siadhail, p. 3)

Until the 1600's Gaelic speaking Scotland viewed Ireland as their ancestral home and the fount of Gaelic culture. Scottish chiefs sent bards and harpists to Ireland to learn the intricacies of their profession. Refugees and mercenaries from the many internecine wars of both nations found the opposite country welcomed them, accounting for some of the names shared by the Irish and Scots. Scottish Gaelic was habitually called "Erse" until about 1800. Although the native language of Ireland is colloquially referred to as "Gaelic", the official name of the language is "Irish". You will never see a course in the Irish language named "Gaelic." That name is reserved for the Scottish language. The two became distinctly separate languages in the 1600's although some dialects are still mutually intelligible with effort.

It was the rebellion of some of earls of Ulster in the late sixteenth century that finally cut off the close relationship between the two nations – and the ready supply of Irish linen. Earls are the same as "Counts" on the continent. They normally rule "counties" and their wives are titled "Countess." There is a modern tendency to confuse Northern Ireland with historic Ulster. Three of Ulster's counties are today part of the Republic of Ireland. (See the list on page five and six.)

The nominal ruler of Ireland at that time, Queen Elizabeth I, reacted quickly. The rebellion was quickly and ruthlessly crushed. Elizabeth forfeited the lands of the earls and replaced them with English nobles. These men in turn populated the forfeited lands with English speaking Protestant settlers, displacing the native Irish. Thus there was a belt of English speakers between the two parts of Gaeldom. The settlers or "Planters" were to a large degree Lowland Scots who were required to be Protestants and had little in common with both the Gaelic Irish Roman Catholic and their own Scottish Gaelic speaking and often Catholic Highlanders.

The proximity of the two nations, the mutual employment of mercenaries and the intrusion of the Plantation account for the large number of Scottish surnames in Ireland and to a lesser number of Irish surnames in Scotland. Irish names in Scotland are largely associated with Clan Donald. The Earl of Antrim is chief of one of the cadet branches of Clan Donald.

IRISH NAMES

The early Irish, living in small villages had no reason for surnames. In a village of a hundred or fewer a man two men named "Brian" might be "Big Brian" (Brian Mór) while the other might be called "Blond Brian" (Brian Bán). This is held in common with many early cultures. In Western Europe the use of surnames was initiated by the Romans. More common were the use of "clan" or "tribal" surnames. For example, most Koreans today have only one of four surnames in use in the entire nation: Kim, Park, Chang and Li/Ri. Icelanders are given "family" surnames only when they travel abroad. In their own culture they are known as "Leif Jacob's son" or "Ingrid Jacob's daughter." The son of "Eric the Red" was "Leif Ericson."

In Ireland the same two patterns developed. Tribal or "sept" names were shown by the prefix **_Ui_** meaning "belonging to the tribe/race of" and anglicized as "O'" as in "O' Day." The possessive apostrophe following the **O** is redundant since the original **_Ui_** carries the meaning "belonging to". **O'** is used in this book since it has become customary to spell names in this fashion.

"Sons of" prefix **_Mac_** as in "Sean Mac Loughlin" and "daughters" prefix **_Ní_** as in "Nora Ní Loughlin." **_Ní_** can be anglicized as either "O'" or "Mac." Even today a brother and a sister can have different Irish surnames as "Seán Mac Loughlin" and "Nóra O' Loughlin."

Ireland was one of the first nations of the British Isles to develop systematic surnames. Some date back before the year 1,000 A. D. However, due to the attempts of the English to spell native Irish names, there is a very great variation among surnames that may have had a common source in Irish.

Among the early Celts, every village had a "headman" who, with other "headmen", sought protection from a stronger **_Ri_** ("king" or more properly "kinglet"). The followers of a **_Ri_** were termed "septs." There would be, at times, more than a hundred persons entitled **_Ri_** across Ireland. Each **_Ri_** in turn would owe allegiance to a more powerful **_Ri_** and at times an **_Ard-Ri_** or "High King." There was never a single **_Ard-Ri_** who governed all of Ireland. At times there was one; at times there was none, at other times two or three but even then each **_Ard-Ri_** still had no control over the totality of the portions of Ireland under their nominal protection. The myth of Ireland as a long term united Celtic nation is just that, a myth. It was just this very fragmentation that allowed Ireland to be conquered.

The Normans, French speaking descendents of the Viking "Northmen" that had settled in northern France, began their conquest of England in 1066. It was not long until they reached Scotland and Ireland. They established a ring of castle fortresses around Dublin, referred to as "The Pale." It was the Pale, the intrusion of the English and Scots into Ulster, called "The Plantation", five hundred years later, and the almost continual infighting, rebellions and shifting alliances that have shaped Irish history.

It is not the purpose of this work to review Irish history, but only to make the point that continual shifting alliances made the Irish relate more to "place" rather than to "sept" or "clan."

For this very reason, expatriate Irish formed "County Societies" rather than "Clan Societies" as did the Scots. Of two "O' Briens", for example, one might belong to a "County Mayo Society" while the other might join the "County Clare" group. In contrast, two Scots surnamed "MacDonald" formed a "Clan MacDonald Society."

In this work you will see that the vast majority of Irish surnames can wear a "place" -- or in more traditional terms -- a "District" tartan.

DIVISIONS OF IRELAND

Ireland was historically divided into a number of locales that shifted back and forth over the past millennium. With English domination came the breakup of the Gaelic order and Brehon Law in the sixteenth century. These variable territorial and tribal names gave way to fixed county and territorial lines. In this work the official modern names are given – "County Laois" for what used to be labeled "County Leix", "Connacht", the Irish spelling of the English spelling "Connaught" and the full "Londonderry" for "Derry."

There is a tartan for each of these five provinces or "states" and a tartan for each of the associated counties:

Connacht: Counties Galway, Leitrim, Mayo, Roscommon, and Sligo.

Leinster: Counties Carlow, Dublin, Kildare, Kilkenny, Laois, Longford. Meath, Offaly, Westmeath, Wexford, and Wicklow.

Oriel: Counties Armagh and Monaghan and parts of south Down, Fermanagh and Louth.

Munster: Cos. Clare, Cork, Kerry, Limmerick, Tipperary, and Waterford.

Ulster: Counties Antrim, Cavan, Donegal, Down, Londonderry, and Tyrone.

In addition, there are a number of tartans intended for all of Ireland or all of those of Irish descent. These include the "Tara", the "Clodagh", the "Eire", the "Irish National", and the "St. Patrick." The oldest of these are the "Tara", originally known as the "Murphy", and the "Clodadh" – sometimes spelled "Cladadh."

Irish families have begun to develop their own tartans following the Scottish model. Early among these were the "Brooke" and the "Forde". Since these early tartans there have been and continue to be additional family designs. Some of these are commissioned by the leaders of individual septs, others by "clan" organizations, and still more by individuals who simply wish their name to "have a tartan."

"SEPTS" AND "CLANS"

The term "sept" is preferred to "clan" when speaking of Irish names and families. The "clan" has a belief in descent from a common, perhaps mythical, ancestor. The "sept" is a family or a group of families from an area that holds its allegiance to a higher authority through traditional, religious, land grant or other means. Membership is more variable than the "clan". As pointed out earlier, a dozen "O' Briens" might follow a dozen different leaders and be considered a part of their "sept" whereas a dozen "Grants" are all part of "Clan Grant" despite their place of residence or any internal wrangling.

Sean Murphy, a professional Irish genealogist who lives in County Wicklow, has written a carefully researched essay for the *Directory of Irish Genealogy*. In Mr. Murphy's "Irish Chiefs" he makes the following statement:

> **Although there is much talk of Irish 'Clans' and 'Clan Chiefs', it is also important to remember that the Irish did not have clan system exactly like the Scots, despite the many elements of Gaelic culture common to both countries. The term 'clan' is best reserved for the Scottish kin-based unit, while the anglicised term 'sept' is more appropriate for the more disparate and less feudalised kingroup system of the Irish. The great authority on Irish surnames, Edward MacLysaght, advised against the use of the term 'clan' in the Irish context, but his words have been little heeded.**

Part of the illusion of Irish "clans" was fostered by the Irish government when it set up an office of "Irish Clans." "Clans" along the Scottish model did not develop in Ireland. The same argument in reverse is made in regard to Scottish clans who claim each dependent surname as a separate "sept." In

Tartan For Me!-7 (Smith, p. 6) it is pointed out that the word "sept" was borrowed from Ireland in the nineteenth century to account for the many names within a clan – but that the preferred nomenclature is not "The Septs of Clan Campbell" but instead "The Names of Clan Campbell."

SPELLING DIFFERENCES

No matter what the pride in a particular spelling, all spelling variations of a surname are just that – spelling variants of that name. A friend named "Kell*ey*" emphasized vehemently that there was very much a difference between his name and that of "Kelly" without the "*e*". No, there isn't. Most Irish surnames were first written by parish priests, census takers, enlistment officers and semi-literate government officials, many of whom did not speak Irish – and those who could had few writing skills.

However, in Ireland different spellings of the same name often indicate that the families ***do come from different counties.***

Edward MacLysaght, the late High Herald of Ireland, points out in his book *The Surnames of Ireland* that he came across six variations within two cemeteries of the same small family's name, ***Mac an Dhéaghanaigh***, "Son of the Dean", usually anglicized as "MacEneany" (MacLysaght, p. xiii). Another example is the Ulster Scots surname "Elliot" which can be spelled with one "l" ("Eliot"), two "l's" ("Elliot"), one "l" and two "t"s ("Eliott") and two of each ("Elliott").

In an 1840 Indiana (USA) census, the Irish names "MacAuliffe" are spelled "McOlive" and "MacCunnion" as "McOnion." There are fourteen spellings of *MacAoidh* in two small neighboring communities of North Carolina (USA). That name is commonly "MacGee" or "MacCoy" in Ireland. The Donegal surname *Mag Congail* has a wide range of spellings from "MacGonigall" to "Magonagle" and "Megunigal."

The very nature of both of Irish pronunciation and spelling may also have an influence on the many spelling variations. A few examples may help to illustrate.

In contrast to English, Celtic languages change on the *beginnings* of words as well as in the middle and on the ends. The two traditional terms for these are "aspiration" (now termed "lenition" or weakening) and "eclipsis" in which an initial consonant takes on some feature of the sound that precedes it.

Prefixing **Mac**, "son of", causes the initial consonant of some words to "weaken" or even disappear completely, thus changing the sound of the original word. In example, the forename "Patrick" will become "MacPhatrick", often spelled "Mac Fattrick." Prefixing **Mac** or **Ó** to a word beginning with a vowel will cause an **h-** to be inserted as in "Hannigan" from the Irish **Annagáin** which then became **Ó hAnnagáin** -- the **Ó** is dropped. Sometimes the final **-c** of **Mac** will be attached to the following word. The name "Arthur" is often shortened to "Art". When **Mac** is attached the name can be "MacArthur", "MacHart", "MacArt" or "MacCart" and even "Hart" after dropping the **Mac**.

"Eclipsis" or "assimilation" is not confined to Irish, witness the common English pronunciation of "butter" as /budder/. Irish *is* unique in that it is spelled out, causing considerable confusion to learners. For example, the word for "stone" is **cloch,** pronounced like English "clock". But "*the* stone" is **an gcloch** /uhn glock/. The combination **gc-** tells you that the original word is **cloch** for "dictionary purposes" but pronounce **gcloch** as if it begins with a /g/ sound, /uhn glock/.

"Eclipsis" is one of the reasons that **Mac Congail** becomes "Mac Gonigale". The other reason is that Irish has an "unwritten" vowel sound between **-ng-** and other consonant combinations, particularly those with "l, r, m, n". This "unwritten" vowel is always pronounced /uh/. This is why you will hear "film" pronounced /fil-uhm/ by some English speakers. **Congail** is pronounced /KON-uh-gahl/, thus "MacGonagle", "MacGonigle", or "Magonugal:, etc.

Just as the "-e-" in "Kell*ey* is meaningless and not pronounced, so is the "g" in names such as "Monaghan/Monahan/" and *-dh* or *-th* on the ends of words.

Many variations are contained in the Surname-Tartan List but not all since they continue to be found by the author. Don't try to reason why, leave that to the linguists and name specialists. Even MacLysaght is at times reduced to saying, "I have not traced the origin of this name" (MacLysaght, p. 145).

"MAC" OR "Mc"

There is absolutely no truth to the widely held belief that "Mac" denotes a name of Scottish origin and "Mc" indicates an Irish name. This myth is especially held in America, ignoring the fact that early census takers were instructed to abbreviate "Mac" as "Mc." "Mc" is *always* an abbreviation of

"Mac" and the two are used interchangeably. In Irish **Mac** is sometimes **Mag** as in **Mag Uidir**, "MacGuire" as "Maguire".

An example is the telephone book where the two are intermixed and alphabetized on the first letters of the following word, usually a forename. The same is true of the prefix **O'**. An example:

MacNab	**J & A**	**McNeill**	**A.**
McNab	**James**	**MacNeill**	**Archibald**
McNab	**John**	**McNeill**	**B.K.**
MacNab	**K.L.**	**MacNeill**	**Colin**
McNab	**L.**	**MacNeill**	**James**
MacNab	**Margaret**	**McNeill**	**Liam**
MacNab	**M.R.**	**McNeill**	**Nora**

The abbreviation of "Mc" for "Mac" is clearly understood in Ireland (and Scotland) but causes confusion elsewhere in the world. Books, files, and rosters of various kinds are sorted alphabetically, especially in the computer age, requiring the query, "Is your name spelled 'Mc' or 'Mac'?" The list will skip from "MacZ" through the "Mad-Maz" before getting to the section that begins with "Mc".

For those two reasons, that "Mc" is always an abbreviation of "Mac" and for sorting purposes, *Tartans For The Irish* only uses the full word "Mac". The almost obsolete **M'** is used now only by people like the author in note taking and **M'** is then later written in full as **Mac**.

In addition, it was the custom to primarily alphabetize names beginning with **Mac/Mc** under the second part of the name, **McArt** under "A" and **MacZeal** under "Z". MacLysaght does this by showing the **Mac** in parentheses where it is optional and sorting on the second name. The same procedure is used for **O'**. Examples from page 39 of MacLysaght include: **Carton, (O) Carty, Cauther, Carruthers, (Mac) Carvey, Mac Carvill**.

THE PREFIX "O'"

The prefix **O'** is typically Irish. There are a very few Scottish names beginning with **O'** and they are largely Hebridean and of clearly Irish origin.

O' is the English version of the Irish **Ui**, meaning "of the race of". With this in mind, the English possessive apostrophe is redundant. Heads of major Irish families such as the **O Connor Don** omit it. However, the practice is so widespread that **O'** is used in this book.

In the movement from a Gaelic society to a predominantly English one during the sixteenth century, many Irish families dropped both the **Mac** and the **O'**. In the nineteenth century with the move toward Irish independence, many families readopted these prefixes. MacLysaght cites the case of the "Sullivans" which had always been known historically as the "O' Sullivans". In 1844 only four percent of the "Sullivans" used the prefix **O'**. By 1944 the number was sixty percent and by 1980 MacLysaght estimated it at eighty-five percent in urban areas (MacLysaght, p. xi).

In some cases the prefixes **Mac** and **O'** were misapplied. Here again MacLysaght points to a "Gorman" adopting an **O'** where the family had earlier dropped the **Mac** and another referred to as added **Mac** when they had originally been **O'** (MacLysaght, p. xi).

The surnames beginning with **Mac** and **O'** are so common that each is given a separate place in *Tartans For The Irish*. If a name cannot be located in one of these sections, look for it in the opposite list or under the name without the prefix.

Another very common element in Irish surnames is a religious one, "Son of the Servant of [a saint's name]", **Mac Giolla ….** These are usually shortened to **Mac 'iolla**, translated into "Mac Il …" or "Mac El…".

The **Mac En...** surnames come from the phrase "Son of *the* ..." where the Irish for "the" is **an** as in "The Son of the Priest", **Mac an tSagairt**, "MacEntaggart". Priests were allowed to marry in the original Celtic church.

In addition to the native Irish and the admixture of Scottish Gaelic surnames, a number of English language names appear. Quite often these are translations or even mistranslations form the original Irish. Others from English settlers of long ago who quickly became Irish. Names like "Pritchard" (**Ap Richard**) and "Hopkins" ("Bobby") come from Wales. All of the "Fitz" names are of Norman origin, from **fils**, French for "son."

THE "ULSTER TARTAN"

Ulster was one of the five states of early Celtic Ireland. It should not be confused with the modern political entity of Northern Ireland which is a part of the United Kingdom. Northern Ireland embraces six of the counties of

"Historic Ulster" – Antrim, Armagh, Down, Fermanagh, Londonderry, and Tyrone. Three of its counties, Cavan, Donegal, and Monaghan remain in the Republic of Ireland.

In April, 1956, Mr. A. W. Dixon discovered a bundle of buried clothing beside a lane leading to a farm about a mile north of Dungiven in County Londonderry. Taken to the Belfast Museum, examination showed that it consisted of a semi-circular woolen cloak, a set of trews or tightly fitted trousers, a tunic, belt and shoes. The trews were made of tartan stained to various shades of brown by the long burial in the soil. The clothing was dated between 1575 and 1650 (Teall and Smith, p. 172). This date makes it ***the second oldest known tartan***. Only the Lennox District tartan from Scotland is older, dated *circa* 1575.

The tartan today is woven in the colours in which it was found, shades of yellowish brown and dark brown with a double red over stripe. It is also woven in the shades that some believe were the original colours – green, red, and with a yellow over stripe. This colour version is called the "'Red' Ulster Tartan". A person should specify which colour combination they prefer.

The "Ulster Tartan" is over four hundred years old — older by a hundred years than the earliest Scottish "clan" tartan; it is older by two to three hundred years than the majority of tartans in use today. This should not be discounted when choosing a tartan.

HOW TO USE THE NAME-TARTAN LIST

The following **Name-Tartan List** contains only "Suggested Tartans" for each surname. There is nothing sacrosanct about this list. It is based upon the best information available to the author at the time of writing (February, 2005).

First, realize that an Irish name can be found in a number of districts. Therefore one or several tartans may be listed for a name.

Most Irish know in which county their family originated. If they do not, or if their surname is not on the **Name-Tartan List**, suggest that they chose one of the "state" tartans – "Connacht", "Leinster", "Munster", "Oriel" or "Ulster". Also suggest one of the "All Irish" tartans listed at the bottom of each page.

Caution persons seeking a tartan that they should see a sample before purchasing. Various mills weave different tartans and none of them weaves all of them. "Connacht" can be spelled in the older English style "Connaught" but this an entirely different tartan, red rather than the traditional green and light brown.

Some family tartans will have to be specially woven. Contact the author in care of Heritage Books or the International Tartan Index maintained on the Tartans Authority web site at **tartansauthority.com** for a list of mills that weave each one.

There are a number of conventions in the **Name-Tartan List**. These include:

> The use of parentheses indicates an optional spelling: "Mona(g)han" indicates that the can be spelled with or without the "g" – "Monahan" or "Monaghan".

> Scottish names introduced to Ulster have suggested the appropriate "clan/family" tartan as well as the Irish tartans.

> In order to "fit" a suggested tartan into the computer, the name may be abbreviated. For example, "MAC DONALD" is sometimes abbreviated "MAC DON" or "M'DON.

Do not use religion as the basis for suggesting a tartan from the "Republican" counties versus the "Northern Ireland" counties". There are both Roman Catholic and Protestant citizens in every county. Many of the great names of the Irish national movement were Protestants—and many converted.

REFERENCES

Bell, Robert. *The Book of Ulster Surnames*. (Belfast: The Blackstaff Press), 1988.

McClintock, H. F. *Old Irish and Highland Dress*. Dunsdale, Scotland: Dundalgan Press, 1943.
Reprinted by Scot Press, Bruceton Mills, WV, 1999.

MacLysaght, Edward. *The Surnames of Ireland, 6th edition*. (Dublin: Irish Academic Press), 1999.

Murphy, Sean. "Irish Chiefs", *Directory of Irish Genealogy*
http://homepage.tinent.ie/~seanjmurphy/ dir/chiefs.htm

Ó Siadhail, Mícheál. *Learning Irish*. (Dublin: Dublin Institute for Advanced Studies), 1980.

Smith, Philip D. *Tartan For Me!-7th edition.* (Bowie, MD: Heritage Books), 1992.

Teall, D. Gordon and Philip D. Smith. *District Tartans* (London: Shepheard-Walwyn Publishers), 1992.

THE SUGGESTED IRISH

SURNAME – TARTAN

LIST

NOTES:

This list is alphabetical. If a surname appears at the bottom of a column, be sure the check the top of the next column even if it is on the following page. Most names have several suggested tartans. You will want to check to see that the surname does not "spill over" to the next column.

The "Clan Cian" (Pronounced /KEE-uhn/) is synonymous with the "O'Carrolls of Ely", Chief of the Sept. "Clan Cian" was one of the first Irish septs to adopt a tartan (1981).

In this list the common spelling "MacNaughton" is spelled "MacNachten". That is the correct spelling of the name according to the Chief (who has resided in Ireland for many generations) and the Clan MacNachten Society.

Similarly, the name "MacPhee" is spelled "MacFie" as that is the name preferred by the clan society.

TARTANS FOR IRISH NAMES

Anyone with a "County" Tartan may substitute one of the major "District" tartans listed below:

Galway, Leitrim, Mayo, Roscommon, Sligo:	**Connacht tartan**
Clare, Cork, Kerry, Limmerick, Tipperary, Waterford:	**Munster tartan**
Armagh, Down, Fermanagh, Louth, Monaghan:	**Oriel tartan**
Carlow, Dublin, Kildare, Kilkenny, Laois, Longford:	
Meath, Offaly, Westmeath, Wexford, Wicklow:	**Leinster tartan**
Antrim, Armagh, Cavan, Donegal, Down, Londonderry, Tyrone:	**Ulster tartan**

SURNAME	TARTAN	SURNAME	TARTAN
A		ANGLIM, ANGLIN	Co. CORK
		ANKETELL	Co. MONAGHAN
		ANNESLEY	AINSLIE
		ANNESLEY	MUNSTER TARTAN
		ANNET(T)	ULSTER TARTAN
		ANNET(T)	Co. DOWN
ACHESON	ULSTER TARTAN	ANSBERY	CONNACHT TARTAN
ACHESON	Co. ARMAGH	ANSBORO	Co. GALWAY
ACHESON	Co. FERMANAGH	ANTHONY	Co. WATERFORD
ACHMUTY	Co. CAVAN	ARAGAN	Co. CORK
ACKLE	ULSTER TARTAN	ARCHBOLD	Co. WICKLOW
ADAIR	ULSTER TARTAN	ARCHDALE	ULSTER TARTAN
ADAIR	Co. ANTRIM	ARCHDALE	Co. FERMANAGH
ADAIR	Co. DOWN	ARCHDEACON	Co. KILKENNEY
ADAMS	ULSTER TARTAN	ARCHER	Co. KILKENNY
ADDIS	ULSTER TARTAN	ARCHIBOLD	Co. WICKLOW
ADLEY	ULSTER TARTAN	ARDAGH	Co. LOUTH
ADLUM	IRISH-SeeFootnote	ARDIFF	IRISH-See Footnote
ADORIAN	Co. DOWN	ARDILL	Co. KILDARE
ADRAIN	ULSTER TARTAN	ARGUE	Co. CAVAN
AGAR	Co. KILKENNY	ARKINS	Co. CLARE
AGARTY	ULSTER TARTAN	ARLAND	Co. WATERFORD
AGNEW	AGNEW	ARMER	ULSTER TARTAN
AGNEW	ULSTER TARTAN	ARMOUR	ULSTER TARTAN
AGNEW	Co. CORK	**ARMSTRONG**	ARMSTRONG
AHARA	ULSTER TARTAN	ARMSTRONG	ULSTER TARTAN
AHERN	Co. CORK	AMSTRONG	Co. FERMANAGH
AIKEN(S)	ULSTER TARTAN	ARNOLD	Co. DUBLIN
AIRY	ULSTER TARTAN	ARNOTT	ULSTER TARTAN
ALDIN(E)	ORIEL TARTAN	ARNOTT	Co. ANTRIM
ALDUFF	IRISH-See Footnote	ARNUL	Co. DUBLIN
ALEXANDER	ALEXANDER	ARRELL	ULSTER TARTAN
ALEXANDER	ULSTER TARTAN	ARRELL	Co. TYRONE
ALEXANDER	Co. ANTRIM	ARRELL	Co. ANTRIM
ALGEE	ULSTER TARTAN	ARTHUR	Co. LIMERICK
ALIMAS	IRISH-See Footnote	ARUNDEL	Co. CORK
ALLAN	ALLAN	ASHE	Co. MEATH
ALLEN	ALLEN	ASHTON	IRISH-See Footnote
ALLEN	ULSTER TARTAN	ASKEY	ULSTER TARTAN
ALLEN	Co. ANTRIM	ASKEY	Co. TYRONE
ALLEN	Co. ARMAGH	ASKEY	Co. LONDONDERRY
ALLEN	Co. OFFALY	ASKIN	CONACHT TARTAN
ALLMAN	Co. LOUTH	ASPEL	LEINSTER TARTAN
ALLY	CLAN CIAN/O'CARROLL	ASPIG	ULSTER TARTAN
ALTIMAS	Co. WEXFORD	ASPIG	Co. TYRONE
ALTON	IRISH-See Footnote	ASTON	IRISH-See Footnote
ALYMER	Co. KILDARE	ATHY	Co. KILDARE
AMBROSE	Co. WEXFORD	ATKINS	Co. CORK
AMOOTY	Co. CAVAN	ATKINSON	ULSTER TARTAN
AMORY	Co. CAVAN	AUBINS	ULSTER TARTAN
ANDERSON	ULSTER TARTAN	AUDLEY	Co. DOWN
ANDERSON	ANDERSON	AUGHER	Co. TIPPERARY
ANDERSON	MAC DONALD	AUGHMUTY	Co. CAVAN
ANGIER	Co. CORK	AUGHMUTY	Co. LONGFORD
ANGLAND	Co. CORK	AUNGIER	Co. DUBLIN

"IRISH" indicates a choice of a general Irish tartan: "All Ireland", "Tara", "Clodagh", "Irish National", "St. Patrick"

TARTANS FOR IRISH NAMES

Anyone with a "County" Tartan may substitute one of the major "District" tartans listed below:

Galway, Leitrim, Mayo, Roscommon, Sligo:	Connacht tartan
Clare, Cork, Kerry, Limmerick, Tipperary, Waterford:	Munster tartan
Armagh, Down, Fermanagh, Louth, Monaghan:	Oriel tartan
Carlow, Dublin, Kildare, Kilkenny, Laois, Longford:	
Meath, Offaly, Westmeath, Wexford, Wicklow:	Leinster tartan
Antrim, Armagh, Cavan, Donegal, Down, Londonderry, Tyrone:	Ulster tartan

SURNAME	TARTAN	SURNAME	TARTAN
AVERELL	ULSTER TARTAN	BANNAN(E)	Co. OFFALY
AYLMER	Co. KILDARE	BANNISTER	Co. CARLOW
AYLWARD	Co. WATERFORD	BANNON	Co. FERMANAGH
		BANNON	Co. MAYO
B		BANNON	Co. OFFALY
		BANVILLE	Co. WEXFORD
BABE	Co. LOUTH	BARBER	ULSTER TARTAN
BACKAS	Co. WATERFORD	BARBOUR	ULSTER TARTAN
BACKHOUSE	ULSTER TARTAN	BARDANE	Co. WATERFORD
BACKHOUSE	Co. LONDONDERRY	BARDEN,BARDON	Co. WEXFORD
BACKUS	Co. WATERFORD	BARKER	LEINSTER TARTAN
BADGER	CONNACHT TARTAN	BARKER	ULSTER TARTAN
BADGER	Co. GALWAY	BARLOW	Co. TIPPERARY
BAGENAL	Co. CARLOW	BARNEVILLE	Co. DUBLIN
BAGGE	IRISH-See Fotnote	BARNWALL,-WELL	Co. MEATH
BAGGOT	Co. DUBLIN	BARON	See BARRON
BAGLEY	See BEGLEY	BARRAGRY	Co. TIPPERARY
BAGNAIL	Co. CARLOW	BARRET(T)	CONNACHT TARTAN
BAGNAL	Co. CARLOW	BARRET(T)	Co. CORK
BAGOT	Co. KERRY	BARRET(T)	Co. DUBLIN
BAGWELL	Co. TIPPERARY	BARRET(T)	Co. MAYO
BAILLIE	ULSTER TARTAN	BARRON	ULSTER TARTAN
BAILLIE	Co. ANTRIM	BARRON	O' NEILL
BAILLEY	ULSTER TARTAN	BARRON	FITZGERALD
BAILLEY	Co. DOWN	BARRON	Co. WATERFORD
BAIRD	BAIRD	BARRY	Co. CORK
BAIRD	ULSTER TARTAN	BARTER	Co. CORK
BAIRD	Co. ANTRIM	BARTON	Co. KILDARE
BAIRD	Co. DOWN	BASKIN	Co. CLARE
BAKER	BAKER	BASNETT	Co. DUBLIN
BALDOON	Co. WATERFORD	BASQUILL	Co. MAYO
BALDWIN	Co. WATERFORD	BASSETT	IRISH-See Footnote
BALFE	Co. MEATH	BASTABLE	Co. CORK
BALL	BALL	BASTABLE	Co. KERRY
BALL	ULSTER TARTAN	BASTICK	Co. OFFALY
BALLAGH	IRISH-See Footnote	BATEMAN	Co. CORK
BALLARD	Co. DUBLIN	BATES	BATES
BALLENGER	Co. CLARE	BATES	LEINSTER TARTAN
BALLESTY	Co. WESTMEATH	BATES	Co. DUBLIN
BALTON	Co. CLARE	BATES	Co. MEATH
BAMBERY	Co. KERRY	BATHE	LEINSTER TARTAN
BAMBRICK	Co. LAOIS	BATTERSBY	Co. FERMANAGH
BAMBURY	Co. KERRY	BATTERSBY	Co. MONAGHAN
BANAGHAN	CONNACHT TARTAN	BATTLE	Co. SLIGO
BANAGHAN	Co. SLIGO	BAWN	CONNACHT TARTAN
BANANE	Co. FERMANAGH	BAWN	Co. CLARE
BANANE	Co. KERRY	BAWN	Co. GALWAY
BANFIELD	Co. WEXFORD	BAXTER	BAXTER
BANIGAN	ULSTER TARTAN	BAXTER	MAC MILLAN
BANIGAN	Co. DONEGAL	BAXTER	ULSTER TARTAN
BANIM	Co. KILKENNY	BAYLY	See BAILIE
BANKS	Co. OFFALY	BAYRES	Co. GALWAY
BANNAN(E)	Co. CORK	BEAGHAN	Co. KILDARE
		BEAMISH	LEINSTER TARTAN
		BEAMISH	Co. CORK

"IRISH" indicates a choice of a general Irish tartan: "All Ireland", "Tara", "Clodagh", "Irish National", "St. Patrick"

TARTANS FOR IRISH NAMES

Anyone with a "County" Tartan may substitute one of the major "District" tartans listed below:

Galway, Leitrim, Mayo, Roscommon, Sligo:	Connacht tartan
Clare, Cork, Kerry, Limmerick, Tipperary, Waterford:	Munster tartan
Armagh, Down, Fermanagh, Louth, Monaghan:	Oriel tartan
Carlow, Dublin, Kildare, Kilkenny, Laois, Longford:	
Meath, Offaly, Westmeath, Wexford, Wicklow:	Leinster tartan
Antrim, Armagh, Cavan, Donegal, Down, Londonderry, Tyrone:	Ulster tartan

SURNAME	TARTAN	SURNAME	TARTAN
BEAMISH	Co. KERRY	BERRELL, BERRALL	See BURRELL
BEARD	BEARD	BERRIGAN	Co. OFFALY
BEARD	Co. LAOIS	BERRY	Co. OFFALY
BEARY	Co. OFFALY	BERTH	Co. CLARE
BEASTY	Co. MAYO	BESLIN	Co. DONEGAL
BEAUMONT	ULSTER TARTAN	BEST	ULSTER TARTAN
BECHER	Co. CORK	BESTON	Co. LIMERICK
BECK	BECK	BETAGH	BEATTY
BECK	ULSTER TARTAN	BETHEL	ULSTER TARTAN
BECKETT	ULSTER TARTAN	BETTY	BEATTY
BEEGAN	LEINSTER TARTAN	BETTY	Co. FERMANAGH
BEGANNE	ULSTER TARTAN	BEUG	Co. CORK
BEGANNE	Co. MONAGHAN	BICKERSTAFF	Co. DOWN
BEGG(E)	Co. CORK	BIGGARS	Co. DOWN
BEGG(E)	LEINSTER TARTAN	BIGGINS	ORIEL TARTAN
BEGGINS	CLAN CIAN/O'CARROLL	BIGGY	Co. MAYO
BEGGS	ULSTER TARTAN	BIGGY	CONNACHT TARTAN
BEGGS	Co. ANTRIM	BIGLEY	Co. CORK
BEGLAN	Co. WESTMEATH	BINANE	Co. CORK
BEGLEY	ULSTER TARTAN	BINCHY	Co. CORK
BEGLEY	MUNSTER TARTAN	BINDON	Co. CLARE
BEGLEY	Co. CORK	BINGHAM	ULSTER TARTAN
BEGLEY	Co. DONEGAL	BINGHAM	Co. DOWN
BEGLEY	Co. KERRY	BINGHAM	Co. ANTRIM
BEGLIN	Co. LONGFORD	BINGHAM	Co. MAYO
BEGNEY	Co. LONGFORD	BINNANE	Co. KERRY
BEHAN	Co. KILDARE	BIRACREA	Co. TIPPERARY
BEHAN	Co. OFFALY	BIRCH	BIRCH
BEIRNE	CONNACHT TARTAN	BIRCH	Co. OFFALY
BELDON	Co. FERMANAGH	BIRD	MAC BYRD
BELL	BELL	BIRD	IRISH-See Footnote
BELL	ULSTER TARTAN	BIRRANE	CONNACHT TARTAN
BELLEW	Co. LOUTH	BIRT	Co. DUBLIN
BELLINGHAM	Co. LOUTH	BISHOP	ULSTER TARTAN
BELTON	Co. FERMANAGH	BISHOP	Co. TYRONE
BENBO	CONNACHT TARTAN	BLACAGH	CONNACHT TARTAN
BENBO	Co. SLIGO	BLACK	ULSTER TARTAN
BENISON	ULSTER TARTAN	BLACK	LAMONT
BENISON	Co. DUBLIN	BLACKALL	Co. DUBLIN
BENNET(T)	BENNET	BLACKBURN(E)	Co. ROSCOMMON
BENNET(T)	Co. KILKENNY	BLACKBYRNE	Co. ROSCOMMON
BENNIS	Co. LIMERICK	BLACKER	ORIEL TARTAN
BENTLEY	Co. CLARE	BLACKER	Co. ARMAGH
BERESFORD	Co. WATERFORD	BLACKHALL	Co. DUBLIN
BERGAN,BERGIN	Co. OFFALY	BLACKNEY	Co. DUBLIN
BERKERY	Co. TIPPERARY	BLACKWELL	Co. CLARE
BERMINGHAM	Co. KILDARE	BLAIR	BLAIR
BERNAL	Co. DUBLIN	BLAIR	ULSTER TARTAN
BERNARD	CLAN CIAN/O'CARROLL	BLAKE	CONNACHT TARTAN
BERNE	ULSTER TARTAN	BLAKE	Co. GALWAY
BERNEVAL	Co. DUBLIN	BLAKELY	Co. CAVAN
BERNEY	ULSTER TARTAN	BLANCHFIELD	Co. KILKENNY
BEROCHRY	Co. TIPPERARY	BLANEY	Co. MONAGHAN
BERRANE	Co. MAYO	BLEAHAN	Co. GALWAY
BERREEN	Co. SLIGO	BLEAKLEY	Co. CAVAN

"IRISH" indicates a choice of a general Irish tartan: "All Ireland", "Tara", "Clodagh", "Irish National", "St. Patrick"

16

Anyone with a "County" Tartan may substitute one of the major "District" tartans listed below:

Galway, Leitrim, Mayo, Roscommon, Sligo:	**Connacht tartan**
Clare, Cork, Kerry, Limmerick, Tipperary; Waterford:	**Munster tartan**
Armagh, Down, Fermanagh, Louth, Monaghan:	**Oriel tartan**
Carlow, Dublin, Kildare, Kilkenny, Laois, Longford:	
Meath, Offaly, Westmeath, Wexford, Wicklow:	**Leinster tartan**
Antrim, Armagh, Cavan, Donegal, Down, Londonderry, Tyrone:	**Ulster tartan**

SURNAME	TARTAN	SURNAME	TARTAN
BLEHEEN	Co. GALWAY	BOLLEN	CLAN CIAN/O'CARROLL
BLENNERHASSET	Co. KERRY	BOLMAR	ULSTER TARTAN
BLESSING	Co. LEITRIM	BOLSTER	Co. CORK
BLEVINS	Co. TYRONE	BOLTON	IRISH-See Footnote
BLEWETT	Co. LIMERICK	BONAR	BONNER
BLIGH(E)	CONNACHT TARTAN	BONAR	Co. DONEGAL
BLIGH(E)	Co. GALWAY	BONAR	ULSTER TARTAN
BLOOD	CLAN CIAN/O'CARROLL	BONASS	CLAN CIAN/O'CARROLL
BLOOD	Co. CLARE	BOND	IRISH-See Footnote
BLOOMER	ULSTER TARTAN	BONES	CLAN CIAN/O'CARROLL
BLOOSE	LYNCH	BONES	CONNACHT TARTAN
BLOWICK	CONNACHT TARTAN	BONFIELD	Co. CLARE
BLUETT	Co. CORK	BONFIELD	Co. LIMERICK
BLUNDEN	Co. KILKENNY	BOOKLE	Co. WICKLOW
BLUNT	IRISH-See Footnote	BOONIZER	Co. LIMERICK
BLY	CONNACHT TARTAN	BOOTH	BOOTH
BLYTHE	CONNACHT TARTAN	BOOTH	Co. DUBLIN
BOAG	Co. CORK	BOOTH	Co. SLIGO
BOAL	ULSTER TARTAN	BORAN	Co. LIMERICK
BOAL	Co. ANTRIM	BORGAR	CLAN CIAN/O'CARROLL
BOAR	Co. SLIGO	BORRIS	ULSTER TARTAN
BODDY	Co. LEITRIM	BOSSHER	Co. WEXFORD
BODELL	ULSTER TARTAN	BOSTOCK	Co. OFFALY
BODELL	ULSTER TARTAN	BOUCHER	Co. WEXFORD
BODEN	Co. KILDARE	BOUGHAN	CONNACHT TARTAN
BODKIN	Co. GALWAY	BOUGHLA	Co. OFFALY
BODKIN	Co. MAYO	BOURKE	CONNACHT TARTAN
BODKIN	CONNACHT TARTAN	BOURNE	Co. DUBLIN
BOG(G)AN	Co. DONEGAL	BOURNE	Co. KILDARE
BOG(G)AN	Co. WEXFORD	BOUVAIRD	ULSTER TARTAN
BOGUE	ORIEL TARTAN	BOVAIRD	Co. DONEGAL
BOHAN(E)	CONNACHT TARTAN	BOVENIZER	Co. LIMERICK
BOHAN(E)	Co. CORK	BOWDEN	Co. KILDARE
BOHAN(E)	Co. GALWAY	BOWDERN	Co. WATERFORD
BOHANNAN	BUCHANAN	BOWDREN	Co. WATERFORD
BOHANNON	Co. CLARE	BOWEN	CLAN CIAN/O'CARROLL
BOHELLY,-HILLY	Co. OFFALY	BOWER	Co. SLIGO
BOHILL	Co. DOWN	BOWLER	Co. KERRY
BOILEAU	Co. LOUTH	BOWMAN	ULSTER TARTAN
BOLAN(D)	CONNACHT TARTAN	BOWMAN	ULSTER TARTAN
BOLAND	CLAN CIAN/O'CARROLL	BOWYER	Co. DUBLIN
BOLAN(D)	Co. CLARE	BOYCE	ULSTER TARTAN
BOLAN(D)	Co. CORK	BOYCE	Co. DONEGAL
BOLAN(D)	Co. SLIGO	BOYD	BOYD
BOLASTY	Co. WESTMEATH	BOYD	ULSTER TARTAN
BOLDWIN	Co. WATERFORD	BOYDELL	Co. MEATH
BOLE(S)	ORIEL TARTAN	BOYER	Co. DUBLIN
BOLEYN	CLAN CIAN/O'CARROLL	BOYES	Co. DOWN
BOLEYN	Co. CORK	BOYHAN	Co. WESTMEATH
BOLGER	Co. CARLOW	BOYLAN	ULSTER TARTAN
BOLGER	Co. CLARE	BOYLAN	Co. DONEGAL
BOLGER	Co. WEXFORD	BOYLAN	Co. KILKENNY
BOLIN	CLAN CIAN/O'CARROLL	BOYLE	ULSTER TARTAN
BOLLARD	Co. DUBLIN	BOYLE	Co. DONEGAL
BOLLARD	Co. WEXFORD	BOYLE	Co. FERMANAGH

"IRISH" indicates a choice of a general Irish tartan: "All Ireland", "Tara", "Clodagh", "Irish National", "St. Patrick"

TARTANS FOR IRISH NAMES

Boyne   *Brohoon*

Anyone with a "County" Tartan may substitute one of the major "District" tartans listed below:

Galway, Leitrim, Mayo, Roscommon, Sligo:	Connacht tartan
Clare, Cork, Kerry, Limmerick, Tipperary, Waterford:	Munster tartan
Armagh, Down, Fermanagh, Louth, Monaghan:	Oriel tartan
Carlow, Dublin, Kildare, Kilkenny, Laois, Longford:	
Meath, Offaly, Westmeath, Wexford, Wicklow:	Leinster tartan
Antrim, Armagh, Cavan, Donegal, Down, Londonderry, Tyrone:	Ulster tartan

SURNAME	TARTAN	SURNAME	TARTAN
BOYNE	Co. LEITRIM	BREDIN	Co. TYRONE
BOYTON	CONNACHT TARTAN	BREE	CONNACHT TARTAN
BRABAZON	IRISH-See Footnote	BREE	Co. MEATH
BRACKEN	BRACKEN	BREE	Co. SLIGO
BRACKEN	Co. KILDARE	BREEN	LEINSTER TARTAN
BRACKEN	Co. DONEGAL	BREEN	Co. ARMAGH
BRADDEN	LEINSTER TARTAN	BREEN	Co. KILKENNY
BRADDEN	ULSTER TARTAN	BREEN	Co. LAOIS
BRADFORD	ULSTER TARTAN	BREHAN	Co. OFFALY
BRADFORD	Co. DOWN	BREHANY	Co. SLIGO
BRADIGAN	Co. ROSCOMMON	BREHON	Co. SLIGO
BRADISH	Co. WICKLOW	BRENNAGH	CONNACHT TARTAN
BRADLEY	ULSTER TARTAN	BRENNAN	Co. FERMANAGH
BRADLEY	Co. DONEGAL	BRENNAN	Co. GALWAY
BRADLEY	Co. LONDONDERRY	BRENNAN	Co. KILKENNY
BRADLEY	Co. KILDARE	BRENNOCK	IRISH-See Footnote
BRADLEY	Co. CORK	BRERETON	Co. TIPPERARY
BRADSHAW	ORIEL TARTAN	BRESLANE	ULSTER TARTAN
BRADSHAW	Co. CORK	BRESLIN	ULSTER TARTAN
BRADY	Co. CAVAN	BRESLIN	Co. DONEGAL
BRAGAN	Co. LOUTH	BRESLIN	Co. ROSCOMMON
BRAHAN	Co. LIMERICK	BRESNAHAN	Co. KERRY
BRAKEY	Co. MONAGHAN	BRESNAN	See BROSNAN
BRAN(N)	Co. CLARE	BRETT	Co. TIPPERARY
BRANAGAN	Co. MAYO	BRETT	Co. WATERFORD
BRANDON	Co. KERRY	BREW	Co. KILKENNY
BRANGAN	ORIEL TARTAN	BRICK	Co. FERMANAGH
BRANIFF	ULSTER TARTAN	BRICK	Co. KERRY
BRANIFF	Co. DOWN	BRICKLEY	Co. CORK
BRANIGAN	ORIEL TARTAN	BRIDGEMAN	Co. CLARE
BRANIGAN	Co. FERMANAGH	BRIDGET	ULSTER TARTAN
BRANLEY	CONNACHT TARTAN	BRIODY	Co. LONGFORD
BRANN	ULSTER TARTAN	BRISCOE	IRISH-See Footnote
BRANNAGH	CONNACHT TARTAN	BRISLAWN	ULSTER TARTAN
BRANNAN	CONNACHT TARTAN	BRISLIN	ULSTER TARTAN
BRANNELLY	CONNACHT TARTAN	BRITT	Co. TIPPERARY
BRANNIGAN	See BRANIGAN	BRITT	Co. WATERFORD
BRANNOCK	IRISH-See Footnote	BRITTAIN	IRISH-See Footnote
BRANSFIELD	Co. WATERFORD	BRITTON	IRISH-See Footnote
BRASSIL	Co. WATERFORD	BROCAS	Co. DUBLIN
BRASSLE	Co. WATERFORD	BROCK	Co. KERRY
BRAWLEY	ULSTER TARTAN	BRODER	Co. KILKENNY
BRAWLEY	Co. LONDONDERRY	BRODER	Co. WATERFORD
BRAWN	CONNACHT TARTAN	BRODERICK	Co. DONEGAL
BRAY	Co. WICKLOW	BRODERICK	Co. KILKENNY
BRAZIL	Co. WATERFORD	BRODIGAN	Co. MEATH
BRAZZLE	Co. WATERFORD	BRODY	BRODIE
BREADON	ULSTER TARTAN	BRODY	Co. CORK
BREADY	See BRADY	BROGAN	CONNACHT TARTAN
BREAKEY	Co. MONAGHAN	BROGAN	Co. CAVAN
BREARTY	ULSTER TARTAN	BROGAN	Co. CLARE
BRECKLEY	Co. CORK	BROHAL	LEINSTER TARTAN
BREDICAN	Co. MAYO	BROHAN	Co. MAYO
BREDICAN	Co. SLIGO	BROHAN	Co. OFFALY
BREDIN	ULSTER TARTAN	BROHOON	Co. SLIGO

"IRISH" indicates a choice of a general Irish tartan: "All Ireland", "Tara", "Clodagh", "Irish National", "St. Patrick"

Anyone with a "County" Tartan may substitute one of the major "District" tartans listed below:

Galway, Leitrim, Mayo, Roscommon, Sligo:	**Connacht tartan**
Clare, Cork, Kerry, Limmerick, Tipperary, Waterford:	**Munster tartan**
Armagh, Down, Fermanagh, Louth, Monaghan:	**Oriel tartan**
Carlow, Dublin, Kildare, Kilkenny, Laois, Longford:	
Meath, Offaly, Westmeath, Wexford, Wicklow:	**Leinster tartan**
Antrim, Armagh, Cavan, Donegal, Down, Londonderry, Tyrone:	**Ulster tartan**

SURNAME	TARTAN	SURNAME	TARTAN
BROILY	See BRAWLEY	BURBAGE	Co. LONGFORD
BROPHY	Co. LAOIS	BURCHILL	Co. CORK
BROPHY	Co. OFFALY	BURGESS	ULSTER TARTAN
BROSNAN	Co. KERRY	BURKE	CONNACHT TARTAN
BROSNAN	Co. LAOIS	BURKE	Co. CORK
BROTHERS	ULSTER TARTAN	BURKE	Co. SLIGO
BROUDIN	Co. CLARE	BURNELL	Co. DUBLIN
BROUGHALL	LEINSTER TARTAN	BURNELL	Co. MEATH
BROWDER	Co. KILKENNY	BURNEY	ULSTER TARTAN
BROWN(E)	BROWN	BURNS	BURNS
BROWN(E)	ULSTER TARTAN	BURNS	ULSTER TARTAN
BROWN(E)	Co. GALWAY	BURNSIDE	ULSTER TARTAN
BROWN(E)	Co. LIMMERICK	BURNSIDE	Co. LONDONDERRY
BROWN(E)	Co. WEXFORD	BURRANE	Co. TIPPERARY
BROWNLEA	IRISH-See Footnote	BURRIS	ULSTER TARTAN
BROWNLEE	IRISH-See Footnote	BURROUGHS	ULSTER TARTAN
BROWNLOW	IRISH-See Footnote	BURROWS	ULSTER TARTAN
BROWNRIGG	IRISH-See Footnote	BURSON	Co. DOWN
BROY	Co. KILKENNY	BURTCHAELL	Co. WICKLOW
BRUEN	Co. ROSCOMMON	BURTCHELL	Co. WICKLOW
BRUNELL	Co. MEATH	BURTON	Co. CORK
BRUNTY	BRONTE	BUSHER	Co. CORK
BRUODIN	Co CLARE	BUSHER	Co. WEXFORD
BRUTON	Co. DUBLIN	BUSTARD	ULSTER TARTAN
BRYAN	BRYANT	BUSTARD	Co. DONEGAL
BRYAN	Co. KILKENNY	BUTLER	BUTLER
BRYANT	BRYANT	BUTLER	CLAN CIAN/O'CARROLL
BRYANT	O' BRIEN	BUTLER	Co. KILLKENNY
BRYSON	BRYSON	BUTT	ULSTER TARTAN
BUCHANAN	BUCHANAN	BUTTERLY	Co. LOUTH
BUCHANAN	ULSTER TARTAN	BUTTIMER	Co. CORK
BUCKLEY	Co. GALWAY	BWEE	ULSTER TARTAN
BUGGLE	Co. DUBLIN	BYERS	ULSTER TARTAN
BUGGY	Co. KILKENNY	BYERS	Co. ARMAGH
BUGGY	Co. WEXFORD	BYERS	Co. CAVAN
BUGLER	Co. CLARE	BYRNE	LEINSTER TARTAN
BUHAN	Co. CORK	BYRTH	Co. LONDONDERRY
BUHILLY	Co. OFFALY		
BULLARD	Co. DUBLIN		
BULLEN	Co. CORK		
BULLIVAN	Co. TIPPERARY	**C**	
BULLMAN	BULLMAN		
BULLMAN	Co. CORK		
BULLOCK	IRISH-See Footnote		
BULMER	ULSTER TARTAN	CADDELL	CONNACHT TARTAN
BUNBURY	Co. CARLOW	CADDO	CONNACHT TARTAN
BUNION	Co. KERRY	CADDO(W)	ULSTER TARTAN
BUNTING	ULSTER TARTAN	CADIGAN	ULSTER TARTAN
BUNTING	Co. ARMAGH	CADOGAN	ULSTER TARTAN
BUNTING	Co. TYRONE	CADOGAN	ULSTER TARTAN
BUNTON	ULSTER TARTAN	CAFFERTY	Co. DONEGAL
BUNTON	Co. ARMAGH	CAFFERTY	Co. LONDONDERRY
BUNWORTH	Co. CORK	CAFFERTY	ULSTER TARTAN
BUNYAN	Co. KERRY	CAFFREY	MAC GUIRE
BURBAGE	Co. LEITRIM	CAGNEY	Co. CORK

"IRISH" indicates a choice of a general Irish tartan: "All Ireland", "Tara", "Clodagh", "Irish National", "St. Patrick"

TARTANS FOR IRISH NAMES

Cague   *Clement*

Anyone with a "County" Tartan may substitute one of the major "District" tartans listed below:

Galway, Leitrim, Mayo, Roscommon, Sligo:	Connacht tartan
Clare, Cork, Kerry, Limmerick, Tipperary, Waterford:	Munster tartan
Armagh, Down, Fermanagh, Louth, Monaghan:	Oriel tartan
Carlow, Dublin, Kildare, Kilkenny, Laois, Longford:	
Meath, Offaly, Westmeath, Wexford, Wicklow:	Leinster tartan
Antrim, Armagh, Cavan, Donegal, Down, Londonderry, Tyrone:	Ulster tartan

SURNAME	TARTAN	SURNAME	TARTAN
CAGUE	ULSTER TARTAN	CARAHER	ORIEL TARTAN
CAHALANE	Co. LIMERICK	CARBERY	Co. FERMANAGH
CAHAN	Co. CLARE	CARBERY	Co. WATERFORD
CAHANY	Co. MAYO	CARDELL	Co. DOWN
CAHEERIN	Co. CAVAN	CARDEN	Co. DUBLIN
CAHERN	Co. CAVAN	CARDEN	Co. MAYO
CAHERTY	Co. DOWN	CARDIFF	LEINSTER TARTAN
CAHILL	CLAN CIAN/O'CARROLL	CARDUFF	ULSTER TARTAN
CAHILL	Co. CLARE	CARDUFF	Co. DONEGAL
CAHIR	Co. CLARE	CARDWELL	Co. DOWN
CAHOON	See COLHOUN	CAREW	Co. TIPPERARY
CAIG	ULSTER TARTAN	CAREY	See KERRY
CAIRNS	ULSTER TARTAN	CARGILL	ULSTER TARTAN
CALDDIN	CLAN CIAN/O'CARROLL	CARKHILL	Co. CLARE
CALDWELL	ULSTER TARTAN	CARKILL	ULSTER TARTAN
CALDWELL	Co. TYRONE	CARLAND	ULSTER TARTAN
CALDWELL	Co. LONDONDERRY	CARLAND	Co. TYRONE
CALDERWOOD	ULSTER TARTAN	CARLETON	ORIEL TARTAN
CALDIN	CLAN CIAN/O'CARROLL	CARLIN	ULSTER TARTAN
CALDWELL	ULSTER TARTAN	CARLIN	Co. TYRONE
CALFE	Co. WATERFORD	CARLISLE	CARLISLE FAMILY
CALLAGHAN	Co. CORK	CARLISLE	ULSTER TARTAN
CALGHAN	Co. MAYO	CARLISLE	Co. ANTRIM
CALLAGY	Co. SLIGO	CARLOS	Co. GALWAY
CALLERY	CONNACHT TARTAN	CARLTON	ORIEL TARTAN
CALLIG(H)AN	Co. CORK	CARMODY	Co. CLARE
CALLINAN	Co. GALWAY	CARNAHAN	ULSTER TARTAN
CALLOW	LEINSTER TARTAN	CARNAHAN	Co. ANTRIM
CALNAN	Co. GALWAY	CARNAHAN	Co. ARMAGH
CALSHENDER	ULSTER TARTAN	CARNEY	CLAN CIAN/O'CARROLL
CALTER	ULSTER TARTAN	CARNEY	CONNACHT TARTAN
CALTER	Co. ARMAGH	CARNEY	ULSTER TARTAN
CALVEY	CONNACHT TARTAN	CAROLAN	ULSTER TARTAN
CALVEY	Co. SLIGO	CAROLAN	Co. LONDONDERRY
CALWAY	Co. MAYO	CAROLL	CLAN CIAN/O'CARROLL
CAMERON	CAMERON	CARRA(G)HER	ORIEL TARTAN
CAMERON	ULSTER TARTAN	CARREEN	Co. WEXFORD
CAMERON	Co. ANTRIM	CARROLL	CLAN CIAN/O'CARROLL
CAMPION	Co. LAOIS	CARVIN	Co. LAOIS
CANALLY	MAC INALLY	CARVOLLE	CLAN CIAN/O'CARROLL
CANAVAN	CONNACHT TARTAN	CASEY	CASEY
CANAVAN	Co. GALWAY	CASEY	CLAN CIAN/O'CARROLL
CANAWAY	ULSTER TARTAN	CASSELLS	CLAN CIAN/O'CARROLL
CANNING	ULSTER TARTAN	CASSEY	CASEY
CANNING	Co. LONDONDERRY	CASSEY	CLAN CIAN/O'CARROLL
CANTILLION	Co. KERRY	CASSIDY	MAC GUIRE
CANTLIN	Co. KERRY	CASTLES	CLAN CIAN/O'CARROLL
CANTRELL	Co. DUBLIN	CATHERWOOD	ULSTER TARTAN
CANTY	Co. CORK	CAULFIELD	Co. DOWN
CAPEL	Co. CARLOW	CAULFIELD	ULSTER TARTAN
CAPLE(S)	Co. CARLOW	CLANC(E)Y	CLAN CIAN/O'CARROLL
CAPLICE	Co. TIPPERARY	CLANTON	CLANTON
CAPLISS	Co. CARLOW	CLEMENT	LAMONT
CAPPOCK	Co. LOUTH	CLEMENT	ULSTER TARTAN
CARABINE	Co. MAYO	CLEMENT	Co. ANTRIM

"IRISH" indicates a choice of a general Irish tartan: "All Ireland", "Tara", "Clodagh", "Irish National", "St. Patrick"

20

TARTANS FOR IRISH NAMES

Clooney   *Creagh*

"County" Tartan may substitute one of the major "District" tartans listed below:

Galway, Leitrim, Mayo, Roscommon, Sligo:	Connacht tartan
Clare, Cork, Kerry, Limmerick, Tipperary, Waterford:	Munster tartan
Armagh, Down, Fermanagh, Louth, Monaghan:	Oriel tartan
Carlow, Dublin, Kildare, Kilkenny, Laois, Longford:	
Meath, Offaly, Westmeath, Wexford, Wicklow:	Leinster tartan
Antrim, Armagh, Cavan, Donegal, Down, Londonderry, Tyrone:	Ulster tartan

SURNAME	TARTAN	SURNAME	TARTAN
CLOON(E)Y	ULSTER TARTAN	COPPINGER	Co. DOWN
CLOON(E)Y	Co. TYRONE	CORCORAN	CORCORAN
CLUSBY	Co. LOUTH	CORCORAN	CLAN CIAN/O'CARROLL
COAKLEY	Co. CORK	CORCORAN	Co. FERMANAGH
COCHRANE	COCHRANE	CORCORAN	Co. KERRY
CODY	Co. KILKENNEY	CORDUFF	ULSTER TARTAN
COEN	CONNACHT TARTAN	COREY	CLAN CIAN/O'CARROLL
COFFEY	Co. CORK	CORISH	Co. GALWAY
COGHRANE	COCORAN	CORISH	Co. TIPPERARY
COGHRANE	CLAN CIAN/O'CARROLL	CORLESS	Co. GALWAY
COGHRANE	COCHRANE	CORMICAN	IRISH-See Footnote
COGHRANE	COCHRANE	CORR	ULSTER TARTAN
COGLEY	Co. WEXFORD	CORR	Co. TYRONE
COHAN, COHEN	CONNACHT TARTAN	CORRA	CLAN CIAN/O'CARROLL
COLGAN	COLGAN	CORRELL	CLAN CIAN/O'CARROLL
COLLEARY	CONNACHT TARTAN	CORRIBEEN	CONNACHT TARTAN
COMBER	Co. MAYO	CORRIGAN	Co. FERMANAGH
CONAGH	CONNACHT TARTAN	CORRIGAN	Co. WEXFORD
CONAGH	Co. GALWAY	CORRILL	CLAN CIAN/O'CARROLL
CONDRICK	Co. CORK	CORRY	MAC GUIRE
CONDRON	Co. CORK	CORRY	Co. FERMANAGH
CONELLEN	Co. MAYO	CORRY	Co. WESTMEATH
CONLAN	O' NEILL	CORY	CLAN CIAN/O'CARROLL
CONLAN	Co. OFFALY	COSGRAVE	CLAN CIAN/O'CARROLL
CONNEGAN	Co. MEATH	COSGRAVE	Co. CORK
CONNELL	MAC CONNELL	COSGRAVE	Co. FERMANAGH
CONNELL	CONNELL	COSTELLO	ULSTER TARTAN
CONNELLEN	O' NEILL	COSTELLO	Co. CORK
CONNELLAN	Co. MEATH	COSTELLO	Co. TYRONE
CONNER	CONNER	COSTIGAN	Co. WICKLOW
CONNIFF	CONNACHT TARTAN	COTTER	Co. MONAGHAN
CONNOLLY	ORIEL TARTAN	COUGHLIN	CLAN CIAN/O'CARROLL
CONNOLLY	Co. FERMANAGH	COUGHLIN	Co. LIMMERICK
CONNOLLY	Co. MONAGHAN	COUGHLIN	Co. MAYO
CONN OLLY	Co. CORK	COULTER	COULTER
CONROY	CLAN CIAN/O'CARROLL	COULTER	ULSTER TARTAN
CONRY	CLAN CIAN/O'CARROLL	COUNTRY	Co. CORK
CONRY	Co. GALWAY	COURTNEY	Co. CORK
CONSIDINE	MAC GUIRE	COWAN	COWAN
CONSIDINE	Co. GALWAY	COWAN	ULSTER TARTAN
CONVEY	Co. SLIGO	COWAN	Co. ARMAGH
CONWAY	Co. CLARE	COWLEY	Co. KILKENNY
CONWAY	Co. LONGFORD	COX	Co. KERRY
CONWAY	Co. SLIGO	COYLE	Co. CORK
COOK	COOK	COYNE	CONNACHT TARTAN
COOK	ULSTER TARTAN	COYNE	Co. KILKENNY
COOK	Co. TYRONE	CRAIG	CRAIG
COOKE	Co. GALWAY	CRAIG	ULSTER TARTAN
COOLAHAN	Co. WICKLOW	CRAIG	Co. CAVAN
COOLEY	Co. GALWAY	CRAMPSEY	Co. DONEGAL
COOMBE(S)	CLAN CIAN/O'CARROLL	CRAWFORD	CRAWFORD
COON(E)Y	CLAN CIAN/O'CARROLL	CRAWFORD	ULSTER TARTAN
COON(E)Y	Co. MAYO	CRAWFORD	Co. ANTRIM
COON(E)Y	Co. TYRONE	CRAWFORD	Co. ROSCOMMON
COPELAND	Co. ROSCOMMON	CREAGH	CLAN CIAN/O'CARROLL

"IRISH indicates a choice of a general Irish tartan: "All Ireland", "Tara", "Clodagh", "Irish National", "St. Patrick"

20B

Anyone with a "County" Tartan may substitute one of the major "District" tartans listed below:

Galway, Leitrim, Mayo, Roscommon, Sligo:	Connacht tartan
Clare, Cork, Kerry, Limmerick, Tipperary, Waterford:	Munster tartan
Armagh, Down, Fermanagh, Louth, Monaghan:	Oriel tartan
Carlow, Dublin, Kildare, Kilkenny, Laois, Longford:	
Meath, Offaly, Westmeath, Wexford, Wicklow:	Leinster tartan
Antrim, Armagh, Cavan, Donegal, Down, Londonderry, Tyrone:	Ulster tartan

SURNAME	TARTAN	SURNAME	TARTAN
CREAGH	Co. DONEGAL	CUSHELEY	Co. TYRONE
CREAGH	Co. MAYO	CUSHLEY	ULSTER TARTAN
CREAL	Co. KERRY	CUSHLY	Co. TYRONE
CREAN	Co. LEITRIM	CUSHNAHANE	ULSTER TARTAN
CREAN	Co. LIMMERICK	CUSKELLY	Co. TYRONE
CREMIN	Co. LIMERICK	CUSKER	MAC GUIRE
CROKE	Co. DONEGAL	CUSKERAN	Co. DOWN
CROKE	Co. SLIGO	CUSKLEY	Co. TYRONE
CROMIE	ULSTER TARTAN	CUSSANE	CONNACHT TARTAN
CRONIN	ULSTER TARTAN	CUSSANE	Co. GALWAY
CRONIN	Co. ANTRIM	CUSSEN	Co. WEXFORD
CRONIN	Co. CORK	CUSTY	Co. CLARE
CROSBY	CROSBY		
CROSBY	Co. TIPPERARY		
CROTTY	Co. KERRY		
CROWE	ULSTER TARTAN		**D**
CROWE	Co. CLARE		
CROWE	Co. CORK		
CROWLEY	Co. LAOIS		
CROWLEY	Co. WATERFORD	D'ESTENE	MUNSTER TARTAN
CROZIER	CROZIER	DACEY	Co. WEXFORD
CROZIER	ULSTER TARTAN	DADY	See DEADY
CROZIER	Co. CAVAN	DAFFY	Co. CLARE
CRUISE	Co. CORK	DAGG	Co. WEXFORD
CULBERTSON	IRISH-See Footnote	DAGG	Co. WICKLOW
CULHNE	Co. ROSCOMMON	DAHILL	Co. TIPPERARY
CULLEN	ORIEL TARTAN	DAHONEY	See DOHENY
CULLEN	Co. FERMANAGH	DAILE	IRISH-See Footnote
CULLEN	Co. DUBLIN	DAILEY	Co. WESTMEATH
CULLIGAN	Co. CORK	DALE	Co. DUBLIN
CULLIGAN	Co. LIMMERICK	DALLAGHAN	CONNACHT TARTAN
CULLINANE	Co. KILDARE	DALLION	See DELANE
CULLY	CONNACHT TARTAN	DALLON	See DELANE
CULLY	Co. GALWAY	DALLY	Co. WESTMEATH
CUNNEEN	Co. MONAGHAN	DALTON	Co. CLARE
CUNNIFF	ULSTER TARTAN	DALTON	Co. WESTMEATH
CURLEY	Co. CLARE	DALY(E)	Co. WESTMEATH
CURRAN	ULSTER TARTAN	DANAGHER	Co. LIMERICK
CURRAN	Co. DONEGAL	DANAHER	Co. LIMERICK
CURRAN	Co. CORK	DANAHY	See DENNEHY
CURRID	Co. SLIGO	DANCEY	Co. CAVAN
CURRIGAN	See CORRIGAN	DANE	Co. ROSCOMMON
CURRIN	See CURRAN	DANGER	Co. OFFALY
CURRY	CURRY	DARBY	Co. LAOIS
CURRY	MAC GUIRE	DARCY	CONNACHT TARTAN
CURRY	CLAN CIAN/O'CARROLL	DARCY	Co. GALWAY
CURTAIN	Co. CORK	DARCY	Co. MAYO
CURTAYNE	Co. CORK	DARCY	Co. WEXFORD
CURTIN	Co. CORK	DARCY	Co. FERMANAGH
CURTIS	LEINSTER TARTAN	DARCY	Co. MEATH
CUSACK	CUSACK	DARDIS	LEINSTER TARTAN
CUSACK	Co. MEATH	DARGAN	Co. CORK
CUSH	Co. LIMERICK	DARGAN	LEINSTER TARTAN
CUSH	Co. TIPPERARY	DARLEY	Co. DUBLIN
CUSHANAN	ULSTER TARTAN	DARLING	ULSTER TARTAN

"IRISH" indicates a choice of a general Irish tartan: **"All Ireland"**, **"Tara"**, **"Clodagh"**, **"Irish National"**, **"St. Patrick"**

Anyone with a "County" Tartan may substitute one of the major "District" tartans listed below:

Galway, Leitrim, Mayo, Roscommon, Sligo:	**Connacht tartan**
Clare, Cork, Kerry, Limmerick, Tipperary, Waterford:	**Munster tartan**
Armagh, Down, Fermanagh, Louth, Monaghan:	**Oriel tartan**
Carlow, Dublin, Kildare, Kilkenny, Laois, Longford:	
Meath, Offaly, Westmeath, Wexford, Wicklow:	**Leinster tartan**
Antrim, Armagh, Cavan, Donegal, Down, Londonderry, Tyrone:	**Ulster tartan**

SURNAME	TARTAN	SURNAME	TARTAN
DARLING	Co. DUBLIN	DEE	CLAN CIAN/O'CARROLL
DARMODY	See DERMODY	DEEGAN	Co. CLARE
DARRAGH	ULSTER TARTAN	DEEGAN	Co. LAOIS
DARRAGH	Co. ANTRIM	DEEHAN	Co. LAOIS
DARREN	See DARRAGH	DEELY	CONNACHT TARTAN
DATON	Co. KILKENNY	DEELY	Co. GALWAY
DAUGHERTY	See DOHERTY	DEENIHAN	Co. KERRY
DAUGHTON	Co. KILKENNY	DEENY	ULSTER TARTAN
DAUNT	Co. CORK	DEER(E)	CONNACHT TARTAN
DAVANE	CONNACHT TARTAN	DEERANE	CONNACHT TARTAN
DAVENPORT	Co. DUBLIN	DEERING	LEINSTER TARTAN
DAVERN	Co. CLARE	DEERY	ULSTER TARTAN
DAVIDSON	DAVIDSON	DEERY	Co. LONDONDERRY
DAVIDSON	ULSTER TARTAN	DEES	CLAN CIAN/O'CARROLL
DAVIDSON	Co. ANTRIM	DEFFELY	See DEVILLY
DAVIDSON	Co. DOWN	DEGIDAN	Co. CLARE
DAVIN	Co. TIPPERARY	DEIGNAN	ORIEL TARTAN
DAVIS	ULSTER TARTAN	DELACOUR	Co. CORK
DAVIS	LEINSTER TARTAN	DELAHANTY	CLAN CIAN/O'CARROLL
DAVITT	Co. MAYO	DELAHUNT	CLAN CIAN/O'CARROLL
DAVOCK	CONNACHT TARTAN	DELAHUNT	Co. OFFALY
DAVOREN	Co. CLARE	DELAHUNTLY	Co. OFFALY
DAVYS	See DAVIS	DELAHUNTY	Co. OFFALY
DAWLEY	Co. WESTMEATH	DELAHYDE	Co. DUBLIN
DAWNEY	See DOHENY	DELAMER	Co. WESTMEATH
DAWSON	DAVIDSON	DELANE	Co. MAYO
DAWSON	ORIEL TARTAN	DELANEY	Co. KERRY
DAWTON	Co. KILKENNY	DELANEY	Co. LAOIS
DAY	CONNACHT TARTAN	DELAP	ULSTER TARTAN
DAY	CLAN CIAN/O'CARROLL	DELAP	Co. ARMAGH
DAY	Co. CLARE	DELARGY	ULSTER TARTAN
DAY	Co. GALWAY	DELARGY	Co. ANTRIM
DAYORAN	Co. CLARE	DELAY	See DUNLEA
De FREYNE	Co. KILKENNY	DELEA	See DUNLEA
DE LA HYDE	LEINSTER TARTAN	DELMERGE	Co. LIMERICK
DE LACY	Co. MEATH	DELOOREY	Co. CORK
DE LARY	Co. MEATH	DELOUGHERY	Co. CORK
DEACON	IRISH-See Footnote	DELVANY	Co. DOWN
DEADY	CLAN CIAN/O'CARROLL	DEMPSEY	Co. LAOIS
DEADY	Co. KERRY	DEMPSEY	Co. OFFALY
DEADY	Co. LIMERICK	DEMPSTER	DEMPSTER
DEAKIN	IRISH-See Footnote	DEMPSTER	Co. DOWN
DEAL(E)	MUNSTER TARTAN	DEMPSTER	MANX NATIONAL
DEALY	Co. CORK	DENEGAN	CONNACHT TARTAN
DEAN(E)	ULSTER TARTAN	DENHAM	IRISH-See Footnote
DEAN(E)	CONNACHT TARTAN	DENIEFFE	Co. KILKENNY
DEAN(E)	Co. GALWAY	DENIHAN	CONNACHT TARTAN
DEANY,-IE	DENNY	DENIHAN	Co. KERRY
DEANY,-IE	ULSTER TARTAN	DENIVAN	Co. WEXFORD
DEASE	Co. WESTMEATH	DENN(E)	Co. KILKENNY
DEASEY	Co. CORK	DENN(E)	Co. WATERFORD
DEASY	Co. WEXFORD	DENNAN(Y),-EN(Y)	Co. CAVAN
DEAVIR	See DEVIR	DENNEHY	Co. CAVAN
DE BRYSON	See BRYSON	DENNEHY	Co. CORK
DECOVECY	Co. CORK	DENNEHY	Co. KERRY

"IRISH" indicates a choice of a general Irish tartan: "All Ireland", "Tara", "Clodagh", "Irish National", "St. Patrick"

22

TARTANS FOR IRISH NAMES

Dennery   *Dix*

"County" Tartan may substitute one of the major "District" tartans listed below:

Galway, Leitrim, Mayo, Roscommon, Sligo:	Connacht tartan
Clare, Cork, Kerry, Limmerick, Tipperary, Waterford:	Munster tartan
Armagh, Down, Fermanagh, Louth, Monaghan:	Oriel tartan
Carlow, Dublin, Kildare, Kilkenny, Laois, Longford:	
Meath, Offaly, Westmeath, Wexford, Wicklow:	Leinster tartan
Antrim, Armagh, Cavan, Donegal, Down, Londonderry, Tyrone:	Ulster tartan

SURNAME	TARTAN	SURNAME	TARTAN
DENNERY	Co. ROSCOMMON	DEVLIN	ULSTER TARTAN
DENNIGAN	CONNACHT TARTAN	DEVLIN	Co. LONDONDERRY
DENNING	Co. CORK	DEVLIN	Co. SLIGO
DENNIS	Co. DUBLIN	DEVON	Co. LOUTH
DENNISON	See DENNY	DEVOY	See DEERY
DENNY	DENNY	DEXTER	IRISH-S EE Footnote
DENNY	ULSTER TARTAN	DEYERMOTT	See DERMOND
DENNY	Co. LONDONDERRY	DIAMINT	ULSTER TARTAN
DENROCHE	CONNACHT TARTAN	DIAMOND	ULSTER TARTAN
DENVER	ULSTER TARTAN	DIAMOND	Co. ANTRIM
DENVER	Co. DOWN	DICK	DICKIE
DENVIR	See DENVER	DICK	ULSTER TARTAN
DERENZY	Co. WEXFORD	DICKIE	DICKIE
DERGAN	LEINSTER TARTAN	DICKSON	See DICK
DERHAM	Co. DUBLIN	DIFFIN	ULSTER TARTAN
DERMODY	Co. CAVAN	DIFFLEY	CONNACHT TARTAN
DERMODY	Co. KILDARE	DIGAN	Co. LAOIS
DERMODY	Co. TIPPERARY	DIGGIN	Co. KERRY
DERMODY	Co. WESTMEATH	DIGNAM, DIGNAN	Co. LOUTH
DERMOND	ULSTER TARTAN	DIGNEY	CONNACHT TARTAN
DERRANE	Co. GALWAY	DILGAN	Co. CLARE
DERRICK	Co. MAYO	DILL	Co. DONEGAL
DERRIG	Co. MAYO	DILLAHAN	ORIEL TARTAN
DERRY	ULSTER TARTAN	DILLANE	Co. LIMERICK
DERRY	Co. DONEGAL	DILLEEN	CONNACHT TARTAN
DERVAN	Co. ROSCOMMON	DILLON	Co. MEATH
DERWIN	Co. ROSCOMMON	DILLWORTH	Co. CORK
DESMOND	Co. CORK	DIMON(D)	ULSTER TARTAN
DEVALLEY	Co. GALWAY	DINAGHAN	Co. LIMERICK
DEVAN	CLAN CIAN/O'CARROLL	DINAHAN	Co. LIMERICK
DEVAN	Co. MEATH	DINAN	CLAN CIAN/O'CARROLL
DEVANE	CLAN CIAN/O'CARROLL	DINAN	Co. CLARE
DEVANE	CONNACHT TARTAN	DINAN	Co. TIPPERARY
DEVANNY	CONNACHT TARTAN	DINERTY	CLAN CIAN/O'CARROLL
DEVANY	CONNACHT TARTAN	DINGEVAN	Co. CORK
DEVANY	Co. MEATH	DINKIN	CONNACHT TARTAN
DEVEEN	Co. TIPPERARY	DINNAHAN	Co. LIMMERICK
DEVEN	Co. LOUTH	DINNEEN	LEINSTER TARTAN
DEVENISH	Co. DUBLIN	DINNEEN	Co. CORK
DEVENNY	CONNACHT TARTAN	DINNEEN	Co. KERRY
DEVENNY	Co. GALWAY	DINNEVAN	Co. CORK
DEVER(S)	CONNACHT TARTAN	DIRANE	CONNACHT TARTAN
DEVER(S)	Co. GALWAY	DIRRANE	Co. GALWAY
DEVER(S)	Co. DONEGAL	DIRREEN	Co. KILKENNY
DEVEREAUX	Co. WEXFORD	DISKIN	CONNACHT TARTAN
DEVEREUX	Co. LOUTH	DISNEY	IRISH-See Footnote
DEVEREUX	Co. WEXFORD	DIVANE	Co. KERRY
DEVERILL	Co. LAOIS	DIVER	CONNACHT TARTAN
DEVERY	Co. OFFALY	DIVER	Co. DONEGAL
DEVESEY	Co. KILDARE	DIVER	Co. SLIGO
DEVILLY	CONNACHT TARTAN	DIVILLY	Co. GALWAY
DEVILLY	Co. GALWAY	DIVINE	See DEVINE
DEVINE	ULSTER TARTAN	DIVIN(E)	Co. LOUTH
DEVINE	Co. TYRONE	DIVINEY	CONNACHT TARTAN
DEVINE	Co. LOUTH	DIX	DICKIE

"IRISH indicates a choice of a general Irish tartan: "All Ireland", "Tara", "Clodagh", "Irish National", "St. Patrick"

TARTANS FOR IRISH NAMES

Dix

Doris

Anyone with a "County" Tartan may substitute one of the major "District" tartans listed below:

Galway, Leitrim, Mayo, Roscommon, Sligo:	**Connacht tartan**
Clare, Cork, Kerry, Limmerick, Tipperary, Waterford:	**Munster tartan**
Armagh, Down, Fermanagh, Louth, Monaghan:	**Oriel tartan**
Carlow, Dublin, Kildare, Kilkenny, Laois, Longford:	
Meath, Offaly, Westmeath, Wexford, Wicklow:	**Leinster tartan**
Antrim, Armagh, Cavan, Donegal, Down, Londonderry, Tyrone:	**Ulster tartan**

SURNAME	TARTAN	SURNAME	TARTAN
DIX	ULSTER TARTAN	DONNAN	Co. DOWN
DIXON	Co. DUBLIN	DONNEGAN	Co. CORK
DIXSON	Co. MAYO	DONNEGAN	Co. TYRONE
DOAG	ULSTER TARTAN	DONNELLY	ULSTER TARTAN
DOAK	ULSTER TARTAN	DONNELLY	O' NEILL
DOAN(E)	CLAN CIAN/O'CARROLL	DONNELLY	ULSTER TARTAN
DOAN(E)	CONNACHT TARTAN	DONNELLY	Co. TYRONE
DOBBIN(S)	ULSTER TARTAN	DONNELLY	Co. DONEGAL
DOBBIN(S)	Co. KILKENNY	DONOGHUE	O' DONOHUE
DOBBS	ULSTER TARTAN	DONOGHUE	LEINSTER TARTAN
DOBSON	Co. LEITRIM	DONOGHUE	Co. CORK
DOCKERY	CONNACHT TARTAN	DONOGHUE	Co. KERRY
DOCKRELL	Co. DUBLIN	DONOHOE	Co. CAVAN
DODD	DODD	DONOVAN	MUNSTER TARTAN
DODDSON	DODD	DONOVAN	Co. CORK
DODWELL	ULSTER TARTAN	DONOVAN	Co. LIMMERICK
DOEY	ULSTER TARTAN	DONWORTH	Co. TIPPERARY
DOGGETT	LEINSTER TARTAN	DOODY	Co. KERRY
DOHENY	Co. CORK	DOOEY	ULSTER TARTAN
DOHERTY	ULSTER TARTAN	DOOG(UE)	LEINSTER TARTAN
DOHERTY	Co. DONEGAL	DOOGAN	ULSTER TARTAN
DOILE	See DOYLE	DOOGHAN	Co. OFFALY
DOLAN	CONNACHT TARTAN	DOOHEY	DUFFY
DOLAN	Co. CAVAN	DOOHIG	DUFFY
DOLAN	Co. MAYO	DOOLADY	Co. LEITRIM
DOLIER	Co. DUBLIN	DOOLAGHTY	Co. CLARE
DOLLAGHAN	CONNACHT TARTAN	DOOLAN	Co. CORK
DOLLAGHER	CONNACHT TARTAN	DOOLE	DOYLE
DOLLARD	Co. DUBLIN	DOOLEY	CLAN CIAN/O'CARROLL
DOLLY	Co. GALWAY	DOOLEY	CLAN CIAN/O'CARROLL
DOLMAGE	Co. LIMERICK	DOOLEY	CLAN CIAN/O'CARROLL
DOLOHAN	CONNACHT TARTAN	DOOLEY	Co. WESTMEATH
DOLOHUNTY	IRISH-See Footnote	DOOLIN	Co. KERRY
DOLPHIN	CONNACHT TARTAN	DOOLING	ORIEL TARTAN
DOMEGAN	LEINSTER TARTAN	DOOLY	CLAN CIAN/O'CARROLL
DONAGHER	Co. ROSCOMMON	DOONA	SULLIVAN
DONAGHY	MAC DONAGH	DOONAN	Co. FERMANAGH
DONALDSON	MAC DONALD	DOONER	Co. LEITRIM
DONALDSON	ULSTER TARTAN	DOONER	Co. ROSCOMMON
DONARTY	Co. TIPPERARY	DOONIGAN	Co. FERMANAGH
DONDON	Co. LIMERICK	DOOREY	Co. ROSCOMMON
DONEGAN	CLAN CIAN/O'CARROLL	DOORISH	ORIEL TARTAN
DONEGAN	Co. CORK	DOORLEY	Co. OFFALY
DONEGAN	Co. TIPPERARY	DOORLY	Co. WEXFORD
DONELEAN	CONNACHT TARTAN	DOORTY	Co. CARE
DONELEAN	Co. GALWAY	DORAN	LEINSTER TARTAN
DONELEAN	Co. ANTRIM	DORAN	Co. LAOIS
DONELEY	Co. DONEGAL	DORCAN	Co. SLIGO
DONEY	Co. KERRY	DORCEY	Co. MAYO
DONGAN	Co. DUBLIN	DORDAN	Co. MAYO
DONGAN	Co. KILDARE	DORE	Co. LIMERICK
DONLAN	Co. ROSCOMMON	DOREY	Co. MAYO
DONLEVY	CONNACHT TARTAN	DORGAN	Co. CORK
DONLEVY	Co. DOWN	DORIAN	Co. DONEGAL
DONLY	O' NEILL	DORIS	ORIEL TARTAN

"IRISH" indicates a choice of a general Irish tartan: "All Ireland", "Tara", "Clodagh", "Irish National", "St. Patrick"

24

TARTANS FOR IRISH NAMES

Anyone with a "County" Tartan may substitute one of the major "District" tartans listed below:

Galway, Leitrim, Mayo, Roscommon, Sligo:	Connacht tartan
Clare, Cork, Kerry, Limmerick, Tipperary, Waterford:	Munster tartan
Armagh, Down, Fermanagh, Louth, Monaghan:	Oriel tartan
Carlow, Dublin, Kildare, Kilkenny, Laois, Longford:	
Meath, Offaly, Westmeath, Wexford, Wicklow:	Leinster tartan
Antrim, Armagh, Cavan, Donegal, Down, Londonderry, Tyrone:	Ulster tartan

SURNAME	TARTAN	SURNAME	TARTAN
DORLAN	Co. DONEGAL	DOWNS	CLAN CIAN/O'CARROLL
DORMAN	Co. DOWN	DOYLE	DOYLE
DORMER	Co. WEXFORD	DOYLE	Co. CARLOW
DORNAN	ULSTER TARTAN	DOYLE	Co. GALWAY
DORNAN	Co. DONEGAL	DOYLE	Co. WICKLOW
DORNEY	Co. TIPPERARY	DOYNE	Co. LAOIS
DORNIN	ULSTER TARTAN	DRADDY	Co. CORK
DORNIN	Co. DONEGAL	DRADDY	CONNACHT TARTAN
DOROHY	Co. KERRY	DRAFFIN	ORIEL TARTAN
DORR	Co. LEITRIM	DRAIN	ULSTER TARTAN
DORRAGH	ULSTER TARTAN	DRAKE	Co. MEATH
DORRAN	LEINSTER TARTAN	DRAPER	ULSTER TARTAN
DORRAN	Co. LAOIS	DRAPER	Co. LONDONDERRY
DORRANE	Co. DOWN	DRAPER	Co. CORK
DORRIAN	Co. DOWN	DRAYCOTT	IRISH-See Footnote
DORRIGAN	Co. CORK	DREA	Co. CLARE
DORRITY	ORIEL TARTAN	DREAN	ULSTER TARTAN
DORSEY	Co. MAYO	DREELAN	LEINSTER TARTAN
DOUGAN	ULSTER TARTAN	DREENAN	See DRENNAN
DOUGHER	CONNACHT TARTAN	DREILAN	Co. KILKENNY
DOUGHTERTY	ULSTER TARTAN	DRENNAN	CONNACHT TARTAN
DOUGHTY	Co. DUBLIN	DRENNAN	DRENNAN
DOUGLAS	DOUGLAS	DREW	Co. CLARE
DOUGLAS	ULSTER TARTAN	DREW(E)RY	Co. CAVAN
DOUGLAS	Co. ANTRIM	DRING	Co. CORK
DOUGLAS	Co. LONDONDERRY	DRISCOLL	Co. CORK
DOUPE	Co. LIMERICK	DRISLANE	Co. CORK
DOWCE	Co. DUBLIN	DROGAN	Co. CORK
DOWD	CONNACHT TARTAN	DROGHAN	Co. CORK
DOWD	Co. MAYO	DROM	Co. CAVAN
DOWD	Co. SLIGO	DROMEY	ORIEL TARTAN
DOWDALL	LEINSTER TARTAN	DROMGOLD	Co. LOUTH
DOWDALL	Co. MEATH	DROMGOOLE	Co. LOUTH
DOWDALL	Co. DUBLIN	DROODY	CONNACHT TARTAN
DOWDICAN	Co. SLIGO	DROOGAN	ULSTER TARTAN
DOWDIE	ULSTER TARTAN	DROUGH	Co. CLARE
DOWDS	ULSTER TARTAN	DROUGHT	Co. CLARE
DOWER	Co. WATERFORD	DRUDY	CONNACHT TARTAN
DOWEY	DUFFY	DRUGAN	Co. ARMAGH
DOWLAND	Co. CORK	DRUMGOOLE	Co. LOUTH
DOWLANE	Co. DOWN	DRUMGOULD	Co. LOUTH
DOWLER	CONNACHT TARTAN	DRURY	DRURIE
DOWLEY	ORIEL TARTAN	DRURY	Co. ROSCOMMON
DOWLING	DOWLING	DRYNAN	Co. CORK
DOWLING	LEINSTER TARTAN	DUAINE	CLAN CIAN/O'CARROLL
DOWLING	Co. LAOIS	DUANE	CONNACHT TARTAN
DOWMAN	IRISH-See Footnote	DUANE	CLAN CIAN/O'CARROLL
DOWNER	See DOONER	DUANE	Co. GALWAY
DOWNES	Co. CLARE	DUANY	CONNACHT TARTAN
DOWNES	Co. LIMERICK	DUARTE	Co. TIGPPERARY
DOWNEY	See O' DOWNEY	DUARTY	Co. TIPPERARY
DOWNEY	CLAN CIAN/O'CARROLL	DUDDY	ULSTER TARTAN
DOWNEY	Co. KERRY	DUDDY	Co. LONDONDERRY
DOWNING	Co. KERRY	DUDDY	Co. SLIGO
		DUDGEON	ORIEL TARTAN

"IRISH" indicates a choice of a general Irish tartan: "All Ireland", "Tara", "Clodagh", "Irish National", "St. Patrick"

TARTANS FOR IRISH NAMES

Early

"County" Tartan may substitute one of the major "District" tartans listed below:

Galway, Leitrim, Mayo, Roscommon, Sligo:	Connacht tartan
Clare, Cork, Kerry, Limmerick, Tipperary, Waterford:	Munster tartan
Armagh, Down, Fermanagh, Louth, Monaghan:	Oriel tartan
Carlow, Dublin, Kildare, Kilkenny, Laois, Longford:	
Meath, Offaly, Westmeath, Wexford, Wicklow:	Leinster tartan
Antrim, Armagh, Cavan, Donegal, Down, Londonderry, Tyrone:	Ulster tartan

SURNAME	TARTAN	SURNAME	TARTAN
DUDICAN	Co. DONEGAL	DUNLOP	ULATER TARTAN
DUDICAN	ULSTER TARTAN	DUNN(E)	LEINSTER TARTAN
DUDIGAN	Co. CLARE	DUNN(E)	Co. KILDARE
DUDLEY	Co. CORK	DUNN(E)	Co. LAOIS
DUFF	DUFFY	DUNN(E)	Co. MEATH
DUFF	MAC FIE	DUNN(E)	Co. OFFALY
DUFF	LEINSTER TARTAN	DUNNIGAN	CONNACHT TARTAN
DUFF	ULSTER TARTAN	DUNNIGAN	Co. CORK
DUFF	Co. LAOIS	DUNNING	ULSTER TARTAN
DUFF	Co. TYRONE	DUNNION	Co. DONEGAL
DUFFERLEY	Co. ROSCOMMON	DUNNY	IRISH-See Footnote
DUFFICEY	CONNACHT TARTAN	DUNPHY	MAC DONOUGH
DUFFIN	Co. WATERFORD	DUNPHY	Co. KILKENNY
DUFFIN	ULSTER TARTAN	DUNROCHE	CONNACHT TARTAN
DUFFLEY	CONNACHT TARTAN	DUNSHEA(TH)	ULSTER TARTAN
DUFFY	DUFFY	DURACK	Co. CLARE
DUFFY	ORIEL TARTAN	DUREY	DURRIE
DUFFY	Co. DONEGAL	DUREY	Co. ROSCOMMON
DUFFY	Co. MAYO	DURHAM	Co. DUBLIN
DUFFY	Co. MONAGHAN	DURIS	ULSTER TARTAN
DUFFY	Co. ROSCOMMON	DURKAN, DURKIN	Co. SLIGO
DUGAN	Co. CORK	DURNEY	Co. CORK
DUGAN	Co. MAYO	DUROSS	ULSTER TARTAN
DUGGAN	CONNACHT TARTAN	DURR	Co. ROSCOMMON
DUGGAN	Co. MAYO	DURRY	DURIE
DUGGAN	Co. CORK	DURRY	Co. LEITRIM
DUHIG	See DUFFY	DURR(A)N	Co. DOWN
DUIGAN	Co. LAOIS	DUVAN(E)	Co. DONEGAL
DUIGAN	Co. ROSCOMMON	DUVANY	Co. TYRONE
DUKE	CONNACHT TARTAN	DUVICK	Co. WESTMEATH
DULANTY	CLAN CIAN/O'CARROLL	DWANE	Co. CORK
DULHUNTY	CLAN CIAN/O'CARROLL	DWYER	Co. TIPPERARY
DULLAGHAN	ORIEL TARTAN	DYER	DYER
DULLAHAN	ORIEL TARTAN	DYER	Co. SLIGO
DULLAHANTY	CLAN CIAN/O'CARROLL	DYERMONTT	See DERMOND
DULLARD	Co. DUBLIN	DYMOND	ULSTER TARTAN
DULLEA	Co. CORK	DYNAN	Co. CLARE
DULLEHANLY	CLAN CIAN/O'CARROLL	DYNAN	Co. CORK
DUMIGAN	Co. DOWN	DYNES	ULSTER TARTAN
DUNDON	Co. LIMERICK	DYRA	Co. MAYO
DUNFORD,-FORT	Co. TIPPERARY		
DUNFY	Co. KILKENNY		
DUNGAN	Co. KILDARE		
DUNICAN	ULSTER TARTAN	**E**	
DUNICAN	Co. OFFALY		
DUNICAN	Co. FERMANAGH		
DUNIGAN	See DUNICAN		
DUNKIN	See DUNCAN	EABLE	Co. LONDONDERRY
DUNLAP	See DUNLOP	EAGAR	Co. KERRY
DUNLEA	Co. CORK	EAKIN(S)	ULSTER TARTAN
DUNLEVY	Co. DONEGAL	EAKIN(S)	Co. DONEGAL
DUNLEVY	CONNACHT TARTAN	EASKIN(S)	Co. LONDONDERRY
DUNLEVY	ULSTER TARTAN	EAMES	MUNSTER TARTAN
DUNLIEF	See DUNLOP	EARLE	IRISH-See Footnote
DUNLOP	DUNLOP	EARLS	Co. GALWAY
		EARLY	Co. LEITRIM

"IRISH indicates a choice of a general Irish tartan: "All Ireland", "Tara", "Clodagh", "Irish National", "St. Patrick"

TARTANS FOR IRISH NAMES

Earner   *Fane*

Anyone with a "County" Tartan may substitute one of the major "District" tartans listed below:

Galway, Leitrim, Mayo, Roscommon, Sligo:	Connacht tartan
Clare, Cork, Kerry, Limmerick, Tipperary, Waterford:	Munster tartan
Armagh, Down, Fermanagh, Louth, Monaghan:	Oriel tartan
Carlow, Dublin, Kildare, Kilkenny, Laois, Longford:	
Meath, Offaly, Westmeath, Wexford, Wicklow:	Leinster tartan
Antrim, Armagh, Cavan, Donegal, Down, Londonderry, Tyrone:	Ulster tartan

SURNAME	TARTAN	SURNAME	TARTAN
EARNER	Co. WESTMEATH	ERVINE	ULSTER TARTAN
EASON	MAC KAY	ERWIN(E)	ULSTER TARTAN
EASTWOOD	ULSTER TARTAN	ESBAL(D)	Co. LONDONDERRY
EATON	ULSTER TARTAN	ESKILDSON	IRISH-See Footnote
EBRILL	ULSTER TARTAN	ESMOND	Co. WEXFORD
ECHLIN	ULSTER TARTAN	ESNOR	See ALEXANDER
EDDERY	Co. MAYO	ETCHINGHAM	Co. WEXFORD
EDGAR	See ADAIR	EURELL	Co. WESTMEATH
EDGEWORTH	Co. LONGFORD	EUSTACE	CLAN CIAN/O'CARROLL
EGAN	Co. GALWAY	EUSTACE	Co. KILDARE
EGAN	Co. KERRY	EUSTACE	Co. WICKLOW
EGAN	Co. TIPPERARY	EVANS	Co. KILKENNY
ELCHINDER	See ALEXANDER	EVATT	ORIEL TARTAN
ELDER	ULSTER TARTAN	EVERARD	Co. MEATH
ELLARD	MUNSTER TARTAN	EVERETT	Co. TIPPERARY
ELLARD	Co. CORK	EVERILL	ULSTER TARTAN
ELLARD	Co. KERRY	EVERS	Co. MEATH
ELLIFFE	Co.WESTMEATH	EVOY	Co. WEXFORD
ELLIOT(T)	ELLIOT	EVOY	Co. WEXFORD
ELLIOT(T)	ORIEL TARTAN	EWART	MUNSTER TARTAN
ELLIS	ULSTER TARTAN	EWING	ULSTER TARTAN
ELLIS	Co. DUBLIN	EYRE(S)	EYRE
ELLISON	IRISH-See Footnote	EYRE(S)	CONNACHT TARTAN
ELMER	ELMORE	EYRE(S)	Co. GALWAY
ELMER	Co. LOUTH		
ELMORE	ELMORE		
ELMORE	Co. LOUTH		
ELSHANDER	See ALEXANDER		
ELSHINDER	See ALEXANDER	**F**	
ELVERS	MAC IVER		
ELVERY	Co. DUBLIN		
ELWARD(S)	Co. MAYO		
ELWOOD	LEINSTER TARTAN	FAGAN	Co. MEATH
ELY	CLAN CIAN/O'CARROLL	FAGGY	MAC FADYEN
EMERSON	MUNSTER TARTAN	FAGHENY	Co. ROSCOMMON
EMISON	MUNSTER TARTAN	FAHERTY	CONNACHT TARTAN
EMMET	Co. TIPPERARY	FAHEY	Co. GALWAY
EMO	ORIEL TARTAN	FAHY	Co. GALWAY
ENGLAND	Co. CORK	FAILOON	ULSTER TARTAN
ENGLISH	ULSTER TARTAN	FAIR	MUNSTER TARTAN
ENGLISH	Co. LIMERICK	FAIRY	ULSTER TARTAN
ENGLISHBY	ULSTER TARTAN	FALAHEE	Co. CLARE
ENGLISHBY	Co. ANTRIM	FALCONER	FALCONER/KEITH
ENNIS	Co. MEATH	FALCONER	ULSTER TARTAN
ENNIS	Co. ANTRIM	FALKINER	See FALCONER
ENNOS, ENOS	Co. WESTMEATH	FALL	CONNACHT TARTAN
ENRIGHT(Y)	Co. CLARE	FALLAHER	Co. CLARE
ENSOR	Co. ARMAGH	FALLON	Co. OFFALY
ERCKE	ULSTER TARTAN	FALLOR	Co. ROSCOMMON
ERLEY	MUNSTER TARTAN	FALLS	ULSTER TARTAN
ERRAUGHT	Co. KERRY	FALSEY	Co. CLARE
ERRINGTON	CONNACHT TARTAN	FALVEY	Co. KERRY
ERRITY	CONNACHT TARTAN	FANAGAN	ORIEL TARTAN
ERSKINE	ERSKINE	FANE	Co. KILKENNY
ERVINE	IRVINE		

"IRISH" indicates a choice of a general Irish tartan: "All Ireland", "Tara", "Clodagh", "Irish National", "St. Patrick"

26

Fanning   *Ferry*

Anyone with a "County" Tartan may substitute one of the major "District" tartans listed below:

Galway, Leitrim, Mayo, Roscommon, Sligo:	**Connacht tartan**
Clare, Cork, Kerry, Limmerick, Tipperary, Waterford:	**Munster tartan**
Armagh, Down, Fermanagh, Louth, Monaghan:	**Oriel tartan**
Carlow, Dublin, Kildare, Kilkenny, Laois, Longford:	
Meath, Offaly, Westmeath, Wexford, Wicklow:	**Leinster tartan**
Antrim, Armagh, Cavan, Donegal, Down, Londonderry, Tyrone:	**Ulster tartan**

SURNAME	TARTAN	SURNAME	TARTAN
FANNIN(G)	Co. LIMERICK	FEENEY	CONNACHT TARTAN
FANNIN(G)	Co. TIPPERARY	FEENEY	Co. GALWAY
FANNON	CONNACHT TARTAN	FEENEY	Co. SLIGO
FANT	Co. GALWAY	FEGAN	ORIEL TARTAN
FANT	Co. LIMERICK	FEGAN	Co. LOUTH
FANTON	Co. KERRY	FEHELLY	Co. ROSCOMMON
FARAUGHER	Co. WATERFORD	FEHILL	Co. LIMERICK
FARDY	Co. WEXFORD	FEHILLY	CONNACHT TARTAN
FARELLY	O' FARRELL	FEHILLY	ULSTER TARTAN
FARELLY	ORIEL TARTAN	FEIGHEY	Co. ROSCOMMON
FARELLY	Co. CAVAN	FEIGHNEY	Co. KERRY
FARKER	FARQUHARSON	FEIGHRY	CONNACHT TARTAN
FARLEY	O" FARRELL	FELAN	Co. KILKENNY
FARLOW	O' FARRELL	FELAN	Co. WATERFORD
FARLOW	Co. LIMERICK	FELAY	Co. LEITRIM
FARMER	Co. FERMANAGH	FELTUS	Co. CARLOW
FARNAN, FARNON	ULSTER TARTAN	FENAGHTY	Co. ROSCOMMON
FARNAN, FARNON	Co. TYRONE	FENELLY	Co. CORK
FARQUHAR	FARQUHARSON	FENELON	Co. WESTMEATH
FARRAHER	CONNACHT TARTAN	FENLON	Co. WESTMEATH
FARRELL, FARRALL	O' FARRELL	FENNELL	Co. DUBLIN
FARRELL, FARRALL	Co. LONGFORD	FENNELLY	LEINSTER TARTAN
FARREN	Co. DONEGAL	FENNELLY	Co. KILKENNY
FARRINGTON	MUNSTER TARTAN	FENNELLY	Co. LAOIS
FARRIS	CONNACHT TARTAN	FENNER	Co. DUBLIN
FARRISSY	Co. LEITRIM	FENNESSY	Co. TIPPERARY
FARRY	CONNACHT TARTAN	FENNESSY	Co. WATERFORD
FARSHIN	Co. CORK	FENNING	ULSTER TARTAN
FAUGHNAN	CONNACHT TARTAN	FENNORS	Co. DUBLIN
FAUGHNAN	Co. KERRY	FENTON	Co. LIMERICK
FAUGHNAN	Co. LONGFORD	FENTON	Co. KERRY
FAULKNER	ULSTER TARTAN	FENTRY	ULSTER TARTAN
FAULKNER	Co. ANTRIM	FEORE	Co. WEXFORD
FAULKNER	Co. LONDONDERRY	FERAN	ORIEL TARTAN
FAVERTY	CONNACHT TARTAN	FERGHNEY	CONNACHT TARTAN
FAWCETT	IRISH-See Footnote	FERGUS	CONNACHT TARTAN
FAWCITT	IRISH-See Footnote	FERGUSON	FERGUSON
FAY	Co. WESTMEATH	FERGUSON	ULSTER TARTAN
FEALTY	Co. DONEGAL	FERICK	CONNACHT TARTAN
FEALY	Co. KERRY	FERLEY	Co. LONGFORD
FEANE	Co. ROSCOMMON	FERNAN	ULSTER TARTAN
FEARON	ORIEL TARTAN	FERNS	Co. OFFALY
FEARON	Co. DONEGAL	FERON	ORIEL TARTAN
FEDDES, FEDDIS	FIDDES	FERRALL	O' FARRELL
FEDDES, FEDDIS	Co. ARMAGH	FERRAR	LEINSTER TARTAN
FEDEGAN	ORIEL TARTAN	FERREN	ORIEL TARTAN
FEE	MAC FIE	FERRIGAN	ULSTER TARTAN
FEE	ORIEL TARTAN	FERRIGAN	Co. LOUTH
FEE	Co. FERMANAGH	FERRIS	FERGUSON
FEEHAN	Co. TIPPERARY	FERRIS	ULSTER TARTAN
FEEHARRY	Co. WEXFORD	FERRIS	Co. ANTRIM
FEEHIN	Co. CORK	FERRIS	Co. KERRY
FEELY	ULSTER TARTAN	FERRITER	Co. KERRY
FEEN	Co. CORK	FERRY	ULSTER TARTAN
FEENAGHTY	Co. ROSCOMMON	FERRY	Co. DONEGAL

"IRISH" indicates a choice of a general Irish tartan: "All Ireland", "Tara", "Clodagh", "Irish National", "St. Patrick"

TARTANS FOR IRISH NAMES

Fetherson   *Fleck*

Anyone with a "County" Tartan may substitute one of the major "District" tartans listed below:

Galway, Leitrim, Mayo, Roscommon, Sligo:	Connacht tartan
Clare, Cork, Kerry, Limmerick, Tipperary, Waterford:	Munster tartan
Armagh, Down, Fermanagh, Louth, Monaghan:	Oriel tartan
Carlow, Dublin, Kildare, Kilkenny, Laois, Longford:	
Meath, Offaly, Westmeath, Wexford, Wicklow:	Leinster tartan
Antrim, Armagh, Cavan, Donegal, Down, Londonderry, Tyrone:	Ulster tartan

SURNAME	TARTAN	SURNAME	TARTAN
FETHERSTON	Co. WESTMEATH	FITZGERALD	LEINSTER TARTAN
FETHERSTON	Co. ROSCOMMON	FITZGERALD	Co. LIMMERICK
FEWER	Co. KILKENNY	FITZGERALD	Co. KILDARE
FEY	CONNACHT TARTAN	FITZGERALD	Co. CORK
FEY	ULSTER TARTAN	FITZGIBBINS	See FITZGIBBONS
FIDDES	FIDDES	FITZGIBBON(S)	Co.. MAYO
FIDDES	ULSTER TARTAN	FITZGIBBON(S)	Co. LIMMERICK
FIDDES	Co. ARMAGH	FITZHARRIS	Co. LIMMERICK
FIDGEON	ORIEL TARTAN	FITZHARRIS	Co. WEXFORD
FIELD(S)	ULSTER TARTAN	FITZHENRY	CONNACHT TARTAN
FIELDING	ULSTER TARTAN	FITZHENRY	LEINSTER TARTAN
FIGGIS	LEINSTER TARTAN	FITZHENRY	Co. KILDARE
FILBIN	Co. MAYO	FITZHENRY	Co. WEXFORD
FILGATE	Co. LOUTH	FITZMAURICE	Co. KERRY
FILLAN	Co. WATERFORD	FITZPATRICK	FITZPATRICK
FINAGHTY	Co. KERRY	FITZPATRICK	Co. LAOIS
FINAGHTY	Co. ROSCOMMON	FITZSIM(M)ON(S)	MUNSTER TARTAN
FINAN	CONNACHT TARTAN	FITZSIM(M)ON(S)	Co. CAVAN
FINCH	ULSTER TARTAN	FITZSIM(M)ON(S)	Co. DOWN
FINDLAY	FARQUHARSON	FITZSIM(M)ON(S)	Co. WESTMEATH
FINEGAN	See FINNEGAN	FITZSTEPHEN(S)	Co. WEXFORD
FINGLAS(S)	Co. DUBLIN	FITZWILLIAM	ULSTER TARTAN
FINLAN	Co. TIPPERARY	FITZWILLIAM	Co. DUBLIN
FINLAY	FARQUHARSON	FITZWILLIAM	Co. WICKLOW
FINLAY	ULSTER TARTAN	FIVEY	Co. DOWN
FINLAY	Co. ANTRIM	FIZZELL	See FITZELLE
FINLAY	Co. DONEGAL	FLACK	LINDSAY
FINN	CONNACHT TARTAN	FLACK	ULSTER TARTAN
FINN	Co. MONAGHAN	FLAHAVAN	Co. WATERFORD
FINN	Co. SLIGO	FLAHER	MUNSTER TARTAN
FINN	Co. LEITRIM	FLAHER	Co. CLARE
FINNAMORE	CONNACHT TARTAN	FLAHER	Co. TIPPERARY
FINNEGAN	FINNEGAN	FLAHERTY	Co. GALWAY
FINNEGAN	CLAN CIAN/O'CARROLL	FLAHERTY	Co. KERRY
FINNEGAN	ORIEL TARTAN	FLAHERTY	Co.OFFALY
FINNEGAN	CONNACHT TARTAN	FLAHIVE	Co. CLARE
FINNEGAN	Co. MAYO	FLAHY	Co. CLARE
FINNELL(Y)	Co. DUBLIN	FLANAG(H)AN	LEINSTER TARTAN
FINNERALL	Co. CLARE	FLANAG(H)AN	CLAN CIAN/O'CARROLL
FINNERAN	CONNACHT TARTAN	FLANAG(H)AN	Co. FERMANAGH
FINNERTY	Co. ROSCOMMON	FLANAG(H)AN	Co. OFFALY
FINNESSY	Co. WATERFORD	FLANAHY	Co. CLARE
FINNEY	ULSTER TARTAN	FLANNAG(H)AN	Co. WATERFORD
FINNING	ULSTER TARTAN	FLANNELLY	Co. SLIGO
FINNUCANE	Co. CLARE	FLANNERY	Co. LIMMERIK
FINURE	Co. KILKENNY	FLANNERY	Co. MAYO
FISHER	IRISH-See Footnote	FLATESBURY	Co. KILDARE
FITCH	ULSTER TARTAN	FLATLEY	Co. SLIGO
FITCH	Co. DOWN	FLATTERY	Co. CLARE
FITTON	IRISH-See Footnote	FLATTERY	Co. OFFALY
FITZELLE	ULSTER TARTAN	FLAVAHAN	Co. WATERFORD
FITZELLE	Co. ANTRIM	FLAVELE	ULSTER TARTAN
FITZERY	LEINSTER TARTAN	FLAVERTY	CONNACHT TARTAN
FITZEUSTACE	LEINSTER TARTAN	FLAVIN	Co. WATERFORD
FITZGERALD	FITZGERALD	FLECK	LINDSAY

"IRISH" indicates a choice of a general Irish tartan: "All Ireland", "Tara", "Clodagh", "Irish National", "St. Patrick"

TARTANS FOR IRISH NAMES

Fleck　　　　　　　　　　　　　　　　　　　　　　　　　　　　　　　　　*Frizelle*

"County" Tartan may substitute one of the major "District" tartans listed below:

Galway, Leitrim, Mayo, Roscommon, Sligo:	Connacht tartan
Clare, Cork, Kerry, Limmerick, Tipperary, Waterford:	Munster tartan
Armagh, Down, Fermanagh, Louth, Monaghan:	Oriel tartan
Carlow, Dublin, Kildare, Kilkenny, Laois, Longford:	
Meath, Offaly, Westmeath, Wexford, Wicklow:	Leinster tartan
Antrim, Armagh, Cavan, Donegal, Down, Londonderry, Tyrone:	Ulster tartan

SURNAME	TARTAN	SURNAME	TARTAN
FLECK	ULSTER TARTAN	FOSSITT	IRISH-See Footnote
FLEETWOOD	Co. WATERFORD	FOSTER	FOSTER
FLEMING	FLEMING	FOSTER	FORESTER
FLEMING	Co. CAVAN	FOSTER	ULSTER TARTAN
FLEMING	Co. LONGFORD	FOTTRELL	Co. DUBLIN
FLEMING	Co. MEATH	FOUDY	Co. MAYO
FLEMING	FLEMING	FOUHY	Co. CORK
FLETCHER	FLETCHER	FOURSIDES	See FORSYTHE
FLETCHER	ULSTER TARTAN	FOWLEY	Co. LEITRIM
FLEURY	Co. GALWAY	FOWLOO	Co. CORK
FLINN	FLYNN	FOX	ULSTER TARTAN
FLINN	ULSTER TARTAN	FOX	Co. TYRONE
FLINT	Co. DUBLIN	FOX	Co. LIMERICK
FLINTER	Co. KILDARE	FOX	Co. WESTMEATH
FLINTER	Co. WICKLOW	FOY	CONNACHT TARTAN
FLOOD	CLAN CIAN/O'CARROLL	FOYLAN	Co. WESTMEATH
FLOOD'	Co. LONGFORD	FOYLE	Co. LAOIS
FLOODY	See FLOOD	FOYNES	Co. MEATH
FLYNN	O' FLYNN	FRAHER	CONNACHT TARTAN
FLYNN	CONNACHT TARTAN	FRAHILL	O' FARRELL
FODAGHAN	ORIEL TARTAN	FRAHY	Co. CLARE
FODHA	IRISH-See Footnote	FRAIN	Co. ROSCOMMON
FOERY	CONNACHT TARTAN	FRAME	FRAME
FOGARTTY	CLAN CIAN/O'CARROLL	FRAME	ULSTER TARTAN
FOGARTY	Co. TIPPERARY	FRANCIS	Co. GALWAY
FOLAN(E)	CONNACHT TARTAN	FRANLKIN	MUNSTER TARTAN
FOLEY	LEINSTER TARTAN	FRANKLIN	Co. LIMMERICK
FOLEY	Co. CORK	FRANKLIN	Co. TIPPERARY
FOLEY	Co. KERRY	FRANKS	Co. LAOIS
FOLEY	Co. WATERFORD	FRANKS	Co. OFFALY
FOLLIN	LEINSTER TARTAN	FRASER	FRASER
FOLLIOT	ULSTER TARTAN	FRASER	ULSTER TARTAN
FOLSEY	Co. CLARE	FRASER	Co. ANTRIM
FONT	Co. GALWAY	FRASER	Co. DOWN
FOODY	ORIEL TARTAN	FRAUL	O' FARRELL
FOODY	Co. MAYO	FRAWLEY	O' FARELL
FOOHY	Co. CORK	FRAYNE	Co. ROSCOMMON
FORAN	Co. GALWAY	FRAZER	See FRASER
FORBES	FORBES	FREE	Co. KILDARE
FORDE	FORDE	FREEBORN(E)	ULSTER TARTAN
FORDE	Co. LEITRIM	FREELY	Co. MAYO
FOERY	CONNACHT TARTAN	FREEMAN	Co. WESTMEATH
FORHAN(E)	Co. CORK	FREEMAN	IRISH-See Footnote
FORKE	Co. KERRY	FREENEY	Co. KILKENNY
FORKE	Co. CORK	FREENEY	Co. WATERFORD
FORKER	FARQUHARSON	FREER	ORIEL TARTAN
FORKIN	Co. KERRY	FREHILL	Co. ROSCOMMON
FORRESTAL	Co. KILKENNY	FREHY	Co. CLARE
FORRESTUAL	Co. KILKENNY	FRENCH	CONNACHT TARTAN
FORREY	CONNACHT TARTAN	FRENCH	Co. GALWAY
FORSYTHE	FORSYTHE	FREW	ULSTER TARTAN
FORSYTHE	ULSTER TARTAN	FREWEN	Co. DUBLIN
FORTIN	Co. WEXFORD	FRIEL	ULSTER TARTAN
FORTUNE	Co. CARLOW	FRIEL	CONNACHT TARTAN
FORTY	Co. CARLOW	FRIZELL(E)	See FRASER

"IRISH indicates a choice of a general Irish tartan: "All Ireland", "Tara", "Clodagh", "Irish National", "St. Patrick"

TARTANS FOR IRISH NAMES

Anyone with a "County" Tartan may substitute one of the major "District" tartans listed below:

Galway, Leitrim, Mayo, Roscommon, Sligo:	Connacht tartan
Clare, Cork, Kerry, Limmerick, Tipperary, Waterford:	Munster tartan
Armagh, Down, Fermanagh, Louth, Monaghan:	Oriel tartan
Carlow, Dublin, Kildare, Kilkenny, Laois, Longford:	
Meath, Offaly, Westmeath, Wexford, Wicklow:	Leinster tartan
Antrim, Armagh, Cavan, Donegal, Down, Londonderry, Tyrone:	Ulster tartan

SURNAME	TARTAN	SURNAME	TARTAN
FROST	Co. CLARE	GALBRAITH	ULSTER TARTAN
FRY	ULSTER TARTAN	GALBRAITH	Co. GALWAY
FRYER	ORIEL TARTAN	GALBRAITH	Co. LAOIS
FUGE	Co. WATERFORD	GALE	LEINSTER TARTAN
FULHAM	Co. DUBLIN	GALL	Co. KILKENNEY
FULLAN,-EN	ULSTER TARTAN	GALLAGHER	ULSTER TARTAN
FULLAN,-EN	Co. TYRONE	GALLAGHER	Co. DONEGAL
FULLER	Co. KERRY	GALLAHUE	Co. CORK
FULLERTON	STUART of BUTE	GALLEN	Co. DONEGAL
FULLERTON	ULSTER TARTAN	GALLERY	Co. CLARE
FULLERTON	Co. ANTRIM	GALLESPY	GILLESPIE
FULMER	CLAN CIAN/O'CARROLL	GALLESPY	MAC PHERSON
FULTON	FULTON	GALLIGAN	Co. CAVAN
FULTON	ULSTER TARTAN	GALLIGAN	Co. SLIGO
FUREY	CLAN CIAN/O'CARROLL	GALLIN,-AN	Co. LEITRIM
FUREY	Co. TIPPERARY	GALLINA(GH)	Co. DONEGAL
FUREY	Co. WESTMEATH	GALLIVAN	Co. KERRY
FURLONG	Co. WEXFORD	GALLOGLY	ULSTER TARTAN
FURLONG	Co. WICKLOW	GALLON	Co. LEITRIM
FURNELL	Co. CORK	GALLOWAY	GALLOWAY DIST
FURNELL	Co. LIMERICK	GALLOWAY	ULSTER TARTAN
FURPHY	ULSTER TARTAN	GALVAN(E)	Co. CLARE
FURREY	Co. WESTMEATH	GALVIN(E)	Co. CLARE
FYAN	Co. MEATH	GALWAY,GALWEY	CONNACHT TARTAN
FYE	CONNACHT TARTAN	GALWAY,GALWEY	Co. GALWAY
FYE	MAC FIE	GAMBLE	ULSTER TARTAN
FYFE(E)	Co. FERMANAGH	GAMBLE	Co. CORK
FYLAN	Co. WATERFORD	GAMMELL	GAMMELL
FYLAND	Co. WESTMEATH	GAMMELL	ULSTER TARTAN
		GAMMON	Co. MAYO
		GAMMON	Co. WATERFORD
		GANLY	Co. LEITRIM
		GANNESSY	Co. CLARE
		GANNON	CONNACHT TARTAN
		GANNON	Co. MAYO
		GANTER	Co. DUBLIN
		GANTLEY	Co. LEITRIM
GABBETT	Co. LIMERICK	GARAHY	Co. OFFALY
GAFF	MAC GAUGH	GARAVAN	Co. MAYO
GAFF	Co. OFFALY	GARDE	Co. CORK
GAFFIGAN	Co. DUBLIN	GARDINER	JARDINE
GAFFNEY	ULSTER TARTAN	GARDINER	ULSTER TARTAN
GAFFNEY	Co. CAVAN	GARETTY	CONNACHT TARTAN
GAGGY	ULSTER TARTAN	GARGAN	Co. CAVAN
GAHAGAN	O' NEILL	GARGAN	Co. LOUTH
GAHAGAN	Co. WESTMEATH	GARIGAN	Co. CAVAN
GAHAN	Co. CARLOW	GARLAND	ORIEL TARTAN
GAHAN	Co. WEXFORD	GARNER	JARDINE
GAHAN	Co. WICKLOW	GARRAG(H)AN	Co. MEATH
GAINE	ULSTER TARTAN	GARRETT	ULSTER TARTAN
GAINOR	Co. LONGFORD	GARRIGAN	Co. CAVAN
GAITENS	ULSTER TARTAN	GARRIGHY	CONNACHT TARTAN
GAITENS	Co. DONEGAL	GARRIHY	Co. CLARE
GALBALLY	Co. KILDARE	GARRITY	CONNACHT TARTAN
GALBRAITH	GALBRAITH	GARRITY	ORIEL TARTAN

G

"IRISH" indicates a choice of a general Irish tartan: "All Ireland", "Tara", "Clodagh", "Irish National", "St. Patrick"

TARTANS FOR IRISH NAMES

Garry

Gillanders

Anyone with a "County" Tartan may substitute one of the major "District" tartans listed below:.

Galway, Leitrim, Mayo, Roscommon, Sligo:	Connacht tartan
Clare, Cork, Kerry, Limmerick, Tipperary, Waterford:	Munster tartan
Armagh, Down, Fermanagh, Louth, Monaghan:	Oriel tartan
Carlow, Dublin, Kildare, Kilkenny, Laois, Longford:	
Meath, Offaly, Westmeath, Wexford, Wicklow:	Leinster tartan
Antrim, Armagh, Cavan, Donegal, Down, Londonderry, Tyrone:	Ulster tartan

SURNAME	TARTAN	SURNAME	TARTAN
GARRY	CONNACHT TARTAN	GEROUGHTY	CONNACHT TARTAN
GARRY	CLAN CIAN/O'CARROLL	GERRY	CLAN CIAN/O'CARROLL
GARTY	CONNACHT TARTAN	GERTY	CONNACHT TARTAN
GARTY	O' CONNOR	GERVAIS	Co. CORK
GARVAN	O' NEILL	GETHIN	Co. WEXFORD
GARVEY	Co. WEXFORD	GETHINGS	Co. WEXFORD
GARVILLE	CLAN CIAN/O'CARROLL	GETIGAN	ULSTER TARTAN
GARVIN	Co. MAYO	GETTINS	ULSTER TARTAN
GARY	CLAN CIAN/O'CARROLL	GETTY	HAY
GASKIN	LEINSTER TARTAN	GETTY	ULSTER TARTAN
GASON	CONNACHT TARTAN	GIBBON(S)	CONNACHT TARTAN
GASTON	LEINSTER TARTAN	GIBBON(S)	Co. MAYO
GATCHELL	Co. WATERFORD	GIBBS	GIBBS
GATELY	Co. ROSCOMMON	GIBBS	ULSTER TARTAN
GATTINS	ULSTER TARTAN	GIBBSON	See GIBBS
GATTINS	Co. DONEGAL	GIBLIN	Co. ROSCOMMON
GAUGHAN	Co. MAYO	GIBNEY	Co. MEATH
GAUGHNEY	ULSTER TARTAN	GIBSON	See GIBBS
GAULE	Co. KILKENNY	GIDERY	Co. TIPPERARY
GAULT	ULSTER TARTAN	GIFFEN	ULSTER TARTAN
GAULT	Co. ANTRIM	GIFFEN	Co. ANTRIM
GAUSSEN	CONNACHT TARTAN	GIFFERTY	ULSTER TARTAN
GAVAG(H)AN	CONNACHT TARTAN	GIFFORD	Co. DOWN
GAVAG(H)AN	Co. MAYO	GIHEN, GIHEEN	Co. ROSCOMMON
GAVIGAN	Co. DUBLIN	GILBERT	Co. LOUTH
GAVIN(E)	CONNACHT TARTAN	GILBERT	Co. WESTMEATH
GAVIN(E)	Co. MAYO	GILBEY	OGILVIE
GAWLEY	MAC AULAY	GILBOY	OGILVIE
GAWLEY	CONNACHT TARTAN	GILBRIDE	ULSTER TARTAN
GAY	CONNACHT TARTAN	GILBRIDE	Co. DONEGAL
GAYER	ULSTER TARTAN	GILCHRIS	ULSTER TARTAN
GAYNARD	CONNACHT TARTAN	GILCHRIST	CONNACHT TARTAN
GAYNOR	Co. LONGFORD	GILDEA	CONNACHT TARTAN
GEANE(Y)	Co. CORK	GILDEA	Co. CLARE
GEANOR	Co. LONGFORD	GILDUFF	Co. GALWAY
GEARAN	Co. MAYO	GILES	GILLIES
GEARY	CLAN CIAN/O'CARROLL	GILES	Co. LOUTH
GEARY	Co. CORK	GILESPIE	See GILLESPIE
GEAVENEY	CONNACHT TARTAN	GILFILLAN	MAC LELLEN
GEEHAN	LEINSTER TARTAN	GILFOYLE	Co. OFFALY
GEEHAN	Co. LOUTH	GILFOYLE	Co. TIPPERARY
GEEHAN	Co. WICKLOW	GILGAN	Co. SLIGO
GEHERAN	CONNACHT TARTAN	GILGAR	CONNACHT TARTAN
GENTY	CONNACHT TARTAN	GILGUNN	GUNN
GEOFFREY	ULSTER TARTAN	GILGUNN	Co. FERMANAGH
GEOGHEGAN	O' NEILL	GILHOOL	Co. SLIGO
GEOGHERY	Co. OFFALY	GILHOOLY	Co. LEITRIM
GEORAVAN	ULSTER TARTAN	GILHOOLY	Co. ROSCOMMON
GEORGAS	ULSTER TARTAN	GILKELLY	Co. GALWAY
GEORGE	ULSTER TARTAN	GILKINSON	See GILCHRIST
GEORGESON	ULSTER TARTAN	GILL	MAC GILL
GERAGHTY	Co. MAYO	GILL	Co. OFFALY
GERAGHTY	CONNACHT TARTAN	GILLAN	MAC LELLAN
GERAN, GERIN	Co. KERRY	GILLAN	ULSTER TARTAN
GERNON	Co. MONAGHAN	GILLANDERS	ORIEL TARTAN

"IRISH" indicates a choice of a general Irish tartan: "All Ireland", "Tara", "Clodagh", "Irish National", "St. Patrick"

31

TARTANS FOR IRISH NAMES

Gilleece   *Godfrey*

"County" Tartan may substitute one of the major "District" tartans listed below:

Galway, Leitrim, Mayo, Roscommon, Sligo:	Connacht tartan
Clare, Cork, Kerry, Limmerick, Tipperary, Waterford:	Munster tartan
Armagh, Down, Fermanagh, Louth, Monaghan:	Oriel tartan
Carlow, Dublin, Kildare, Kilkenny, Laois, Longford:	
Meath, Offaly, Westmeath, Wexford, Wicklow:	Leinster tartan
Antrim, Armagh, Cavan, Donegal, Down, Londonderry, Tyrone:	Ulster tartan

SURNAME	TARTAN	SURNAME	TARTAN
GILLEECE	Co. FERMANAGH	GLADDERY	Co. TYRONE
GILLEEN	CONNACHT TARTAN	GLAFFY	CONNACHT TARTAN
GILLEN	CONNACHT TARTAN	GLANCEY	CLAN CIAN/O'CARROLL
GILLEN	Co. MAYO	GLANCY	CLAN CIAN/O'CARROLL
GILLERAN	Co. ROSCPMMON	GLANDERS	Co. MONAGHAN
GILLESPIE	GILLESPIE	GLANFIELD	Co. CORK
GILLESPIE	ULSTER TARTAN	GLANNY	GLENN
GILLESPIE	Co. DONEGAL	GLANVILLE	Co. CORK
GILLHOON	ULSTER TARTAN	GLASCOE	GLASGOW DIST
GILLIARD	Co. DOWN	GLASGOW	ULSTER TARTAN
GILLICE	Co. FERMANAGH	GLASHAN	MAC GLASHAN
GILLIGAN	Co. SLIGO	GLASHAN	ULSTER TARTAN
GILLILAND	MAC LELLAN	GLASHBY	GILLESPIE
GILLMAN	Co. CORK	GLASHBY	Co. LOUTH
GILLOOLY	Co. LEITRIM	GLASHEEN	MAC GLASHAN
GILLORAN	Co. ROSCOMMON	GLASHEEN	Co. TIPPERARY
GILMARTIN	Co. LEITRIM	GLASPEY	GILLESPIE
GILMER	ULSTER TARTAN	GLASS	ULSTER TARTAN
GILMARTIN	O' NEILL	GLASSCOCK	Co. KILDARE
GILMORE	MORRISON	GLAVIN	ULSTER TARTAN
GILMORE	ORIEL TARTAN	GLAZIER	Co. KERRY
GILMORE	ULSTER TARTAN	GLEASON	CLAN CIAN/O'CARROLL
GILMORE	Co. LOUTH	GLEASON	Co. TIPPERARY
GILNAGH	Co. LONGFORD	GLEASURE	Co. KERRY
GILOWLY	Co. LEITRIM	GLEESE	Co. GALWAY
GILPATRICK	Co. LAOIS	GLEESON	CLAN CIAN/O'CARROLL
GILPIN	ORIEL TARTAN	GLEESON	Co. TIPPERARY
GILPIN	Co. SLIGO	GLENAGHAN	ULSTER TARTAN
GILRAIN	Co. LEITRIM	GLENANE	Co. TIPPERARY
GILREA	Co. SLIGO	GLENDENNING	ULSTER TARTAN
GILREEVY	ULSTER TARTAN	GLENDON	Co. KILKENNY
GILROY	ULSTER TARTAN	GLENN	GLENN
GILROY	Co. MONAGHAN	GLENNON	LEINSTER TARTAN
GILSENAN	ULSTER TARTAN	GLENNON	Co. LAOIS
GILSHENAN	ULSTER TARTAN	GLENNON	Co. WESTMEATH
GILSON	Co. OFFALY	GLENNY	GLENN
GILTENAN	Co. CLARE	GLINDON	Co. TIPPERARY
GILTRAP	Co. DUBLIN	GLINN	GLENN
GILVANE	CONNACHT TARTAN	GLINN	CLAN CIAN/O'CARROLL
GILVANY	ULSTER TARTAN	GLISSANE	Co. KERRY
GIN(N)A	Co. KERRY	GLMORE	Co. DOWN
GINNANE	Co. CLARE	GLOAG	CLAN CIAN/O'CARROLL
GINNAW	Co. KERRY	GLOAKS	CLAN CIAN/O'CARROLL
GINNELL	Co. WESTMEATH	GLORNEY	Co. KILKENNY
GINNEVAN	Co. CORK	GLOSTER	Co. LIMMERICK
GINNEVAN	Co. WATERFORD	GLOVER	ULSTER TARTAN
GINTY	CONNACHT TARTAN	GLYNN	GLENN
GIPSEY	GIBBS	GLYNN	CONNACHT TARTAN
GIREY	Co. LIMERICK	GLYNN	CLAN CIAN/O'CARROLL
GIRTY	CONNACHT TARTAN	GOAGAN	Co. CORK
GIRVAN	ULSTER TARTAN	GOALEY	Co. GALWAY
GISSANE	Co. KERRY	GOAN	ULSTER TARTAN
GIVEEN(S)	Co. DONEGAL	GOBBAN	ULSTER TARTAN
GIVEN(S)	Co. DONEGAL	GOBBAN	SMITH
GLACKEN	ULSTER TARTAN	GODFREY	MAC GUIRE

"IRISH indicates a choice of a general Irish tartan: "All Ireland", "Tara", "Clodagh", "Irish National", "St. Patrick"

TARTANS FOR IRISH NAMES

Godsell   *Grear*

Anyone with a "County" Tartan may substitute one of the major "District" tartans listed below:.

Galway, Leitrim, Mayo, Roscommon, Sligo:	**Connacht tartan**
Clare, Cork, Kerry, Limmerick, Tipperary, Waterford:	**Munster tartan**
Armagh, Down, Fermanagh, Louth, Monaghan:	**Oriel tartan**
Carlow, Dublin, Kildare, Kilkenny, Laois, Longford:	
Meath, Offaly, Westmeath, Wexford, Wicklow:	**Leinster tartan**
Antrim, Armagh, Cavan, Donegal, Down, Londonderry, Tyrone:	**Ulster tartan**

SURNAME	TARTAN	SURNAME	TARTAN
GODSELL	Co. LIMMERICK	GOSLING	Co. CORK
GODWIN	ULSTER TARTAN	GOSNELL	Co. CORK
GODWIN	CONNACHT TARTAN	GOSSAN	CONNACHT TARTAN
GODWIN	Co. MAYO	GOUGH	MAC GAUGH
GOFF	MAC GAUGH	GOULD	Co. CORK
GOGAN	Co. CORK	GOULDING	Co. CORK
GOGARTY	Co. MEATH	GOURLEY	ULSTER TARTAN
GOGGIN(S)	Co. CORK	GOVERN(E)Y	Co. CARLOW
GOHERY	MAC GUIRE	GOW	GOW
GOHERY	Co. OFFALY	GOW	Co. CAVAN
GOING	Co. TIPPERARY	GRACE	GRACIE
GOLDEN	Co. CORK	GRACE	Co. KILKENNY
GOLDIE	Co. OFFALY	GRACE	CLAN CIAN/O'CARROLL
GOLDSMTH	ULSTER TARTAN	GRACEN	ORIEL TARTAN
GOLDSMITH	Co. DOWN	GRACIE,GRACEY	GRACIE
GOLIGHER	Co. DONEGAL	GRACIE,GRACEY	Co. KILKENNY
GOLIGHTLY	ORIEL TARTAN	GRADY	GRADY
GOLOGLY	Co. MONAGHAN	GRADY	CONNACHT TARTAN
GOLY	Co. CORK	GRADY	ULSTER TARTAN
GOLY	Co. KERRY	GRADY	Co. CLARE
GONNE	GUNN	GRAECEN	ORIEL TARTAN
GONOUDE	MAC NACHTEN	GRAHAM	GRAHAM
GOOD	CLAN CIAN/O'CARROLL	GRAHAM	ORIEL TARTAN
GOOD	Co. LAOIS	GRAHAM	Co. DOWN
GOODALL	Co. WEXFORD	GRAHAM	Co. FERMANAGH
GOODBODY {1}	Co. OFFALY	GRAHAM	ULSTER TARTAN
GOODFELLOW	ULSTER TARTAN	GRAHAN	GRAHAM
GOODMAN	Co. WICKLOW	GRAILLS	ULSTER TARTAN
GOODWIN	ULSTER TARTAN	GRAINGER	GRAINGER
GOOGIN	Co. CORK	GRAINGER	ULSTER TARTAN
GOOLD	Co. CORK	GRAINGER	Co. ANTRIM
GOOLEY	Co. CORK	GRALTON	Co. ROSCOMMON
GOOLY	Co. KERRY	GRANEY	ULSTER TARTAN
GOONAN(E)	Co. CLARE	GRANFIELD	Co. KERRY
GOONEY	Co. CLARE	GRANNY	ULSTER TARTAN
GORDON	"Red" GORDON	GRANT	GRANT
GORDON	ULSTER TARTAN	GRANT	ULSTER TARTAN
GORDON	CONNACHT TARTAN	GRANVILLE	Co. KERRY
GORDON	LEINSTER TARTAN	GRATTAN	Co. TIPPERARY
GORDON	MUNSTER TARTAN	GRAVES	ULSTER TARTAN
GORE	CONNACHT TARTAN	GRAVES	Co. CORK
GOREY	Co. CAVAN	GRAVES	Co. OFFALY
GOREY	LEINSTER TARTAN	GRAY	GRAY
GORGES	ULSTER TARTAN	GRAY	CONNACHT TARTAN
GORHAM	Co. KERRY	GRAYHAN	GRAHAM
GORISH	ORIEL TARTAN	GRAYSON	GRAY
GORMALLY	ULSTER TARTAN	GRAYSON	OREL TARTAN
GORMAN	ORIEL TARTAN	GREACEN	ORIEL TARTAN
GORMAN	Co. MAYO	GREADY	GRADY
GORMANGAN	Co. GALWAY	GREADY	Co. MAYO
GORMELY	CONNACHT TARTAN	GREAGH	CLAN CIAN/O'CARROLL
GORMICAN	Co. GALWAY	GREAGHAN	CONNACHT TARTAN
GORRY	MAC GUIRE	GREALISH	CONNACHT TARTAN
GORRY	LEINSTER TARTAN	GREALLY	CONNACHT TARTAN
GOSLIN	LEINSTER TARTAN	GREAR	See GREER

"IRISH" indicates a choice of a general Irish tartan: "All Ireland", "Tara", "Clodagh", "Irish National", "St. Patrick"

33

Anyone with a "County" Tartan may substitute one of the major "District" tartans listed below:

Galway, Leitrim, Mayo, Roscommon, Sligo:	Connacht tartan
Clare, Cork, Kerry, Limmerick, Tipperary, Waterford:	Munster tartan
Armagh, Down, Fermanagh, Louth, Monaghan:	Oriel tartan
Carlow, Dublin, Kildare, Kilkenny, Laois, Longford:	
Meath, Offaly, Westmeath, Wexford, Wicklow:	Leinster tartan
Antrim, Armagh, Cavan, Donegal, Down, Londonderry, Tyrone:	Ulster tartan

SURNAME	TARTAN	SURNAME	TARTAN
GREAVES	See GRAVES	GUINRVAN	Co. WATERFORD
GREEHY.	Co. WATERFORD	GUIREY	Co. LIMERICK
GREEN(E)	GREENE	GUISSANE	Co. CLARE
GREEN(E)	ULSTER TARTAN	GULHAN	Co. ROSCOMMON
GREEN(E)	Co. TYRONE	GULHE(E)N	Co. ROSCOMMON
GREEN(E)	O' SULLIVAN	GULLEN	Co. DONEGAL
GREEN(E)	ULSTER TARTAN	GUNNELL	Co. LOUTH
GREENAN	Co. SLIGO	GUNNING	ULSTER TARTAN
GREENAWAY	ULSTER TARTAN	GUNNING	CONNACHT TARTAN
GREENHAY	ULSTER TARTAN	GUNNING	Co. CLARE
GREER	MAC GREGOR	GUNNING	Co. KERRY
GREER	ULSTER TARTAN	GUNSHENAN	Co. LONGFORD
GREEVES	See GRAVES	GURKIN	CLAN CIAN/O'CARROLL
GREGAN	LEINSTER TARTAN	GURKIN	CONNACHT TARTAN
GREGG	MAC GREGOR	GURRY	LEINSTER TARTAN
GREGORY	Co. GALWAY	GUTHRIE	GUTHRIE
GREGORY	Co. KERRY	GUTHRIE	ULSTER TARTAN
GREHAN	CONNACHT TARTAN	GUY	ULSTER TARTAN
GREW	Co. ARMAGH	GWEEHIN	IRISH-See Footnote
GREW	ULSTER TARTAN	GWYNN	Co. DUBLIN
GREY	See GRAY		
GRIBBEN	ULSTER TARTAN		
GRIER	See GREER		
GRIERSON I]	MAC GREGOR		
GRIEVE(S)	See GRAVES	**H**	
GRIFFIN	MUNSTER TARTAN		
GRIFFIN	Co. CLARE		
GRIFFIN	Co. KERRY		
GRIFFITH	Co. KILKENNY	HABERLIN	Co. KILKENNY
GRIMES	ULSTER TARTAN	HACKETT	ULSTER TARTAN
GRIMLEY	Co. ARMAGH	HACKETT	Co. KILDARE
GRODEN, GRODIN	CONNACHT TARTAN	HACKETT	Co. KILKENNY
GROGAN	Co. ROSCOMMON	HADDEN,-ON	Co. LOUTH
GROGGAN	ULSTER TARTAN	HADDEN,-ON	ULSTER TARTAN
GROMMELL	Co. LIMMERICK	HADDOCK	Co. ARMAGH
GRONAN	Co. ARMAGH	HADE	Co. CARLOW
GROOGAN	Co. ROSCOMMON	HADIAN	Co. ROSCOMMON
GROWNEY	Co. WESTMEATH	HADIGAN	Co. CLARE
GRUBB	Co. WATERFORD	HADNETT	Co. CORK
GRUGAN	See GROGAN	HADSOR	Co. LOUTH
GRUMLEY	LEINSTER TARTAN	HAFFEY	ULSTER TARTAN
GUBBINS	ULSTER TARTAN	HAFFORD	Co. DUBLIN
GUBBINS	Co. LIMMERICK	HAFFORD	Co. WESTMEATH
GUDA	CLAN CIAN/O'CARROLL	HAGAN	ORIEL TARTAN
GUERAN	Co. LIMERICK	HAGAN	ULSTER TARTAN
GUFF	See MAC GAUGH	HAGGERTY	ULSTER TARTAN
GUIDER(A)	Co. TIPPERARY	HAGHTIR	Co. TIPPERARY
GUIHAN	Co. ROSCOMMON	HAHER	Co. CLARE
GUIHEN,-EEN	Co. ROSCOMMON	HAHERNEY	CONNACHT TARTAN
GUINA	See GINA	HAHESSY	Co. GALWAY
GUINANE	Co. OFFALY	HAIDE	Co. CARLOW
GUINEVAN	Co. CORK	HAIER	Co. CLARE
GUINEY	Co. KERRY	HAIGNEY	ORIEL TARTAN
GUINNESS	ULSTER TARTAN	HAINES	Co. CORK
GUINNEVAN	Co. WATERFORD	HAINEY	ORIEL TARTAN

"IRISH" indicates a choice of a general Irish tartan: "All Ireland", "Tara", "Clodagh", "Irish National", "St. Patrick"

TARTANS FOR IRISH NAMES

Anyone with a "County" Tartan may substitute one of the major "District" tartans listed below:

Galway, Leitrim, Mayo, Roscommon, Sligo:	Connacht tartan
Clare, Cork, Kerry, Limmerick, Tipperary, Waterford:	Munster tartan
Armagh, Down, Fermanagh, Louth, Monaghan:	Oriel tartan
Carlow, Dublin, Kildare, Kilkenny, Laois, Longford:	
Meath, Offaly, Westmeath, Wexford, Wicklow:	Leinster tartan
Antrim, Armagh, Cavan, Donegal, Down, Londonderry, Tyrone:	Ulster tartan

SURNAME	TARTAN	SURNAME	TARTAN
HAIRT	ULSTER TARTAN	HANNA(H)	HANNA
HALDEN	ORIEL TARTAN	HANNA(H)	ULSTER TARTAN
HALE(S)	ULSTER TARTAN	HANNAY	See HANNA
HALE(S)	Co. CORK	HANNON	Co. GALWAY
HALFERTY	ULSTER TARTAN	HANRAHAN	CLAN CIAN/O'CARROLL
HALFERTY	Co. DONEGAL	HANRAHAN	Co. CLARE
HALFPENNY	Co. MONAGHAN	HANSBERY	CONNACHT TARTAN
HALL	HALL	HANVEY	Co. DOWN
HALL	ULSTER TARTAN	HARAN	See HERRON
HALL	Co. ANTRIM	HARE	ORIEL TARTAN
HALL	Co. ARMAGH	HARE	CLAN CIAN/O'CARROLL
HALLAHAN	Co. CORK	HARFORD	Co. KILKENNY
HALLEY	MUNSTER TARTAN	HARGADAN	Co. SLIGO
HALLEY	CLAN CIAN/O'CARROLL	HARGAN	ULSTER TARTAN
HALLEY	Co. CLARE	HARKAN	ULSTER TARTAN
HALLEY	Co. WATERFORD	HARKIN(S)	Co. DONEGAL
HALLEY	Co. TIPPERARY	HARKNESS	ULSTER TARTAN
HALLGHAN	Co. WATERFORD	HARLAND	Co. ARMAGH
HALLIDAY	ULSTER TARTAN	HARLEY	CLAN CIAN/O'CARROLL
HALLIGAN	ORIEL TARTAN	HARLEY	Co. CORK
HALLIHY	Co. WATERFORD	HARMAN	LEINSTER TARTAN
HALLIN	Co. KILKENNY	HARMER	HARMER
HALLINAN	MUNSTER TARTAN	HARMER	ULSTER TARTAN
HALLINAN	Co. LIMMERICK	HARMON	Co. LOUTH
HALLINAN	Co. TIPPERARY	HARNEDY	Co. CORK
HALLION	Co. KILKENNY	HARNET(T)	Co. LIMMERICK
HALLISSEY	Co. KERRY	HARNEY	CONNACHT TARTAN
HALLORAN	CONNACHT TARTAN	HAROLD	Co. DUBLIN
HALLORAN	Co. GALWAY	HAROLD	Co. LIMMERICK
HALLY	CLAN CIAN/O'CARROLL	HAROUGHTEN	Co. ROSCOMMON
HALLY	Co. WATERFORD	HARPER	Co. WATERFORD
HALPENY	Co. MONAGHAN	HARPER	Co. WEXFORD
HALPIN	Co. LIMERICK	HARPUR	Co. WEXFORD
HALTAGHAN	ULSTER TARTAN	HARRIGAN	MUNSTER TARTAN
HALTON	ULSTER TARTAN	HARRILY	Co. CORK
HALVERTY	ULSTER TARTAN	HARRINGTON	CONNACHT TARTAN
HALVERTY	Co. DONEGAL	HARRIS	LEINSTER TARTAN
HALY	Co. CORK	HARRIS	MUNSTER TARTAN
HALY	Co. LIMERICK	HARRISON	ULSTER TARTAN
HAMBERY	Co. GALWAY	HARRISON	Co. DOWN
HAMBERY	CONNACHT TARTAN	HARRON	ORIEL TARTAN
HAMBOURGH	Co. CLARE	HARRON	Co. CORK
HAMBURGH	CONNACHT TARTAN	HARROT	ULSTER TARTAN
HAMILL	HAMILTON	HART(E)	HART
HAMILL	ORIEL TARTAN	HART(E)	ULSTER TARTAN
HAMILL	ULSTER TARTAN	HARTIGAN	Co. CORK
HAMILTON	HAMILTON	HARTLEY	Co. WEXFORD
HAMILTON	ULSTER TARTAN	HARTNET(T)	Co. CORK
HANAGAN	See HANNIGAN	HARTPOOL	ULSTER TARTAN
HANBURY	CONNACHT TARTAN	HARTRY	CONNACHT TARTAN
HANBURY	Co. GALWAY	HARTY	Co. TIPERRARY
HAND	Co. MEATH	HARVEY	ULSTER TARTAN
HANDRICK	Co. WEXFORD	HARWOOD	Co. CORK
HANERTY	Co. GALWAY	HASELDEN	Co. DOWN
HANLY	Co. WESTEATH	HASKIN(S)	CONNACHT TARTAN

"IRISH" indicates a choice of a general Irish tartan: "All Ireland", "Tara", "Clodagh", "Irish National", "St. Patrick"

TARTANS FOR IRISH NAMES

Haslan   *Helley*

Anyone with a "County" Tartan may substitute one of the major "District" tartans listed below:

Galway, Leitrim, Mayo, Roscommon, Sligo:	Connacht tartan
Clare, Cork, Kerry, Limmerick, Tipperary, Waterford:	Munster tartan
Armagh, Down, Fermanagh, Louth, Monaghan:	Oriel tartan
Carlow, Dublin, Kildare, Kilkenny, Laois, Longford:	
Meath, Offaly, Westmeath, Wexford, Wicklow:	Leinster tartan
Antrim, Armagh, Cavan, Donegal, Down, Londonderry, Tyrone:	Ulster tartan

SURNAME	TARTAN	SURNAME	TARTAN
HASLAN	LEINSTER TARTAN	HEALY	CLAN CIAN/O'CARROLL
HASLAN	Co. LAOIS	HEALY	Co. CORK
HASLAN	Co. OFFALY	HEALY	Co. KERRY
HASLIP	See HYSLOP	HEANAHAN	Co. MAYO
HASSAN	Co. LONDONDERRY	HEANEY	ORIEL TARTAN
HASSARD	LEINSTER TARTAN	HEANEY	Co. LOUTH
HASSETT	Co. CLARE	HEAPHY	Co. WATERFORD
HASSON	Co. WEXFORD	HEAPHY	LEINSTER TARTAN
HASTIE	MAC DERMOT	HEAR	ULSTER TARTAN
HASTING(S)	MAC DERMOT	HEARLD	ULSTER TARTAN
HATTON	Co. ANTRIM	HEARNE	CLAN CIAN/O'CARROLL
HATTON	Co. LONDONDERRY	HEARNE	Co. WATERFORD
HATTON	ULSTER TARTAN	HEARON	Co. WEXFORD
HAUGH	Co. CLARE	HEARST	ULSTER TARTAN
HAUGHEY	ULSTER TARTAN	HEARTY	ORIEL TARTAN
HAUGHLAN(D)	Co. TIPPERARY	HEARTY	Co. CORK
HAUGHTER	Co. TIPPERARY	HEARY	Co. MEATH
HAUGHTON	Co. TIPPERARY	HEATH	Co. DUBLIN.
HAVEN	Co. WESTMEATH	HEATHERINGTON	Co. LAOIS
HAVENTY	ULSTER TARTAN	HEATHERMAN	Co. LAOIS
HAVERAN	ULSTER TARTAN	HEATLEY	Co. ARMAGH
HAVLIN	Co. DONEGAL	HEATON	Co. OFFALY
HAVRON	ULSTER TARTAN	HEAVEN(S)	Co. OFFALY
HAWTHORNE	MAC DONALD	HEAVY	ORIEL TARTAN
HAWTHORNE	ULSTER TARTAN	HEAVY	Co. MONAGHAN
HAY	HAY	HEDERMAN	Co. CLARE
HAY	ULSTER TARTAN	HEDIAN	Co. ROSCOMMON
HAYBURN	HEPBURN	HEDIGAN	Co. CLARE
HAYBURN	ULSTER TARTAN	HEDIVAN	Co. WESTMEATH
HAYDAN	Co. CARLOW	HEDNAN	Co. WESTMEATH
HAYDE	Co. CARLOW	HEDUVAN	Co. WESTMEATH
HAYDEN	Co. CARLOW	HEELAN(D)	Co. CORK
HAYDOCK	Co. ARMAGH	HEENAN	Co. OFFALY
HAYES	HAYES	HEENEY	ORIEL TARTAN
HAYES	Co. DONEGAL	HEERY	Co. CAVAN
HAYES	LEINSTER TARTAN	HEEVER	MAC IVER
HAYES	Co. MEATH	HEFFERNAN	CLAN CIAN/O'CARROLL
HAYES	Co. WEXFORD	HEFFERNAN	MUNSTER TARTAN
HAYLES	Co. CORK	HEFFERNAN	Co. LIMMERICK
HAYNE	Co. KILKENNY	HEFFERNAN	Co. TIPPERARY
HAYNES	Co. CORK	HEFFRON	Co. MAYO
HAZETON	Co. ARMAGH	HEGAN	Co. ARMAGH
HAZLETT	ULSTER TARTAN	HEGARTY	ULSTER TARTAN
HEA	Co. CORK	HEGHER	Co. CLARE
HEAD(E)	Co. MEATH	HEGNEAY	ORIEL TARTAN
HEAD(E)	Co. TIPPERARY	HEGNEY	ORIEL TARTAN
HEADON	Co. WEXFORD	HEHIR	CLAN CIAN/O'CARROLL
HEADY	ULSTER TARTAN	HEHIR	Co. CLARE
HEAFY	Co. WATERFORD	HELEHAN	Co. WATERFORD
HEAGNEY	ORIEL TARTAN	HELLEN	Co. CORK
HEALAN(D)	Co. CORK	HEL(L)Y	CONNACHT TARTAN
HEALIHY	CONNACHT TARTAN	HEL(L)Y	Co. SLIGO
HEALY	HEALY	HEL(L)Y	CLAN CIAN/O'CARROLL
HEALY	MUNSTER TARTAN	HEL(L)Y	Co. LAOIS
		HEL(L)Y	Co. LIMMERICK

"IRISH" indicates a choice of a general Irish tartan: "All Ireland", "Tara", "Clodagh", "Irish National", "St. Patrick"

36

Anyone with a "County" Tartan may substitute one of the major "District" tartans listed below:

Galway, Leitrim, Mayo, Roscommon, Sligo:	**Connacht tartan**
Clare, Cork, Kerry, Limmerick, Tipperary, Waterford:	**Munster tartan**
Armagh, Down, Fermanagh, Louth, Monaghan:	**Oriel tartan**
Carlow, Dublin, Kildare, Kilkenny, Laois, Longford:	
Meath, Offaly, Westmeath, Wexford, Wicklow:	**Leinster tartan**
Antrim, Armagh, Cavan, Donegal, Down, Londonderry, Tyrone:	**Ulster tartan**

SURNAME	TARTAN	SURNAME	TARTAN
HEMPERHALL	Co. WICKLOW	HERR	Co. CLARE
HEMPHILL	AYRSHIRE DIST.	HERRAN	ORIEL TARTAN
HEMPHILL	Co. LONDONDERRY	HERRERAN	ULSTER TARTAN
HEMPHILL	SEMPILL	HERRON	ULSTER TARTAN
HENAGHAN	See HENNIGAN	HERRON	CLAN CIAN/O'CARROLL
HENANUE	Co. MAYO	HERRON	Co. ARMAGH
HENCHY	Co. CLARE	HERRICK	ULSTER TARTAN
HENDERSON	HENDERSON	HESKIN	CONNACHT TARTAN
HENDERSON	ULSTER TARTAN	HESLIN	LEINSTER TARTAN
HENDRICK	Co. WEXFORD	HESLIP	See HYSLOP
HENDRON	HENDERSON	HESLITT	ULSTER TARTAN
HENDRON	ULSTER TARTAN	HESSLON	CONNACHT TARTAN
HENDRON	Co. ARMAGH	HESTER	Co. MAYO
HENDRY,-IE	MAC NACHTEN	HESTON	HESTON
HENDRY,-IE	ULSTER TARTAN	HESTON	Co. MAYO
HENDY	Co. KILDARE	HESTON	MAC DERMAID
HENEBRY	Co. KILDARE	HEUSSON	MAC KAY
HENEBRY	Co. WATERFORD	HEUSTAN,-ON	See HOUSTON
HENEHAN	CLAN CIAN/O'CARROLL	HEVER	MAC IVER
HENERY	ULSTER TARTAN	HEVER	Co. SLIGO
HENIHAN	Co. MAYO	HEVERIN	Co. MAYO
HENLEY	CONNACHT TARTAN	HEVIGAN	CONNACHT TARTAN
HENNELLY	Co. MAYO	HEVIGAN	Co. GALWAY
HENNERSON	See HENDERSON	HEVIGAN	Co. ROSCOMMON
HENNERTY	Co. MAYO	HEVIN	Co. MAYO
HENNESSY	LEINSTER TARTAN	HEWITT	MUNSTER TARTAN
HENNESSY	Co. CORK	HEWLETT	Co. WEXFORD
HENNESSY	Co. DUBLIN	HEWSON	MAC KAY
HENNESSY	Co. MEATH	HEWSTON	See HOUSTON
HENNESSY	Co. OFFALY	HEYBURN	HEPBURN
HENNIGAN	HENNIGAN	HEYBURN	ULSTER TARTAN
HENNIGAN	Co. CORK	HEYDOCK	Co. KILDARE
HENNIGAN	Co. MAYO	HEYES	See HAYES
HENNING	ULSTER TARTAN	HEYFRON	CLAN CIAN/O'CARROLL
HENRICK	Co. WEXFORD	HEYNE	Co. GALWAY
HENRIGHT	Co. CLARE	HICKEY	CLAN CIAN/O'CARROLL
HENRION	Co. WESTMEATH	HICKEY	Co. CLARE
HENRY	See HENDERSON	HICKEY	Co. TIPPERARY
HENRY	ULSTER TARTAN	HICKMAN	Co. KERRY
HENRY	Co. LIMERICK	HIFFERTY	Co. LIMMERICK
HENRY	Co. LONDONDERY	HIGERTY	ULSTER TARTAN
HENRY	Co. TYRONE	HIGGINS	O' NEIL
HENSAY	Co. DUBLIN	HIGGINS	ULSTER TARTAN
HENSON	CONNACHT TARTAN	HIGGINS	CONNACHT TARTAN
HEPENSTALL	Co. WICKLOW	HIGGINSON	CONNACHT TARTAN
HERAGHTY	CONNACHT TARTAN	HIGHLAN(D)	CONNACHT TARTAN
HERAN	ORIEL TARTAN	HILAN(D)	LEINSTER TARTAN
HERATY	CONNACHT TARTAN	HILAN(D)	Co. KILDARE
HERBERT	Co. KERRY	HILAN(D)	Co. KILKENNY
HERDMAN	Co. ANTRIM	HILFERTY	Co. DONEGAL
HERLEY	Co. CORK	HILFERTY	ULSTER TARTAN
HERLIHY	Co. CORK	HILL	ULSTER TARTAN
HERLY	CLAN CIAN/O'CARROLL	HILLAN(D)	ULSTER TARTAN
HERNON	CONNACHT TARTAN	HILLAS, HILLIS	MAC KERREL
HERON	See HERRON	HILLAS, HILLIS	ULSTER TARTAN

"IRISH" indicates a choice of a general Irish tartan: "All Ireland", "Tara", "Clodagh", "Irish National", "St. Patrick"

TARTANS FOR IRISH NAMES

Hillee   *Hourican*

Anyone with a "County" Tartan may substitute one of the major "District" tartans listed below:.

Galway, Leitrim, Mayo, Roscommon, Sligo:	Connacht tartan
Clare, Cork, Kerry, Limmerick, Tipperary, Waterford:	Munster tartan
Armagh, Down, Fermanagh, Louth, Monaghan:	Oriel tartan
Carlow, Dublin, Kildare, Kilkenny, Laois, Longford:	
Meath, Offaly, Westmeath, Wexford, Wicklow:	Leinster tartan
Antrim, Armagh, Cavan, Donegal, Down, Londonderry, Tyrone:	Ulster tartan

SURNAME	TARTAN	SURNAME	TARTAN
HILLEE	Co. KERRY	HOGGAN	See HOGAN
HILLEN	ULSTER TARTAN	HOINS	Co. FERMANAGH
HILLERY	Co. CLARE	HOLACHAN	CONNACHT TARTAN
HILLY	Co. KERRY	HOLAHAN	Co. CLARE
HILTON	ULSTER TARTAN	HOLDEN,-DIN	Co. KILKENNY
HILTON	Co. DUBLIN	HOLDEN,-DIN	Co. WEXFORD
HINAGHAN	See HENNIGAN	HOLEY	Co. CORK
HINAN	Co. LIMMERICK	HOLIAN	CONNACHT TARTAN
HINAN	Co. TIPPERARY	HOLIAN	Co. GALWAY
HINCHIN,-AN	Co. CORK	HOLLAND	Co. LIMMERICK
HINCHY	Co. CLARE	HOLLEGAN	CONNACHT TARTAN
HINDS	CONNACHT TARTAN	HOLLIGAN	CONNACHT TARTAN
HINDS	Co. GALWAY	HOLLOWAY	CONNACHT TARTAN
HINES	CONNACHT TARTAN	HOLLY	ULSTER TARTAN
HINES	Co. GALWAY	HOLLY	Co. KERRY
HINGERDELL	Co. KERRY	HOLMER	ULSTER TARTAN
HINGERTY	Co. KERRY	HOLMES	ULSTER TARTAN
HINNEGAN	See HENNIGAN	HOLOHAN	Co. KERRY
HINNEGAN	CLAN CIAN/O'CARROLL	HOLOHAN	Co. OFFALY
HIPWELL	Co. LAOIS	HOLT	ULSTER TARTAN
HIRELLY	Co. CLARE	HOLWAY	CONNACHT TARTAN
HIRL	Co. DONEGAL	HOLYWOOD	ORIEL TARTAN
HIRRELL	Co. DONEGAL	HOMAN	WESTMEATH
HISHAM	Co. TIPPERARY	HONAHAN	Co. LIMMERICK
HISKY	CONNACHT TARTAN	HONAN	MUNSTER TARTAN
HISTON	HESTON	HONAN	Co. CLARE
HISTON	Co. MAYO	HONAN	Co. TIPPERARY
HITCHINS	ULSTER TARTAN	HONE	Co. MONAGHAN
HOADE	Co. CLARE	HONEEN	GREENE
HOARE	Co. CORK	HONEEN	Co. FERMANAGH
HOBAGAN	CONNACHT TARTAN	HOOBAN	LEINSTER TARTAN
HOBAN	HOBEN	HOOLAHAN	MUNSTER TARTAN
HOBAN	Co. MAYO	HOOLAHAN	Co. CLARE
HOBART	Co. KERRY	HOONAHAN	Co. LIMMERICK
HOBBIKIN(S)	CONNACHT TARTAN	HOONEY	Co. CLARE
HOBEN	HOBEN	HOONIHAN	MUNSTER TARTAN
HOBIKIN	Co. LONGFORD	HOORISKEY	MUNSTER TARTAN
HOBSON	ULSTER TARTAN	HOPE	Co. WESTMEATH
HOCHTON	Co. TIPPERARY	HOPKINS	CONNACHT TARTAN
HOCTOR	Co. TIPPERARY	HORA	Co. MAYO
HODDER	Co. CORK	HORAN	CONNACHT TARTAN
HODE	Co. GALWAY	HORE	Co. WEXFORD
HODGES	LEINSTER TARTAN	HORGAN	Co. CORK
HODKINS	LEINSTER TARTAN	HORISH	LEINSTER TARTAN
HODNETT	Co. CORK	HORISH	ULSTER TARTAN
HOEY	MAC KAY	HORISKY	ULSTER TARTAN
HOEY	ULSTER TARTAN	HORKAN	See HARKIN
HOGAN	CLAN CIAN/O'CARROLL	HOSTY	Co. MAYO
HOGAN	Co. CLARE	HOSTY	CONNACHT TARTAN
HOGAN	Co. CORK	HOUGH	Co. LIMMERICK
HOGAN	Co. TIPPERARY	HOULIGAN	Co. LIMMERICK
HOGART	ULSTER TARTAN	HOULIHAN	Co. DUBLIN
HOGARTY	CONNACHT TARTAN	HOUNEEN	GREEN
HOGG	HOGG	HOUNIHAN	Co. LIMMERICK
HOGG	ULSTER TARTAN	HOURICAN	Co. LONGFORD

"IRISH" indicates a choice of a general Irish tartan: "All Ireland", "Tara", "Clodagh", "Irish National", "St. Patrick"

38

TARTANS FOR IRISH NAMES

Anyone with a "County" Tartan may substitute one of the major "District" tartans listed below:

Galway, Leitrim, Mayo, Roscommon, Sligo:	Connacht tartan
Clare, Cork, Kerry, Limmerick, Tipperary, Waterford:	Munster tartan
Armagh, Down, Fermanagh, Louth, Monaghan:	Oriel tartan
Carlow, Dublin, Kildare, Kilkenny, Laois, Longford:	
Meath, Offaly, Westmeath, Wexford, Wicklow:	Leinster tartan
Antrim, Armagh, Cavan, Donegal, Down, Londonderry, Tyrone:	Ulster tartan

SURNAME	TARTAN	SURNAME	TARTAN
HOURIGAN	Co. TIPPERARY	HUSTY	Co. MAYO
HOURIHAN(E)	Co. CORK	HUTCH	Co. MEATH
HOURISKY	ULSTER TARTAN	HUTCHINSON	MAC DONALD
HOUSTON	MAC DONALD	HUTTAGHAN	Co. FERMANAGH
HOUSTON	ULSTER TARTAN	HUTTON	ORIEL TARTAN
HOVENDON	ULSTER TARTAN	HYDE	Co. KILKENNY
HOWARD	Co. CLARE	HYLAN(D)	HYLAND
HOWELL(S)	Co. MAYO	HYLAN(D)	CONNACHT TARTAN
HOWEN	Co. FERMANAGH	HYNAM	Co. LIMMERICK
HOWLETT	Co. WEXFORD	HYNAN	Co. LIMMERICK
HOWLEY	CONNACHT TARTAN	HYNDMAN	HYNDMAN
HOWLEY	Co. SLIGO	HYNES	Co. CORK
HOY	MAC KAY	HYNES	Co. GALWAY
HOY	ULSTER TARTAN	HYNIE	Co. GALWAY
HOYLE	Co. DONEGAL	HYSLIP	HYSLOP
HUBAN	LEINSTER TARTAN	HYSLOP	HYSLOP
HUDDY	Co. CORK	HYSLOP	ULSTER TARTAN
HUDSON	HUDSON		
HUDSON	Co. DUBLIN		
HUEY	MAC KAY	**I**	
HUEY	ULSTER TARTAN		
HUGGARD	Co. KERRY		
HUGGARD	ULSTER TARTAN		
HUGHES	HUGHES	IGOE	Co. ROSCOMMON
HUGHES	ULSTER TARTAN	INGLIS	INGLIS
HUGHES	Co. ARMAGH	INGLIS	Co. LIMMERICK
HUGHES	Co. MONAGHAN	INGOLDSBY	ULSTER TARTAN
HUGHES	Co. TYRONE	INGOLDSBY	Co. ANTRIM
HUGHY	ULSTER TARTAN	INGRAM	Co. LIMMERICK
HULEATT	Co. CLARE	IRELAND	ULSTER TARTAN
HULLINGSWORTH	IRISH–See Footnote	IRONS	Co. TIPPERARY
HULNANE	Co. CORK	IRVINE	IRVINE of DRUM
HULTAHAN	ULSTER TARTAN	IRVINE	ULSTER TARTAN
HUME	HOME	IRWIN(E)	See IRVINE
HUME	ULSTER TARTAN	ITCHINGHAM	Co. WEXFORD
HUMPHRAY(S)	HUMPHRIES	IVERS	MAC IVER
HUMPHRIES	HUMPHRIES	IVERS	Co. CLARE
HUNEEN	GREENE	IVERS	Co. TYRONE
HUNEEN	Co. CLARE	IVIS	Co. CLARE
HUNGERFORD	Co. CORK	IVORY	Co. WATERFORD
HUNT	CONNACHT TARTAN		
HUNTER	HUNTER		
HUNTER	HUNTER of H'STON		
HUNTER	ULSTER TARTAN	**J**	
HUONYN	See HUNEEN		
HURLEY	CLAN CIAN/O'CARROLL		
HURLEY	Co. CORK	JACK	ULSTER TARTAN
HURNEY	Co. GALWAY	JACKSON	JACKSON
HURRELL	Co. DONEGAL	JACKSON	ULSTER TARTAN
HURST	ULSTER TARTAN	JACOB(S)	Co. LAOIS
HUSSEY	MAC GUIRE		
HUSSEY	ORIEL TARTAN		
HUSSEY	Co. MEATH		
HUSSEY	Co. TRONE		
HUSTON	See HOUSTON		

"IRISH" indicates a choice of a general Irish tartan: "All Ireland", "Tara", "Clodagh", "Irish National", "St. Patrick"

Anyone with a "County" Tartan may substitute one of the major "District" tartans listed below:

Galway, Leitrim, Mayo, Roscommon, Sligo:	Connacht tartan
Clare, Cork, Kerry, Limmerick, Tipperary, Waterford:	Munster tartan
Armagh, Down, Fermanagh, Louth, Monaghan:	Oriel tartan
Carlow, Dublin, Kildare, Kilkenny, Laois, Longford:	
Meath, Offaly, Westmeath, Wexford, Wicklow:	Leinster tartan
Antrim, Armagh, Cavan, Donegal, Down, Londonderry, Tyrone:	Ulster tartan

SURNAME	TARTAN	SURNAME	TARTAN
JAFFERY,-IE(S)	Co. WESTMEATH	KAVANA(U)GH	Co. SLIGO
JAGO	Co. CORK	KEADIAN	Co. ROSCOMMON
JAMES	JAMES	KEADY	Co. CORK
JAMES	Co. CARLOW	KEADY	Co. LAOIS
JAMES	Co. WICKLOW	KEAGHNEY	Co. HERMANAGH
JAM(I)ESON	ULSTER TARTAN	KEAGHRY	Co. TYRONE
JARDINE	JARDINE	KEAGUE	ULSTER TARTAN
JARETY	CONNACHT TARTAN	KEAHAN	Co. CLARE
JARRETY	CONNACHT TARTAN	KEAHERY	Co. TYRONE
JARVIS	Co.CORK	KEAL(L)Y	Co. KILKENNY
JEFFERIES	Co. WESTMEATH	KEAL(L)Y	Co. MEATH
JEFFERSON	See SHAFFREY	KEALAGHAN	ORIEL TARTAN
JENKINS	ULSTER TARTAN	KEAN(E)	MAC KEAN
JENKINS	Co. ANTRIM	KEAN(E)	Co. GALWAY
JENNINGS	Co. GALWAY	KEAN(E)	Co. CLARE
JENNINGS	CONNACHT TARTAN	KEANY	ULSTER TARTAN
JEPHSON	Co. CORK	KEARNEY	LEINSTER TARTAN
JERETY	Co. WESTMEATH	KEARNEY	CLAN CIAN/O'CARROLL
JERMYN	Co. CORK	KEARNEY	Co. MAYO
JERVIS	Co. CORK	KEARNEY	Co. MEATH
JERVOIS	Co. CORK	KEARNEY	Co. OFFALY
JOHNSON	O' NEILL	KEARNEY	Co. WESTMEATH
JOHNSON	ULSTER TARTAN	KEARNS	Co. MAYO
JOHNSTON(E)	JOHNSTON	KEARNS	CONNACHT TARTAN
JOHNSTON(E)	ULSTER TARTAN	KEARNY	CLAN CIAN/O'CARROLL
JOLLEY	LEINSTER TARTAN	KEARON	Co. WICKLOW
JOLY	LEINSTER TARTAN	KEARY	See KERRY
JONES	JONES	KEATING	LEINSTER TARTAN
JONES	ULSTER TARTAN	KEATING	Co. WEXFORD
JORDAN	CONNACHT TARTAN	KEATING	Co. MAYO
JORDAN	Co. DOWN	KEATLY	Co. ROSCOMMON
JOY	Co. KERRY	KEATY	Co. LIMMERICK
JOY	Co. WATERFORD	KEAVENEY	CONNACHT TARTAN
JOYCE	CONNACHT TARTAN	KEAVENEY	ULSTER TARTAN
JOYCE	Co. GALWAY	KEAVY	CONNACHT TARTAN
JOYNT	Co. LIMMERICK	KEDIAN	Co. ROSCOMMON
JUDGE	CONNACHT TARTAN	KEE	MAC KAY
JUDGE	Co. SLIGO	KEE	ULSTER TARTAN
JUDGE	Co. LONDONDERRY	KEEFE	O' KEEFE
		KEEFE	Co. CORK
		KEEGAN	Co. DUBLIN
		KEEGAN	Co. ROSCOMMON
		KEEGHAN	Co. CLARE
		KEEHAM	Co. CLARE
		KEELAGHAN	ORIEL TARTAN
		KEELAHAN	ORIEL TARTAN
		KEELAN	ORIEL TARTAN
		KEELTY	CONNACHT TARTAN

K

SURNAME	TARTAN
KANE	ULSTER TARTAN
KANGLEY	Co. CAVAN
KARLEY	ORIEL TARTAN
KARRELL	CLAN CIAN/O'CARROLL
KARWELL	CLAN CIAN/O'CARROLL
KAVANA(U)GH	ULSTER TARTAN
KAVANA(U)GH	Co. ANTRIM

SURNAME	TARTAN
KEELY	CLAN CIAN/O'CARROLL
KEELY	Co. LOUTH
KEENA	Co. WESTMEATH
KEENAHAN	See KINAHAN
KEENAM	MAC GUIRE
KEERICAN	LEINSTER TARTAN
KEESHAM	Co. CLARE

"IRISH" indicates a choice of a general Irish tartan: "All Ireland", "Tara", "Clodagh", "Irish National", "St. Patrick"

Anyone with a "County" Tartan may substitute one of the major "District" tartans listed below:

Galway, Leitrim, Mayo, Roscommon, Sligo:	Connacht tartan
Clare, Cork, Kerry, Limmerick, Tipperary, Waterford:	Munster tartan
Armagh, Down, Fermanagh, Louth, Monaghan:	Oriel tartan
Carlow, Dublin, Kildare, Kilkenny, Laois, Longford:	
Meath, Offaly, Westmeath, Wexford, Wicklow:	Leinster tartan
Antrim, Armagh, Cavan, Donegal, Down, Londonderry, Tyrone:	Ulster tartan

SURNAME	TARTAN	SURNAME	TARTAN
KEETAGH	Co. DOWN	KENDILLION	Co. LOUTH
KEEVAN	Co. SLIGO	KENDRICK	Co. CORK
KEEVEEN	CONNACHT TARTAN	KENDRICK	ULSTER TARTAN
KEEVEY	O' KEEFE	KENDROGAN	Co. CLARE
KEEVEY	Co. CLARE	KENDRY	See MAC HENRY
KEGLEY	Co. MEATH	KENEALY	Co. LIMMERICK
KEGNEY	Co. FERMANAGH	KENEALY	MAC KINLAY
KEHEERIN	Co. CAVAN	KENEFICHE	Co. OFFALY
KEHER	CONNACHT TARTAN	KENEHAN	Co. OFFALY
KEHERNEY	CONNACHT TARTAN	KENERNEY	Co. OFFALY
KEHIGAN	ULSTER TARTAN	KENERY	Co. OFFALY
KEHILLY	Co. CORK	KENIFECK	IRISH-See Footnote
KEHIR	CONNACHT TARTAN	KENIRONS	Co. TIPPERARY
KEHOE	KEOGH	KENIRY	Co. CLARE
KEHOE	CLAN CIAN/O'CARROLL	KENLAN	Co. MEATH
KEHOE	CO. WICKLOW	KENNAGH	ORIEL TARTAN
KEIGHRY	Co. GALWAY	KENNANE	Co. TIPPERARY
KEIGHTLEY	Co. ROSCOMMON	KENNAW	Co. CLARE
KEILY	Co. LIMMERICK	KENNEALLY	Co. LIMMERICK
KEIRNAN	Co. ARMAGH	KENNEDY	KENNEDY [Irish]
KEIRSEY	Co. WATERFORD	KENNEDY	Co. CLARE
KELEGHAN	Co. MONAGHAN	KENNEDY	Co. TIPPERARY
KELL(S)	ULSTER TARTAN	KENNELLY	Co. MEATH
KELLEDY	ORIEL TARTAN	KENNING	MAC GUIRE
KELLEHER	MUNSTER TARTAN	KENNION	MAC GUIRE
KELLEHER	Co. KERRY	KENNY	LEINSTER TARTAN
KELLEHER	Co. TIPPERARY	KENNY	Co. DONEGAL
KELLER	CLAN CIAN/O'CARROLL	KENNY	Co. GALWAY
KELLER	Co. KERRY	KENNY	Co. LEITRIM
KELLETT	Co. CAVAN	KENNY	Co. LOUTH
KELLETT	Co. MEATH	KENNY	Co. ROSCOMMON
KELLEY	See KELLY	KENYON	MAC GUIRE
KELLOG(G)	ULSTER TARTAN	KEOAUGH	See KEOGH
KELLOPS	ULSTER TARTAN	KEOGAN	Co. CAVAN
KELLOUGH	ULSTER TARTAN	KEOGH	KEOGH
KELLY,Thormond	MUNSTER TARTAN	KEOGH	CLAN CIAN/O'CARROLL
KELLY,Thormond	Co. CLARE	KEOGH	Co. TIPPERARY
KELLY,Thormond	Co.TIPPERARY	KEOGH	Co. WEXFORD
KELLY,Ui Maine	CONNACHT TARTAN	KEOHANE	IRISH-See Footnote
KELLY,Ui Malne	ULSTER TARTAN	KEONAN	Co. FERMANAGH
KELLY,Ui Maine	Co. GALWAY	KEONAN	Co. LONDONDERRY
KELLY,Ui Maine	Co. ROSCOMMON	KEOWN	Co. FERMANAGH
KELLY of Sleat	KELLY of SLEAT	KEPPEL	Co. CARLOW
KELLY of Sleat	MAC DONALD of Sleat	KEPPOCK,KEPPOCH	MAC DON of KEPPOCH
KELSO	Co. DOWN	KEPPOCK, KEPPOCH	Co. LOUTH
KELSO	Co. GALWAY	KERBY	KIRBY
KELSO	Co. KILDARE	KERDIFF	Co. DONEGAL
KELSO	Co. MEATH	KEREVAN	Co. LAOIS
KELSO	Co. TYRONE	KERIN(S)	CONNACHT TARTAN
KELSO	ULSTER TARTAN	KERLIN	Co. DONEGAL
KEMMIN(S)	See KIMMONS	KERMODY,-MODE	MAC DIARMAID
KEMP	ULSTER TARTAN	KERNAGHAN	ULSTER TARTAN
KEMP	Co. DUBLIN	KERNAGHAN	Co. ARMAGH
KEMPLE	Co. GALWAY	KERNAN	ORIEL TARTAN
KEMPLIN	ULSTER TARTAN	KERNEY	ULSTER TARTAN

"IRISH" indicates a choice of a general Irish tartan: "All Ireland", "Tara", "Clodagh", "Irish National", "St. Patrick"

Anyone with a "County" Tartan may substitute one of the major "District" tartans listed below:

Galway, Leitrim, Mayo, Roscommon, Sligo:	Connacht tartan
Clare, Cork, Kerry, Limmerick, Tipperary, Waterford:	Munster tartan
Armagh, Down, Fermanagh, Louth, Monaghan:	Oriel tartan
Carlow, Dublin, Kildare, Kilkenny, Laois, Longford:	
Meath, Offaly, Westmeath, Wexford, Wicklow:	Leinster tartan
Antrim, Armagh, Cavan, Donegal, Down, Londonderry, Tyrone:	Ulster tartan

SURNAME	TARTAN	SURNAME	TARTAN
KERNOHAN	ULSTER TARTAN	KILCAWLEY	Co. SLIGO
KERNOHAN	Co. ANTRIM	KILCHRIST	See GILCHRIST
KERNY	CLAN CIAN/O'CARROLL	KILCOMMON(S)	Co. GALWAY
KERR	KERR	KILCOOLEY	Co. CLARE
KERR	ULSTER TARTAN	KILCOURSE	Co. MAYO
KERRANE	Co. MAYO	KILCOYLE	ULSTER TARTAN
KERRICK	KIRBY	KILCULLEN	Co. SLIGO
KERRIGAN	Co. MAYO	KILDARE	Co. CLARE
KERRIN	Co. DONEGAL	KILDEA	CONNACHT TARTAN
KERRISK	Cu. KERRY	KILDERRY	Cu. CLARE
KERRNAHAN	See CARNAHAN	KILDUFF	CONNACHT TARTAN
KERRY	LEINSTER TARTAN	KILDUFF	Co. GALWAY
KERRY	O' NEILL	KILDUNN	Co. SLIGO
KERVAN	Co. CORK	KILELINE	Co. ROSCOMMON
KERVAN	Co. LAOIS	KILEY	Co. LIMMERICK
KERVERNEY	CONNACHT TARTAN	KILFEATHER	CONNACHT TARTAN
KERVON	Co. CORK	KILFEDDER	Co. SLIGO
KERVON	Co. LAOIS	KILFEDRICK	ULSTER TARTAN
KESHAM	Co. CLARE	KILGALHAN	LEINSTER TARTAN
KESSIDY	Co. FERMANAGH	KILGALLEN	Co. MAYO
KETT	Co. CLARE	KILGANNON	Co. SLIGO
KETTLE	Co. DUBLIN	KILGAR	CONNACHT TARTAN
KEVANE	Co. KERRY	KILGAR	ULSTER TARTAN
KEVANY	CONNACHT TARTAN	KILGORE	KILGORE
KEVINE(E)	ULSTER TARTAN	KILGORE	ULSTER TARTAN
KEVLEHAN	Co. WESTMEATH	KILGOUR	See KILGORE
KEYES	See MAC KEY	KILGREW	CONNACHT TARTAN
KEYSE	See MAC KEY	KILGROVE	Co. WATERFORD
KIAR	CLAN CIAN/O'CARROLL	KILHRGAN	ULSTER TARTAN
KIARON	CLAN CIAN/O'CARROLL	KILKENNY	CONNACHT TARTAN
KIDD	KIDD	KILKY	Co. LONDONDERRY
KIDD	ULSTER TARTAN	KILLACKY	Co. OFFALY
KIDNEY	Co. CORK	KILLAHY	Co. OFFALY
KIELTY	CLAN CIAN/O'CARROLL	KILLARD	Co. WESTMEATH
KIELTY	CONNACHT TARTAN	KILLEEN	CLAN CIAN/O'CARROLL
KIELY	Co. LIMMERICK	KILLEEN	Co. MAYO
KIEREN	CLAN CIAN/O'CARROLL	KILLEGAR	ULSTER TARTAN
KIERNAN	KIERNAN	KILLEN	ORIEL TARTAN
KIERNAN	CONNACHT TARTAN	KILLERAN	Co. ROSCOMMON
KIERNAN	Co. CAVAN	KILLERLEAN	Co. SLIGO
KIERON	CLAN CIAN/O'CARROLL	KILLIAN	Co. CLARE
KIERRON	CLAN CIAN/O'CARROLL	KILLIARD	Co. WESTMEATH
KIERSE	Co. CLARE	KILLIGRAW	CONNACHT TARTAN
KIERSEY	Co. WATERFORD	KILLIGREW	CONNACHT TARTAN
KIGGAN(S)	CONNACHT TARTAN	KILLIGREW	Co. WATERFORD
KIGGIN(S)	CONNACHT TARTAN	KILLILEA	Co. GALWAY
KIHEGAN	ULSTER TARTAN	KILLIMET	Co. WESTMEATH
KILBANE	CONNACHT TARTAN	KILLION	Co. WESTMEATH
KILBANE	Co. SLIGO	KILLIPS	MAC KILLOP
KILBOY	Co. DONEGAL	KILLIPS	ULSTER TARTAN
KILBOY	Co. MAYO	KILLORAN	Co. SLIGO
KILBRIDE	CONNACHT TARTAN	KILLOUGHREY	Co. CLARE
KILCARR	ULSTER TARTAN	KILMAINE	Co. MAYO
KILCARR	Co. DONEGAL	KILMARTIN	CONNACHT TARTAN
KILCASH	Co. SLIGO	KILMARTIN	O' NEILL

"IRISH" indicates a choice of a general Irish tartan: "All Ireland", "Tara", "Clodagh", "Irish National", "St. Patrick"

TARTANS FOR IRISH NAMES

Kilmary   *Knowd*

Anyone with a "County" Tartan may substitute one of the major "District" tartans listed below:.

Galway, Leitrim, Mayo, Roscommon, Sligo:	**Connacht tartan**
Clare, Cork, Kerry, Limmerick, Tipperary, Waterford:	**Munster tartan**
Armagh, Down, Fermanagh, Louth, Monaghan:	**Oriel tartan**
Carlow, Dublin, Kildare, Kilkenny, Laois, Longford:	
Meath, Offaly, Westmeath, Wexford, Wicklow:	**Leinster tartan**
Antrim, Armagh, Cavan, Donegal, Down, Londonderry, Tyrone:	**Ulster tartan**

SURNAME	TARTAN	SURNAME	TARTAN
KILMARY	ULSTER TARTAN	KINNEEN	CONNACHT TARTAN
KILMARY	Co. LONDONDERRY	KINNEGAN	CUNNINGHAM
KILMET	Co. WESTMEATH	KINNEGAN	Co. LOUTH
KILMORE	Co. SLIGO	KINNELLAN	See KINELLEN
KILMURRAY	Co. LONDONDERRY	KINNEN	CONNACHT TARTAN
KILPATRICK	ULSTER TARTAN	KINNERK	Co. CLARE
KILRAIN	Co. ROSCOMMON	KINNERNEY	Co. CLARE
KILRANE	Co. ROSCOMMON	KINNEY	ULSTER TARTAN
KILROE	ROSCOMMON	KINNIFF	CONNACHT TARTAN
KILROY	CONNACHT TARTAN	KINNIFF	Co. CORK
KILROY	Co. ROSCOMMON	KINNINGHAM	CUNNINGHAM
KILVANT	Co. WESTMEATH.	KINNINGHAM	ULSTER TARTAN
KILWEE	Co. SLIGO	KINNIREY	Co. CLARE
KIM(M)	FRASER	KINNIRY	Co. CLARE
KIM(M)	ULSTER TARTAN	KINOCANE	Co. CLARE
KIMMONS	CUMMING	KINOLE	Co. SLIGO
KIMMONS	ORIEL TARTAN	KINOULTY	Co. DOWN
KINAGAN	Co. MONAGHAN	KINSANE	Co. KERRY
KINAHAM	ULSTER TARTAN	KINSELLA	LEINSTER TARTAN
KINAHAN	CUNNINGHAM	KINSELLA	Co. CARLOW
KINAHAN	ULSTER TARTAN	KINSELLA	Co. WEXFORD
KINAHAN	Co. OFFALY	KINUCANE	Co. CLARE
KINALLY	Co. TIPPERARY	KINURE	Co. LONGFORD
KINCAID	KINCAID	KIRBY	KIRBY
KINCAID	ULSTER TARTAN	KIRBY	Co. LIMMERICK
KINCART	Co. MAYO	KIRBY	Co. MAYO
KINCH	LEINSTER TARTAN	KIREA	Co. SLIGO
KINCH	MANX NATIONAL	KIRIVANE	Co.GALWAY
KINCHELLA	Co. WEXFORD	KIRK	KIRK
KINDELAN(D)	Co. MEATH	KIRK	ULSTER TARTAN
KINDELLAN	See KINDELLEN	KIRKPATRICK	KIRKPATRICK
KINDELLEN	O' NEILL	KIRKPATRICK	ULSTER TARTAN
KINDELLEN	LEINSTER TARTAN	KIRLIN	Co. LONDONDERRY
KINDELLEN	Co. LOUTH	KIRRANE	Co. MAYO
KINE	CONNACHT TARTAN	KIRWAN(E)	Co. GALWAY
KINEALY	Co. LIMMERICK	KIRWAN(E)	CONNACHT TARTAN
KINEL	Co. DOWN	KISSANE	Co. CORK
KING	Co. GALWAY	KITCHEN	MAC DONALD
KINGERTY	Co. DONEGAL	KITCHEN	ULSTER TARTAN
KINGSLEY	Co. CARLOW	KITSON	Co. CLARE
KINGSTON	Co. CORK	KITTERICK	ORIEL TARTAN
KINIGAN	CUNNINGHAM	KIVLEHAN	Co. WESTMEATH
KINIRY	Co. LIMMERICK	KLISHAM	Co. CLARE
KINKEAD	See KINCAID	KNALLY	MAC INALLY
KINLAN(D)	Co. MEATH	KNALLY	ORIEL TARTAN
KINLOCH	ULSTER TARTAN	KNAPP	Co. CORK
KINLOUGH	ULSTER TARTAN	KNARESBOURGH	Co. KILKENNY
KINNALLY	TIPPERARY	KNAVIN	See MAC NIVEN
KINNANE	Co. TIPPERARY	KNEAFSEY	Co. DONEGAL
KINNARNEY	Co. OFFALY	KNEE	Co. GALWAY
KINNAVANE	Co. CLARE	KNIGHTLY	Co. KERRY
KINNAWE	CONNACHT TARTAN	KNIPE	ORIEL TARTAN
KINNEALLY	Co. LIMMERICK	KNOCKTON	MAC NACHTEN
KINNEAR	ULSTER TARTAN	KNOTT	Co. DUBLIN
KINNEAVY	CONNACHT TARTAN	KNOWD	Co. KILDARE

"IRISH" indicates a choice of a general Irish tartan: "All Ireland", "Tara", "Clodagh", "Irish National", "St. Patrick"

43

Knoweles   *Lauder*

Anyone with a "County" Tartan may substitute one of the major "District" tartans listed below:

Galway, Leitrim, Mayo, Roscommon, Sligo:	Connacht tartan
Clare, Cork, Kerry, Limmerick, Tipperary, Waterford:	Munster tartan
Armagh, Down, Fermanagh, Louth, Monaghan:	Oriel tartan
Carlow, Dublin, Kildare, Kilkenny, Laois, Longford:	
Meath, Offaly, Westmeath, Wexford, Wicklow:	Leinster tartan
Antrim, Armagh, Cavan, Donegal, Down, Londonderry, Tyrone:	Ulster tartan

SURNAME	TARTAN	SURNAME	TARTAN
KNOWELES	Co. KILDARE	LAMONT	LAMONT
KNOWELL	See NEWELL	LAMONT	ULSTER TARTAN
KNOWLAN(D)	Co. WESTMEATH	LAMOUR	ULSTER TARTAN
KNOWLES	See NEWALL	LAMPORT	Co. WEXFORD
KNOX	KNOX	LANDER(S)	Co. KILKENNY
KNOX	ULSTER TARTAN	LANDRA	Co. KILKENNY
KOEN	CONNACHT TARTAN	LANDRIGAN	MUNSTER TARTAN
KOUGH	See KEOGH	LANDRIGAN	Co. TIPPERARY
KRISHAM	Co. GALWAY	LANDRY	Co. KILKENNY
KUFFE	Co. CORK	LANDY	Co. KILKENNY
KYAN	Co. WICKLOW	LANE	MUNSTER TARTAN
KYLE	KYLE	LANEY	CLAN CIAN/O'CARROLL
KYLE	ULSTER TARTAN	LANG	See LAING
KYNE	CONNACHT TARTAN	LANGAN	Co. MAYO
		LANGAN	Co. MEATH
		LANGFORD	CONNACHT TARTAN
		LANGFORD	MUNSTER TARTAN
L		LANGFORD	ULSTER TARTAN
		LANGFORD	Co. KERRY
		LANGTON	Co. KILKENNY
		LANIGAN	LENAGHAN
		LANIGAN	CLAN CIAN/O'CARROLL
		LANIGAN	Co. KILKENNY
LACKAN(D)	CONNACHT TARTAN	LANNAGAN	LENAGHAN
LACKEN(D)	CONNACHT TARTAN	LANNAGAN	CLAN CIAN/O'CARROLL
LACKEY	See LECKY	LANNIGAN	Co. TIPPERARY
LACY	Co. LIMMERICK	LANNON	Co. KILKENNY
LADE	Co. KILDARE	LAPHIN(E)	ULSTER TARTAN
LADEN	Co. LEITRIM	LAPORTE	LAPORTE
LADRIGAN	Co. TIPPERARY	LAPPIN(E)	ULSTER TARTAN
LADRIGAN	MUNSTER TARTAN	LAPPIN(E)	Co. DONEGAL
LAFFERTY	ULSTER TARTAN	LARACY	Co. KILKENNY
LAFFEY	Co. GALWAY	LARDNER	Co. GALWAY
LAGAN	See LOGAN	LARGAN	ORIEL TARTAN
LAHART	Co. KILKENNY	LARGE	CONNACHT TARTAN
LAHART	Co. TIPPERARY	LARKIN	ORIEL TARTAN
LAHEEN	Co. WATERFORD	LARKIN	CONNACHT TARTAN
LAHERTY	Co. KILKENNY	LARKIN	Co. GALWAY
LAHIFF	CONACHT TARTAN	LARKIN	Co. MONAGHAN
LAHIFF	Co. CLARE	LARKIN	Co. WEXFORD
LAHIFF	Co. GALWAY	LARMER	ULSTER TARTAN
LAHIVE	Co. KERRY	LARMINIE	Co. MAYO
LAHY	Co. KILKENNY	LARMOUR	ULSTER TARTAN
LAID	Co. KILDARE	LARNER	Co, GALWAY
LAING	LAING	LARNEY	ORIEL TARTAN
LAING	LESLIE	LARRISSEY	Co. KILKENNY
LAING	ULSTER TARTAN	LARRISSEY	Co. WEXFORD
LAIRD	ULSTER TARTAN	LASTLY	Co. DONEGAL
LALEE	Co. WESTMEATH	LASTY	Co. DONEGAL
LALLY	CONNACHT TARTAN	LATCHFORD	Co. KERRY
LALLY	Co. MAYO	LATIMER	ORIEL TARTAN
LALOR	Co. LAOIS	LATOUCHE	Co. DUBLIN
LAMB(E)	ORIEL TARTAN	LATTIN	Co. KILDARE
LAMBERT	CONNACHT TARTAN	LAUDER	LAUDER
LAMMON	See LAMONT	LAUDER	LEINSTER TARTAN

"IRISH" indicates a choice of a general Irish tartan: "All Ireland", "Tara", "Clodagh", "Irish National", "St. Patrick"

Anyone with a "County" Tartan may substitute one of the major "District" tartans listed below:

Galway, Leitrim, Mayo, Roscommon, Sligo:	**Connacht tartan**
Clare, Cork, Kerry, Limmerick, Tipperary, Waterford:	**Munster tartan**
Armagh, Down, Fermanagh, Louth, Monaghan:	**Oriel tartan**
Carlow, Dublin, Kildare, Kilkenny, Laois, Longford:	
Meath, Offaly, Westmeath, Wexford, Wicklow:	**Leinster tartan**
Antrim, Armagh, Cavan, Donegal, Down, Londonderry, Tyrone:	**Ulster tartan**

SURNAME	TARTAN	SURNAME	TARTAN
LAUGHERAN	MAC LACHLAN	LEDWICH	Co. WEATMEATH
LAUGHERAN	Co. TYRONE	LEE	LEE
LAUGHNANE	ORIEL TARTAN	LEE	Co. GALWAY
LAUGHRAN	MAC LACHLAN	LEE	Co. LAOIS
LAUNDRY	Co. KILKENNY	LEECH	See LEACH
LAURENCE	IRISH-See Footnote	LEEN	Co. KERRY
LAVALLIN	Co. CORK	LEEPER	ULSTER TARTAN
LAVAN	Co. ROSCOMMON	LEESON	Co. TIPPERARY
LAVELLE	CONNACHT TARTAN	LEEVY	Co. LONGFORD
LAVELLE	Co. MAYO	LEFANCE	Co. DUBLIN
LAVERTY	ULSTER TARTAN	LEGEAR	Co. LIMMERICK
LAVERTY	Co. DONEGAL	LEGG(E)	ULSTER TARTAN
LAVERY	ULSTER TARTAN	LEHAN(E)	Co. CORK
LAVEY	Co. WESTMEATH	LEHAYNE	Co. CORL
LAVON	Co. ROSCOMMON	LEIGH	See LEE
LAW(E)	ULSTER TARTAN	LEITCH	LEACH
LAWDER	See LAUDER	LEITCH	ULSTER TARTAN
LAWDER	LEINSTER TARTAN	LEMASNEY	Co. TIPPERARY
LAWELL	ULSTER TARTAN	LEMASS	Co. CARLOW
LAWLEE	ULSTER TARTAN	LEMM	ULSTER TARTAN
LAWLEE	Co. WESTMEATH	LENAGHAN	Co. ROSCOMMON
LAWLER	Co. LAOIS	LENANE	Co. ROSCOMMON
LAWLESS	See LAWLIS	LENANE	MUNSTER TARTAN
LAWLIS	LAWLIS	LENDRUM	ORIEL TARTAN
LAWLIS	Co. KILKENNY	LENIHAN	LENAGHAN
LAWLIS	MUNSTER TARTAN	LENIHAN	Co. ROSCOMMON
LAWLOR	Co. DOWN	LENNAN	Co. FERMANAGH
LAWLOR	Co. LAOIS	LENNANE	MUNSTER TARTAN
LAWN	Co. SLIGO	LENNON	ULSTER TARTAN
LAWRENCE	IRISH-See Footnote	LENNON	LEINSTER TARTAN
LAWSON	ULSTER TARTAN	LENNON	Co. GALWAY
LAWTON	ULSTER TARTAN	LENNOX	LENNOX DIST.
LE POER	CLAN CIAN/O'CARROLL	LENNOX	ULSTER TARTAN
LEACH	LEACH	LEO	Co. LIMMERICK
LEACH	CONNACHT TARTAN	LEONARD	LEONARD
LEACKY	See LECKY	LEONARD	CONNACHT TARTAN
LEACY	Co. LIMMERICK	LEONARD	LEINSTER TARTAN
LEADER	Co. CORK	LERHIVAN	Co. CLARE
LEAHY	MUNSTER TARTAN	LERNIHAN	LENAGHAN
LEAHY	Co. CORK	LERNIHAN	Co. CLARE
LEAHY	Co. KERRY	LESLEY	See LESLIE
LEAMY	Co. TIPPERARY	LESLIE	LESLIE
LEANE	Co. KERRY	LESLIE	ORIEL TARTAN
LEANY	Co. TIPPERARY	LESTER	MAC ALISTER
LEARY	Co. CORK	LESTRANGE	Co. WESTMEATH
LEARY	Co. CORK	LETT	Co. WEXFORD
LEATHAN,-AM	IRISH-See Footnote	LEVALLIN	Co. CORK
LECKY	LECKIE	LEVENS	Co. LOUTH
LECKY	MAC GREGOR	LEVIN(E)	Co. LOUTH
LECKY	ULSTER TARTAN	LEVINGE	Co. LOUTH
LEDDAN	MUNSTER TARTAN	LEVINSTONE	See LIVINGSTONE
LEDDY	CLAN CIAN/O'CARROLL	LEVIS	Co. CORK
LEDDY	Co. CAVAN	LEVITT	LEINSTER TARTAN
LEDGER	Co. LIMMERICK	LEVY	Co. LONGFORD
LEDLIE	LESLIE	LEWIS	IRISH-See Footnote

"IRISH" indicates a choice of a general Irish tartan: "All Ireland", "Tara", "Clodagh", "Irish National", "St. Patrick"

TARTANS FOR IRISH NAMES

Ley   *Lyvett*

Anyone with a "County" Tartan may substitute one of the major "District" tartans listed below.

Galway, Leitrim, Mayo, Roscommon, Sligo:	Connacht tartan
Clare, Cork, Kerry, Limmerick, Tipperary, Waterford:	Munster tartan
Armagh, Down, Fermanagh, Louth, Monaghan:	Oriel tartan
Carlow, Dublin, Kildare, Kilkenny, Laois, Longford:	
Meath, Offaly, Westmeath, Wexford, Wicklow:	Leinster tartan
Antrim, Armagh, Cavan, Donegal, Down, Londonderry, Tyrone:	Ulster tartan

SURNAME	TARTAN	SURNAME	TARTAN
LEY	Co. KILKENNY	LOVE	ULSTER TARTAN
LEYNE	Co. LIMMERICK	LOVE	Co. LONDONDERRY
LEYNE	LYNN	LOVE	Co. TYRONE
LIDDANE	ULSTER TARTAN	LOWRY	LOWRY
LIDDY	CLAN CIAN/O'CARROLL	LOWRY	GORDON
LIDDY	Co. CLARE	LOWRY	ULSTER TARTAN
LIFFE	Co. WESTMEATH	LOWRY	Co. DOWN
LILLY	MAC GUIRE	LUCY	Co. CORK
LILLY	Co. FERMANAGH	LUFFAN	Co. TIPPERARY
LINDEN	LINDEN	LUFTAN	Co. WICKLOW
LINDON	LINDEN	LUFFNAN	Co. WEXFORD
LINDON	ULSTER TARTAN	LUNDY	LUNDY
LINDSAY	LINDSAY	LUNIN	Co. FERMANAGH
LINDSAY	ULSTER TARTAN	LUNNERGAN	CLAN CIAN/O'CARROLL
LINDSEY	See LINDSAY	LUNN(E)Y	ULSTER TARTAN
LING	LEINSTER TARTAN	LUNN(E)Y	Co. FERMANAGH
LINNANE	MUNSTER TARTAN	LUNN(E)Y	Co. TYRONE
LINTON	ULSTER TARTAN	LUNN(E)	Co. TYRONE
LISTER	MAC ALISTER	LUSTY	Co. DONEGAL
LISTER	ULSTER TARTAN	LUTHERAN	ULSTER TARTAN
LISTER	Co. KILKENNY	LYNAGH	Co. MAYO
LITTLE	LITTLE	LYNAM	Co. WEXFORD
LITTLE	ULSTER TARTAN	LYNAS	ULSTER TARTAN
LITTLE	Co. ANTRIM	LYNCH	LYNCH
LITTLE	Co. FERMANAGH	LYNCH	ULSTER TARTAN
LIVINGSTON(E)	LIVINGSTONE	LYNCH	Co. DONEGAL
LIVINGSTON(E)	ULSTER TARTAN	LYNCH	Co. DOWN
LOAN(E)	ORIEL TARTAN	LYNCH	Co. GALWAY
LOAN(E)	Co. TYRONE	LYNCH	Co. TIPPERARY
LOCHRAN	ULSTER TARTAN	LYNE	See LYNN
LOFTUS	CLAN CIAN/O'CARROLL	LYNE	Co. KERRY
LOFTUS	Co. MAYO	LYNESS	ULSTER TARTAN
LOGAN	LOGAN	LYNG(E)	LEINSTER TARTAN
LOGAN	ULSTER TARTAN	LYNHAN	IRISH-See Footnote
LOGUE	ULSTER TARTAN	LYNN	LYNN
LOMASNEY	Co. TIPPERARY	LYNN	See FLYNN
LOMBARD	Co. WICKLOW	LYNON	Co. CORK
LONDRIGAN	Co. TIPPERARY	LYNON	Co. GALWAY
LONERGAN	CLAN CIAN/O'CARROLL	LYNOTT	Co. MAYO
LONERGAN	Co. TIPPERARY	LYONS	LYONS
LONG	Co. KERRY	LYONS	Co. CORK
LOOBY	Co. TIPPERARY	LYONS	Co. GALWAY
LOONEY	Co. CORK	LYSAGHT	O' BRIEN
LORRASEY	Co. TIPPERARY	LYSAGHT	Co. CLARE
LOSTY	Co. DONEGAL	LYSTER	MAC ALISTER
LOUGHLIN	MAC LACHLAN	LYVET(T)	LEINSTER TARTAN
LOUGHLIN	Co. CLARE		
LOUGHNAN	CLAN CIAN/O'CARROLL		
LOUGHNAN	Co. DOWN		
LOUGHNAN	Co. KILKENNY		
LOUGHNAN	Co. MAYO		
LOUGHNANE	ORIEL TARTAN		
LOUGHNANE	Co. MEATH		
LOUGHRAN	Co. TYRONE		
LOUGHRAN	ULSTER TARTAN		

"IRISH" indicates a choice of a general Irish tartan: "All Ireland", "Tara", "Clodagh", "Irish National", "St. Patrick"

46

Anyone with a "County" Tartan may substitute one of the major "District" tartans listed below:.

Galway, Leitrim, Mayo, Roscommon, Sligo:	**Connacht tartan**
Clare, Cork, Kerry, Limmerick, Tipperary, Waterford:	**Munster tartan**
Armagh, Down, Fermanagh, Louth, Monaghan:	**Oriel tartan**
Carlow, Dublin, Kildare, Kilkenny, Laois, Longford:	
Meath, Offaly, Westmeath, Wexford, Wicklow:	**Leinster tartan**
Antrim, Armagh, Cavan, Donegal, Down, Londonderry, Tyrone:	**Ulster tartan**

SURNAME	TARTAN	SURNAME	TARTAN
		MAC ARTAN	ULSTER TARTAN
		MAC ARTHUR	MAC ARTHUR
		MAC ARTHUR	Co. LIMMERICK
		MAC ASEY	Co. KILDARE
		MAC ASEY	Co. MEATH
		MAC ASHINAGH	Co. ARMAGH
		MAC ASHINAH	Co. OFFALY
		MAC ASKIE	MAC ASKILL
		MAC ASKIE	ULSTER TARTAN
		MAC ASKIE	Co. LONDONDERRY
		MAC ASKIE	Co. TYRONE
		MAC ASPARRAN	MAC SPORRAN
		MAC ASPARRAN	ULSTER TARTAN
		MAC ASPARRAN	Co. LONDONDERRY
		MAC ASTOCKER	ULSTER TARTAN
		MAC ATAMNEY	Co. LONDONDERRY
		MAC ATASNEY	ULSTER TARTAN
		MAC ATASNEY	Co. ARMAGH
		MAC ATASNEY	Co. TYRONE
		MAC ATAVY	Co. MONAGHAN
MAC ADAM	ULSTER TARTAN	MAC ATEE	ORIEL TARTAN
MAC ADOO	CONNACHT TARTAN	MAC ATEER	ULSTER TARTAN
MAC AIG	ULSTER TARTAN	MAC ATEER	Co. ARMAGH
MAC ALARY	CLAN CIAN/O'CARROLL	MAC ATILLA	ULSTER TARTAN
MAC ALINDEN	ULSTER TARTAN	MAC ATTEGART	MAC TAGGART
MAC ALINDEN	Co. ARMAGH	MAC ATTEGART	ULSTER TARTAN
MAC AL(L)ISTER	MAC ALLISTER	MAC AUGHNEY	Co. CARLOW
MAC AL(L)ISTER	ULSTER TARTAN	MAC AULAY	MAC AULAY
MAC AL(L)ISTER	Co. ANTRIM	MAC AULAY	MAC GUIRE
MAC ALOAN	Co. LONDONDERRY	MAC AULAY	Co. OFFALY
MAC ALOAN	ULSTER TARTAN	MAC AULAY	Co. WEST MEATH
MAC ALONAN	Co. ANTRIM	MAC AULEY	Co. FERMANAGH
MAC ALONAN	ULSTER TARTAN	MAC AULEY	See MAC AULAY
MAC AMBROSE	Co. WEXFORD	MAC AULIFFE	Co. MUNSTER TARTAN
MAC ANABB	MAC NAB	MAC AULIFFE	Co. CORK
MAC ANABB	Co. CAVAN	MAC AUSTIN	CONNACHT TARTAN
MAC ANALLEN	Mc INALLY	MAC AVADDY	CONNACHT TARTAN
MAC ANALLEN	ULSTER TARTAN	MAC AVEALLY	Co. MAYO
MAC ANALLY	Mc INALLY	MAC AVEIGH	CONNACHT TARTAN
MAC ANALLY	ORIEL TARTAN	MAC AVEIN	Co. DONEGAL
MAC ANDLES	MAC CANDLISH	MAC AVERY	Co. DOWN
MAC ANDREW	ANDERSON	MAC AVEY	CONNACHT TARTAN
MAC ANDREW	Co. MAYO	MAC AVIN	ULSTER TARTAN
MAC ANEAVE	Co. ROSCOMMON	MAC AVIN(S)	Co. DONEGAL
MAC ANENEY	ORIEL TARTAN	MAC AVINNA	Co. CAVAN
MAC ANENEY	ULSTER TARTAN	MAC AVINNEY	Co. LONDONDERRY
MAC ANERNEY	ULSTER TARTAN	MAC AVINUE	Co. CAVAN
MAC ANESPIE	Co. TYRONE	MAC AVISH	Co. CAVAN
MAC ANESPIE	GILLESPIE	MAC AVOY	Co. LAOIS
MAC ANESPIE	ULSTER TARTAN	MAC AWARD	ULSTER TARTAN
MAC ANIFF	CONNACHT TARTAN	MAC AWARD	Co. DONEGAL
MAC ANTHONY	Co. WATERFORD	MAC AWARD	Co. GALWAY
MAC ANULLA	ULSTER TARTAN	MAC AWEENY	Co. LEITRIM
MAC ANULLY	ULSTER TARTAN	MAC BARRAGRY	Co. TIPPERARY
MAC ARDELL	See MAC ARDLE	MAC BENNETT	BENNETT
MAC ARDLE	ORIEL TARTAN		
MAC ARDLE	Co. MONAGHAN		
MAC AREADY	Co. LONDONDERRY		
MAC AREADY	MAC CREARY		
MAC AREE	Co. MONAGHAN		
MAC ART	ULSTER TARTAN		
MAC ARTAN	MAC DONALD		

Mac - Mc

As explained earlier in the preceding text portion, "Mc" is *always* an abbreviaton of "Mac."

"IRISH" indicates a choice of a general Irish tartan: "All Ireland", "Tara", "Clodagh", "Irish National", "St. Patrick"

TARTANS FOR IRISH NAMES

Anyone with a "County" Tartan may substitute one of the major "District" tartans listed below:

Galway, Leitrim, Mayo, Roscommon, Sligo:	**Connacht tartan**
Clare, Cork, Kerry, Limmerick, Tipperary, Waterford:	**Munster tartan**
Armagh, Down, Fermanagh, Louth, Monaghan:	**Oriel tartan**
Carlow, Dublin, Kildare, Kilkenny, Laois, Longford:	
Meath, Offaly, Westmeath, Wexford, Wicklow:	**Leinster tartan**
Antrim, Armagh, Cavan, Donegal, Down, Londonderry, Tyrone:	**Ulster tartan**

SURNAME	TARTAN	SURNAME	TARTAN
MAC BENNETT	ORIEL TARTAN	MAC CAHILL	Co. DONEGAL
MAC BERKERY	Co. OFFALY	MAC CAHON	Co. CLARE
MAC BERKERY	Co. TIPPERARY	MAC CAIG	CONNACHT TARTAN
MAC BEROCHRY	Co. TIPPERARY	MAC CAIG	Co. GALWAY
MAC BIRACREA	Co. TIPPERARY	MAC CAINSH	ULSTER TARTAN
MAC BIRNEY	ULSTER TARTAN	MAC CALDEN	ULSTER TARTAN
MAC BOYHEEN	Co. LEITRIM .	MAC CALLAN	ORIEL TARTAN
MAC BRADY	CLAN CIAN/O'CARROLL	MAC CALLELY	See LILLY
MAC BRADY	Co. CAVAN	MAC CALLILLY	See LILLY
MAC BRAN(N)	Co. CLARE	MAC CALLION	MAC CALLUM
MAC BRANNAN	CONNACHT TARTAN	MAC CALLION	ULSTER TARTAN
MAC BRANNAN	Co. ROSCOMMON	MAC CALLION	Co. DONEGAL
MAC BRATNEY	MUNSTER TARTAN	MAC CALLION	Co. LONDONDERRY
MAC BREARTY	Co. DONEGAL	MAC CALVEY	Co. SLIGO
MAC BREARTY	ULSTER TARTAN	MAC CALWAY	Co. MAYO
MAC BREEN	MAC BRINE	MAC CAMLEY	MAC AULAY
MAC BREEN	Co. KILKENNY	MAC CAMLEY	ULSTER TARTAN
MAC BREEN	Co. TYRONE	MAC CANCE	ULSTER TARTAN
MAC BREHANY	Co. SLIGO	MAC CANLISS	MAC CANDLISH
MAC BREHON	Co. SLIGO	MAC CANN	ULSTER TARTAN
MAC BRIDE	MAC BRIDE	MAC CANN	Co. ARMAGH
MAC BRIDE	ULSTER TARTAN	MAC CANNON	ORIEL TARTAN
MAC BRIDE	Co. DONEGAL	MAC CAPPIN	MAC ALPINE
MAC BRIN(N)	Co. DOWN	MAC CARKHILL	MAC CORQUODALE
MAC BRINE	MAC BRINE	MAC CARKHILL	Co. CLARE
MAC BRODIN	CLAN CIAN/O'CARROLL	MAC CARL	CLAN CIAN/O'CARROLL
MAC BRODY	CLAN CIAN/O'CARROLL	MAC CARMODY	Co. CLARE
MAC BRODY	O' BRIEN	MAC CARN	Co. MONAGHAN
MAC BROHOON	Co. SLIGO	MAC CARNEY	ULSTER TARTAN
MAC BRUDDIIN	CLAN CIAN/O'CARROLL	MAC CARO	CLAN CIAN/O'CARROLL
MAC BRYAN	BRYANT	MAC CARRA(G)HER	ORIEL TARTAN
MAC BRYAN	O' BRIEN	MAC CARRIGLE	O' FERRELL
MAC BRYAN	Co. FERMANAGH	MAC CARROLL	CLAN CIAN/O'CARROLL
MAC BURNEY	ULSTER TARTAN	MAC CARRON	ULSTER TARTAN
MAC CABE	Co. CAVAN	MAC CARRY	IRISH-See Footnote
MAC CADDEN	ULSTER TARTAN	MAC CART	ULSTER TARTAN
MAC CADDEN	Co. ARMAGH	MAC CARTAN	ULSTER TARTAN
MAC CAFFELLY	ULSTER TARTAN	MAC CARTHY	MUNSTER TARTAN
MAC CAFFELLY	Co. DOWN	MAC CARTNEY	ULSTER TARTAN
MAC CAFFERKY	Co. MAYO	MAC CARTNIE	ULSTER TARTAN
MAC CAFFERTY	ULSTER TARTAN	MAC CARVILL(E)	ULSTER TARTAN
MAC CAFFERTY	Co. DONEGAL	MAC CARVILLE	CLAN CIAN/O'CARROLL
MAC CAFFERTY	Co. LONDONDERRY	MAC CASEY	CASEY
MAC CAFFREY	Co. FERMANAGH	MAC CASEY	Co. MEATH
MAC CAGHERY	MAC GUIRE	MAC CASEY	Co. KILDARE
MAC CAFFREY	MAC GUIRE	MAC CAUGHERTY	Co. DOWN
MAC CAGHEY	ULSTER TARTAN	MAC CAUGHRAN	MAC CAUGHRAN
MAC CAGHEY	Co. DONEGAL	MAC CAUGHRAN	Co. CAVAN
MAC CAGUE	ORIEL TARTAN	MAC CAUL	MAC COLL
MAC CAGUE	ULSTER TARTAN	MAC CAUL	ULSTER TARTAN
MAC CAHAN(E)	Co. CLARE	MAC CAVANA	Co. ANTRIM
MAC CAHERN	Co. CAVAN	MAC CAVISH	Co. CAVAN
MAC CAHERTY	Co. DOWN	MAC CAVOCK	CONNACHT TARTAN
MAC CAHERY	MAC GUIRE	MAC CLAMON	See CLEMENT
MAC CAHILL	ULSTER TARTAN		

"IRISH" indicates a choice of a general Irish tartan: "All Ireland", "Tara", "Clodagh", "Irish National", "St. Patrick"

TARTANS FOR IRISH NAMES

Mac Clanaghan   *Mac Dougall*

Anyone with a "County" Tartan may substitute one of the major "District" tartans listed below:

Galway, Leitrim, Mayo, Roscommon, Sligo:	Connacht tartan
Clare, Cork, Kerry, Limmerick, Tipperary, Waterford:	Munster tartan
Armagh, Down, Fermanagh,Louth, Monaghan:	Oriel tartan
Carlow, Dublin, Kildare, Kilkenny, Laois, Longford, Meath, Offaly, Westmeath, Wexford, Wicklow:	Leinster tartan
Antrim, Armagh, Cavan, Donegal, Down, Londonderry, Tyrone:	Ulster tartan

SURNAME	TARTAN	SURNAME	TARTAN
MAC CLANAGHAN	CLAN CIAN	MAC CURDY	See MAC KIRDY
MAC CLANAHAN	CLAN CIAN	MAC CUREEN	Co. LEITRIM
MAC CLANCY	CLAN CIAN	MAC CURRY	MAC GUIRE
MAC CLARNON	See MAC LARNON	MAC CURRY	MAGUIRE
MAC CLARY	ULSTER TARTAN	MAC CURRY	CURRIE
MAC CLANTON	CLANTON	MAC CURRY	CURRY
MAC CLATTON	Co. ANTRIM	MAC CURTIN	Co. CORK
MAC CLATTON	Co. DERRY	MAC CURTIN	Co. LIMMERICK
MAC CLATTON	ULSTER TARTAN	MAC CUSACK	CUSACK
MAC CLEARY	CLAN CIAN	MAC CUSACK	Co. MEATH
MAC CLELLANAN(D)	See MAC LELLEN	MAC CUSHELEY	Co. TYRONE
MAC CLEMENT	See CLEMENT	MAC CUSHLY	ULSTER TARTAN
MAC CLENATHAN,-EN,-IN	CLAN CIAN	MAC CUSHLY	Co. TYRONE
MAC CLINCHY	ULSTER TARTAN	MAC CUSKER	MAC GUIRE
MAC CLINCHY	CLAN CIAN/O'CARROLL	MAC CUSKERAN	Co. DOWN
MAC CLOSKEY	ULSTER TARTAN	MAC CUSTY	Co. CLARE
MAC CLOSKEY	Co. LONDONDERRY	MAC DACKER	ORIEL TARTAN
MAC CLOSKEY	Co. DONEGAL	MAC DAGNEY	ULSTER TARTAN
MAC CLOY	ORIEL TARTAN	MAC DARA	See DARRAGH
MAC CLOY	Co. ARMAGH	MAC DARBY	Co. TIPPERARY
MAC COLE	ULSTER TARTAN	MAC DARRAGH	See DARRAGH
MAC COLE	Co. DONEGAL	MAC DAVETT	See MAC DEVITT
MAC COMLEY	See MAC AULAY	MAC DAVETT	Co. DONEGAL
MAC COMLEY	ULSTER TARTAN	MAC DAVID	MAC DERMAID
MAC CONE	Co. LOUTH	MAC DAVIE,-Y	CONNACHT TARTAN
MAC CONMEE	Co. TYRONE	MAC DAVOCK	CONNACHT TARTAN
MAC CONNON	ORIEL TARTAN	MAC DAVYMORE	CONNACHT TARTAN
MAC CONRY	CLAN CIAN/O'CARROLL	MAC DERMOT(T)	MAC DERMAID
MAC CONSIDINE	CLAN CIAN/O'CARROLL	MAC DERMOT(T)	ULSTER TARTAN
MAC COOK	COOK	MAC DERMOT(T)	CONNACHT TARTAN
MAC COOK	Co. DONEGAL	MAC DERMOT(T)	Co. ROSCOMMON
MAC COOKE	CONNACHT TARTAN	MAC DERMOT(T)	Co. SLIGO
MAC COOL	ULSTER TARTAN	MAC DEVER	CONNACHT TARTAN
MAC COOL	Co. DONEGAL	MAC DEVER	Co. GALWAY
MAC CORCORAN	CORCORAN	MAC DEVER	Co. MAYO
MAC CORCORAN	CLAN CIAN/O'CARROLL	MAC DEVITT	MAC DEVITT
MAC CORL	CLAN CIAN/O'CARROLL	MAC DEVITT	CONNACHT TARTAN
MAC CORL	Co. LEITRIM	MAC DIGANY	CONNACHT TARTAN
MAC CORMAC(K)	MAC CORMACK	MAC DOCKERY	CONNACHT TARTAN
MAC CORMAC(K)	Co. LONGFORD	MAC DONAGH	See MAC DONOUGH
MAC CORRA	CLAN CIAN/O'CARROLL	MAC DONAGHY	ULSTER TARTAN
MAC CORRY	MAC GUIRE	MAC DONALD	MAC DONALD
MAC CORRY	MAGUIRE	MAC DONALD	ULSTER TARTAN
MAC COUGHLAN	CLAN CIAN/O'CARROLL	MAC DONALD	Co. ANTRIM
MAC COURT	Co. TYRONE	MAC DONALD	Co. LONDONDERRY
MAC CRACKEN	MAC NACHTEN	MAC DONEGAN	Co. MONAGHAN
MAC CRACKEN	ULSTER TARTAN	MAC DONELL	See MAC DONALD
MAC CRACKEN	Co. LONDONDERRY	MAC DONNELL	See MAC DONALD
MAC CRIBBEN	CONNACHT TARTAN	MAC DONOUGH	MAC DONOUGH
MAC CRILLY	Co. LONDONDERRY	MAC DONOUGH	Co. CORK
MAC CROSSAN	Co. DONEGAL	MAC DONOUGH	Co. SLIGO
MAC CROSSNAN	Co. TYRONE	MAC DOOL	MAC DOUGALL
MAC CUE	MAC KAY	MAC DORCY	Co. LEITRIM
MAC CUE	ULSTER TARTAN	MAC DOUGAL(L)	MAC DOUGALL
MAC CUNE	Co. DOWN	MAC DOUGAL(L)	Co. ANTRIM

"IRISH" indicates a general Irish tartan: "All Ireland:, "Tara", "Clodagh", Irish National", "St. Patrick"

TARTANS FOR IRISH NAMES

Mac Dowell   *MacFie*

Anyone with a "County" Tartan may substitute one of the major "District" tartans listed below:.

Galway, Leitrim, Mayo, Roscommon, Sligo:	**Connacht tartan**
Clare, Cork, Kerry, Limmerick, Tipperary, Waterford:	**Munster tartan**
Armagh, Down, Fermanagh, Louth, Monaghan:	**Oriel tartan**
Carlow, Dublin, Kildare, Kilkenny, Laois, Longford:	
Meath, Offaly, Westmeath, Wexford, Wicklow:	**Leinster tartan**
Antrim, Armagh, Cavan, Donegal, Down, Londonderry, Tyrone:	**Ulster tartan**

SURNAME	TARTAN	SURNAME	TARTAN
MAC DOWELL	MAC DOUGALL	MAC ENCHROE	Co. CLARE
MAC DOWELL	Co. ROSCOMMON	MAC ENDOO	CONNACHT TARTAN
MAC DUNLEAVY	ULSTER TARTAN	MAC ENEANY	ORIEL TARTAN
MAC DUNLEVY	CONNACHT TARTAN	MAC ENERY	Co. LIMERICK
MAC DUNPHY	MAC DONOUGH	MAC ENHILL	ULSTER TARTAN
MAC DURKAN	Co. SLIGO	MAC ENIRY	Co. LIMERICK
MAC DYER	DYER	MAC ENNY	ORIEL TARTAN
MAC DYER	ULSTER TARTAN	MAC ENRIGHT(Y)	Co. CLARE
MAC DYER	Co. DONEGAL	MAC ENROE	Co. CAVAN
MAC EAGAN	CONNACHT TARTAN	MAC ENROW	Co. CAVAN
MAC EAGAN	Co. GALWAY	MAC ENTAGGART	MAC TAGGART
MAC EAGAN	CLAN CIAN/O'CARROLL	MAC ENTAGGART	ULSTER TARTAN
MAC EAVEIGH	Co. MAYO	MAC ENTEE	ORIEL TARTAN
MAC EGAN	See MAC EAGAN	MAC ENTEE	Co. MONAGHAN
MAC EGO	Co. CORK	MAC ENTYRE	MAC INTYRE
MAC ELDERRY	ULSTER TARTAN	MAC EOIN	Co. ROSCOMMON
MAC ELDERRY	Co. ANTRIM	MAC ERLEAN	ORIEL TARTAN
MAC ELDOWNEY	Co. CLARE	MAC ERLEAN	Co. LONDONDERRY
MAC ELDUFF	DUFFY	MAC ERRIGLE	See MAC GIRL
MAC ELDUFF	CONNACHT TARTAN	MAC ERVELLE,-VILLE	ULSTER TARTAN
MAC ELDUFF	Co. GALWAY	MAC ETTIGAN	See MAC GETTIGAN
MAC ELEAVY	ULSTER TARTAN	MAC ETIGAN	Co. TYRONE
MAC ELEAVY	Co. DOWN	MAC ETTIGAN	See MAC GETTIGAN
MAC ELFATRICK	Co. LAOIS	MAC EVADDY	CONNACHT TARTAN
MAC ELGUNN	GUNN	MAC EVANNY	Co. MAYO
MAC ELGUNN	Co. FERMANAGH	MAC EVATT	ORIEL TARTAN
MAC ELHAIR	ULSTER TARTAN	MAC EVEIGH	Co. MAYO
MAC ELHAIR	Co. DONEGAL	MAC EVEY	ULSTER TARTAN
MAC ELHARGY	ULSTER TARTAN	MAC EVILLY	Co. MAYO
MAC ELHERON	ULSTER TARTAN	MAC EVIN	ULSTER TARTAN
MAC ELHILL	ULSTER TARTAN	MAC EVINNEY	Co. CAVAN
MAC ELHILL	Co. TYRONE	MAC EVINNEY	Co. LONDONDERRY
MAC ELHOYLE	See MAC ILHOYLE	MAC EVOY	Co. LAOIS
MAC ELI	Co. MAYO	MAC EVOY	Co. WESTMEATH
MAC ELLEN	MAC LELLEN	MAC EWEY	ULSTER TARTAN
MAC ELLIGOTT	Co. KERRY	MAC FADDEN	Co. DONEGAL
MAC ELLIN	MAC LELLEN	MAC FALL	MACKINTOSH
MAC ELLIN	Co. ROSCOMMON	MAC FALL	ULSTER TARTAN
MAC ELLISTRUM	Co. KERRY	MAC FARLAND	MAC FARLANE
MAC ELMEEL	ORIEL TARTAN	MAC FATRIDGE	MAC LEAN of DUART
MAC ELMOYLE	ULSTER TARTAN	MAC FAUL, FAWL	MACKINTOSH
MAC ELMURRAY	ORIEL TARTAN	MAC FAUL, MAC FAWL	ULSTER TARTAN
MAC ELNAY	Co. MONAGHAN	MAC FEE	MAC FIE
MAC ELROY	ULSTER TARTAN	MAC FEELY	ULSTER TARTAN
MAC ELSHANDER	See ALEXANDER	MAC FEERICK	Co. MAYO
MAC ELVANEY	ULSTER TARTAN	MAC FEETERS	ULSTER TARTAN
MAC ELVEEN(A)	ULSTER TARTAN	MAC FEHILLY	ULSTER TARTAN
MAC ELVEEN(A)	Co. DOWN	MAC FERGUS	FERGUSON
MAC ELVEEN(Y)	Co. ANTRIM	MAC FERGUS	Co. LEITRIM
MAC ELVOGUE	Co. TYRONE	MAC FERRAN	ULSTER TARTAN
MAC ELWAIN	ULSTER TARTAN	MAC FERRAN	Co. ANTRIM
MAC ELWEE	ULSTER TARTAN	MAC FERREN	Co. DOWN
MAC ENALLY	Mc INALLY	MAC FETRICK	Co. ANTRIM
MAC ENCAHA	Co. SLIGO	MAC FETTRIDGE	MAC LEAN of DUART
MAC ENCALIS	Co. DONEGAL	MAC FIE	MAC FIE

"IRISH" indicates a choice of a general Irish tartan: "All Ireland", "Tara", "Clodagh", "Irish National", "St. Patrick"

TARTANS FOR IRISH NAMES

Mac Finnucane   *Mac Gill*

Anyone with a "County" Tartan may substitute one of the major "District" tartans listed below:

Galway, Leitrim, Mayo, Roscommon, Sligo:	Connacht tartan
Clare, Cork, Kerry, Limmerick, Tipperary, Waterford:	Munster tartan
Armagh, Down, Fermanagh, Louth, Monaghan:	Oriel tartan
Carlow, Dublin, Kildare, Kilkenny, Laois, Longford:	
Meath, Offaly, Westmeath, Wexford, Wicklow:	Leinster tartan
Antrim, Armagh, Cavan, Donegal, Down, Londonderry, Tyrone:	Ulster tartan

SURNAME	TARTAN	SURNAME	TARTAN
		MAC GEEVER	ULSTER TARTAN
MAC FINNUCANE	Co. CLARE	MAC GEGAN	Co. WESTMEATH
MAC FIRBIS	CONNACHT TARTAN	MAC GEHERAN	CONNACHT TARTAN
MAC FIRBIS	Co. SLIGO	MAC GENIS(S)	MAC INNES
MAC GAFFEY	CONNACHT TARTAN	MAC GENTY	Co. MONAGHAN
MAC GAGH	MAC GAUGH	MAC GEOGHEGAN	Co. WESTMEATH
MAC GAHEY	ORIEL TARTAN	MAC GEOGHEGAN	O' NEILL
MAC GAHEY	Co. WESTMEATH	MAC GEON	ORIEL TARTAN
MAC GALE	Co. TYRONE	MAC GEORGE	ULSTER TARTAN
MAC GALL	MAC CALL	MAC GEOUGH	MAC GAUGH
MAC GALLERY	Co. CLARE	MAC GEOWN	ORIEL TARTAN
MAC GALLOGLY	ULSTER TARTAN	MAC GEOWN	Co. DOWN
MAC GAMMON	Co. CLARE	MAC GEOWN	Co. ROSCOMMON
MAC GANLY	Co. LEITRIM	MAC GERAHTY	Co. SLIGO
MAC GANN	CONNACHT TARTAN	MAC GERAHTY	CONNACHT TARTAN
MAC GANTLEY	Co. LEITRIM	MAC GERETTY	CONNACHT TARTAN
MAC GARAHAN	Co. FERMANAGH	MAC GERL	LEINSTER TARTAN
MAC GARR	ULSTER TARTAN	MAC GERL	ULSTER TARTAN
MAC GARRELL	ULSTER TARTAN	MAC GERN	CLAN CIAN/O'CARROLL
MAC GARRIGAN	Co. CAVAN	MAC GERNY	CLAN CIAN/O'CARROLL
MAC GARRIHY	CONNACHT TARTAN	MAC GERRELL	O' FARRELL
MAC GARRITY	ORIEL TARTAN	MAC GERRY	CONNACHT TARTAN
MAC GARRY	CONNACHT TARTAN	MAC GERRY	Co. CAVAN
MAC GARRY	ULSTER TARTAN	MAC GETRICK	Co. SLIGO
MAC GARRY	LEINSTER TARTAN	MAC GETTIGAN	Co. DONEGAL
MAC GARTLAN(D)	O' NEILL	MAC GETTIGAN	ULSTER TARTAN
MAC GARTLAN(D)	ULSTER TARTAN	MAC GIBBONS	CONNACHT TARTAN
MAC GARTY	See GARTY	MAC GIBBONS	Co. SLIGO
MAC GARVEY	ULSTER TARTAN	MAC GIBBONS	Co. CAVAN
MAC GARVEY	Co. DONEGAL	MAC GIBBONS	Co. DONEGAL
MAC GARY	Co. MAYO	MAC GIBBONY	Co. MAYO
MAC GATELY	Co. ROSCOMMON	MAC GIDDERY	Co. LONDONDERRY
MAC GAUGHEY	Co. MONAGHAN	MAC GIFF	CONNACHT TARTAN
MAC GAUGHRAN	Co. CAVAN	MAC GIFFEN	ULSTER TARTAN
MAC GAUREN	Co. CAVAN	MAC GIFFEN	Co. ANTRIM
MAC GAVIGAN	Co. DUBLIN	MAC GIFFEN	Co. LONDONDERRY
MAC GAW	MAC GAUGH	MAC GIFFIE	CONNACHT TARTAN
MAC GAW	ULSTER TARTAN	MAC GIFFORD	Co. DOWN
MAC GAWLEY	MAC AULAY	MAC GIFFY	CONNACHT TARTAN
MAC GAYNOR	Co. LONGFORD	MAC GILBANE	CONNACHT TARTAN
MAC GEADY	ULSTER TARTAN	MAC GILBRIDE	ULSTER TARTAN
MAC GEADY	Co. DONEGAL	MAC GILCHRIST	CONNACHT TARTAN
MAC GEAGH	MAC GAUGH	MAC GILDEA	CONNACHT TARTAN
MAC GEAGHAN	Co. WESTMEATH	MAC GILDOWNEY	Co. LONDONDERRY
MAC GEARN	Co. DONEGAL	MAC GILDOWNEY	ULSTER TARTAN
MAC GEARTY	CONNACHT TARTAN	MAC GILEA	CONNACHT TARTAN
MAC GEARY	CONNACHT TARTAN	MAC GILFLLAN	MAC LELLEN
MAC GEARY	Co. ROSCOMMON	MAC GILFOYLE	CLAN CIAN/O'CARROLL
MAC GEE	MAC KAY	MAC GILFOYLE	Co. OFFALY
MAC GEE	Co. WESTMEATH	MAC GILGAR	CONNACHT TARTAN
MAC GEEHAN	ULSTER TARTAN	MAC GILGUNN	GUNN
MAC GEEHAN	Co. DONEGAL	MAC GILHEANY	Co. CAVAN
MAC GEENEY	Co. CORK	MAC GILHOOLY	Co. ROSCOMMON
MAC GEER	LEINSTER TARTAN	MAC GILHOON	ULSTER TARTAN
MAC GEEVER	MAC IVER	MAC GILL	MAC GILL
		MAC GILL	ULSTER TARTAN

"IRISH" indicates a choice of a general Irish tartan: "All Ireland", "Tara", "Clodagh", "Irish National", "St. Patrick"

51

TARTANS FOR IRISH NAMES

Anyone with a "County" Tartan may substitute one of the major "District" tartans listed below:.

Galway, Leitrim, Mayo, Roscommon, Sligo:	Connacht tartan
Clare, Cork, Kerry, Limmerick, Tipperary, Waterford:	Munster tartan
Armagh, Down, Fermanagh, Louth, Monaghan:	Oriel tartan
Carlow, Dublin, Kildare, Kilkenny, Laois, Longford:	
Meath, Offaly, Westmeath, Wexford, Wicklow:	Leinster tartan
Antrim, Armagh, Cavan, Donegal, Down, Londonderry, Tyrone:	Ulster tartan

SURNAME	TARTAN	SURNAME	TARTAN
MAC GILLAND	MAC LELLAN	MAC GIRL	ULSTER TARTAN
MAC GILLANDERS	ORIEL TARTAN	MAC GIRL	Co. CLARE
MAC GILLEECE	Co. FERMANAGH	MAC GIRR	LEINSTER TARTAN
MAC GILLEREAGH	Co. CLARE	MAC GIVEEN(S)	ULSTER TARTAN
MAC GILLHOON	ULSTER TARTAN	MAC GIVEENS	Co. DONEGAL
MAC GILLIAN	MAC LEAN	MAC GIVEN(S)	ULSTER TARTAN
MAC GILLIAN	ULSTER TARTAN	MAC GIVEN(S)	Co. DONEGAL
MAC GILLICAN	Co. LONDONDERRY	MAC GIVERN	ORIEL TARTAN
MAC GILLICAN	Co. LONGFORD	MAC GIVNEY	Co. CAVAN
MAC GILLICUDDY	Co. KERRY	MAC GLADDERY	Co. TYRONE
MAC GILLICUDDY	See O' SULLIVAN	MAC GLADE	MAC LEOD
MAC GILLIMEN	Co. FERMANAGH	MAC GLADE	ULSTER TARTAN
MAC GILLOOY	Co. LEITRIM	MAC GLAFFY	CONNACHT TARTAN
MAC GILLORAN	Co. ROSCOMMON	MAC GLANCHY	Co. CAVAN
MAC GILLOWAY	Co. DOWN	MAC GLASGOW	ULSTER TARTAN
MAC GILLY	Co. ROSCOMMON	MAC GLASHAN	MAC GLASHAN
MAC GILLYCUDDY	See O' SULLIVAN	MAC GLASHAN	ULSTER TARTAN
MAC GILMARTIN	O' NEILL	MAC GLAUGHLIN	ULSTER TARTAN
MAC GILMER	ULSTER TARTAN	MAC GLAVE	CONNACHT TARTAN
MAC GILMORE	ULSTER TARTAN	MAC GLAVEY	CONNACHT TARTAN
MAC GILMOORE	ULSTER TARTAN	MAC GLAVIN	ULSTER TARTAN
MAC GILOWLY	Co. LEITRIM	MAC GLEEN	MAC LEAN
MAC GILPATRICK	CLAN CIAN/O'CARROLL	MAC GLEEN	CONNACHT TARTAN
MAC GILPATRICK	Co. LAOIS	MAC GLEENAN	Co. ARMAGH
MAC GILREA	ULSTER TARTAN	MAC GLENAGHAN	ULSTER TARTAN
MAC GILREEVY	ULSTER TARTAN	MAC GLENNON	Co. OFFALY
MAC GILROY	ULSTER TARTAN	MAC GLEW	ORIEL TARTAN
MAC GILSENAN	ULSTER TARTAN	MAC GLINCHY	ULSTER TARTAN
MAC GILSHENAN	ULSTER TARTAN	MAC GLOIN(E)	ULSTER TARTAN
MAC GILTENAN	Co. CLARE	MAC GLONE	ULSTER TARTAN
MAC GILTON	ULSTER TARTAN	MAC GLOON	ULSTER TARTAN
MAC GILVANY	ULSTER TARTAN	MAC GLORY	ULSTER TARTAN
MAC GILVARRY	MAC GILLIVARY	MAC GLOUGHLIN	MAC LACHLAN
MAC GILVARRY	Co. DONEGAL	MAC GLOWRY	ULSTER TARTAN
MAC GILVARRY	CONNACHT TARTAN	MAC GLYNN	MAC GLYNN
MAC GILVIE	CAMPBELL	MAC GLYNN	CONNACHT TARTAN
MAC GILWAY	Co. DONEGAL	MAC GOEY	Co. LEITRIM
MAC GILWEE	Co. DONEGAL	MAC GOEY	Co. LONGFORD
MAC GIMPSEY	Co. DOWN	MAC GOFF	MAC GAUGH
MAC GING	Co. MAYO	MAC GOFF	ORIEL TARTAN
MAC GINLEY	MAC KINLAY	MAC GOFF	MAC GAW
MAC GINLEY	ULSTER TARTAN	MAC GOFFERY	MAC GUIRE
MAC GINLEY	Co. DONEGAL	MAC GOGARTY	Co. MEATH
MAC GINLEY	Co. LONDONDERRY	MAC GOLDRICK	Co. LEITRIM
MAC GINN	ULSTER TARTAN	MAC GOLRICK	Co. FERMANAGH
MAC GINN	Co. TYRONE	MAC GOMORY	MONTGOMERY
MAC GINNELL	Co. WESTMEATH	MAC GONIGLE	ULSTER TARTAN
MAC GINNELLY	Co. MAYO	MAC GONIGAL	Co. DONEGAL
MAC GINNIS	MAC INNES	MAC GONNELL	MAC CONNELL
MAC GINNIS	ULSTER TARTAN	MAC GONNELL	MAC DONALD
MAC GINTY	ORIEL TARTAN	MAC GONNELL	ORIEL TARTAN
MAC GINTY	Co. MONAGHAN	MAC GOOGAN	ULSTER TARTAN
MAC GINTY	ULSTER TARTAN	MAC GOOHAN	Co. LEITRIM
MAC GINTY	Co. DONEGAL	MAC GOOKIN	ULSTER TARTAN
MAC GINVER	Co. LONGFORD	MAC GOORTY	Co. LEITRIM

"IRISH" indicates a choice of a general Irish tartan: "All Ireland", "Tara", "Clodagh", "Irish National", "St. Patrick"

TARTANS FOR IRISH NAMES

Mac Gorish   *Mac Harg*

Anyone with a "County" Tartan may substitute one of the major "District" tartans listed below:

Galway, Leitrim, Mayo, Roscommon, Sligo:	Connacht tartan
Clare, Cork, Kerry, Limmerick, Tipperary, Waterford:	Munster tartan
Armagh, Down, Fermanagh, Louth, Monaghan:	Oriel tartan
Carlow, Dublin, Kildare, Kilkenny, Laois, Longford:	
Meath, Offaly, Westmeath, Wexford, Wicklow:	Leinster tartan
Antrim, Armagh, Cavan, Donegal, Down, Londonderry, Tyrone:	Ulster tartan

SURNAME	TARTAN	SURNAME	TARTAN
MAC GORISH	ORIEL TARTAN	MAC GREGAN	LEINSTER TARTAN
MAC GORLEY	ULSTER TARTAN	MAC GRELLIS	ULSTER TARTAN
MAC GORLEY	Co. DONEGAL	MAC GRENAHAN	Co. DONEGAL
MAC GORLICK	Co. LEITRIM	MAC GRIBBEN	CONNACHT TARTAN
MAC GORMAN	ORIEL TARTAN	MAC GRILLAN	MAC NEILL
MAC GORRY	MAC GUIRE	MAC GRILLIS	MAC NEIL
MAC GORRY	Co. CAVAN	MAC GRILLIS	ULSTER TARTAN
MAC GORTY	Co. LEITRIM	MAC GRISKIN	Co. LEITRIM
MAC GOUGH	MAC GAUGH	MAC GROARK(E)	O' NEILL
MAC GOUGH	ORIEL TARTAN	MAC GROARTY	Co. DONEGAL
MAC GOURKEY	Co. LEITRIM	MAC GROD(D)Y	Co. DONEGAL
MAC GOURNESON	Co. DOWN	MAC GRONAN	Co. ARMAGH
MAC GOURTEY	Co. LEITRIM	MAC GRORY	MAC RAE
MAC GOURTY	Co. LEITRIM	MAC GRORY	ULSTER TARTAN
MAC GOVERAN	ORIEL TARTAN	MAC GROTTY	ULSTER TARTAN
MAC GOVERAN	Co. CAVAN	MAC GROURKE	O' NEILL
MAC GOVERN	ORIEL TARTAN	MAC GROWDER	ORIEL TARTAN
MAC GOVERN	Co. CAVAN	MAC GRUDDER	ORIEL TARTAN
MAC GOWAN	SMITH	MAC GRUDDY	Co. DONEGAL
MAC GOWAN	GOW	MAC GUANE	Co. CLARE
MAC GOWAN	ULSTER TARTAN	MAC GUCKI(A)N	Co. LEITRIM
MAC GOWAN	Co. CAVAN	MAC GUCKIAN	ULSTER TARTAN
MAC GOWAN	Co. DONEGAL	MAC GUCKIN	ULSTER TARTAN
MAC GOWAN	Co. LEITRIM	MAC GUFF	MAC GAUGH
MAC GOWRAN	Co. CAVAN	MAC GUFF	ORIEL TARTAN
MAC GRADE	ULSTER TARTAN	MAC GUFF	CONNACHT TARTAN
MAC GRADE	CLAN CIAN/O'CARROLL	MAC GUFFIN	ULSTER TARTAN
MAC GRADY	GRADY	MAC GUIGAN	ULSTER TARTAN
MAC GRADY	Co. CLARE	MAC GUIGAN	Co. FERMANAGH
MAC GRAIL	MAC NEILL	MAC GUILFOYLE	CLAN CIAN/O'CARROLL
MAC GRAILLS	MAC NEILL	MAC GUILL	Co. ARMAGH
MAC GRAN(N)	LEINSTER TARTAN	MAC GUINESS	MAC INNES
MAC GRANAHAN	Co. DONEGAL	MAC GUINESS	ORIEL TARTAN
MAC GRANE	LEINSTER TARTAN	MAC GUINESS	CONNACHT TARTAN
MAC GRANEY	M' DON CLANRANALD	MAC GUINESS	Co. DOWN
MAC GRANN	ULSTER TARTAN	MAC GUINEST	See MAC GUINESS
MAC GRANNELL	Co. WEXFORD	MAC GUINEY	Co. CAVAN
MAC GRANNON	Co. MAYO	MAC GUINN	CONNACHT TARTAN
MAC GRANNY	M' DON CLANRANALD	MAC GUIRE	MAC GUIRE
MAC GRATH	MAC GRATH	MAC GUIRE	Co.FERMANAGH
MAC GRATH	ULSTER TARTAN	MAC GUIRK	ULSTER TARTAN
MAC GRATH	Co. WATERFORD	MAC GULLIAN	Co. LEITRIM
MAC GRATH	Co. FERMANAGH	MAC GURK	ULSTER TARTAN
MAC GRATH	Co. TIPPERARY	MAC GUSHEN	Co. MEATH
MAC GRATTAN	ULSTER TARTAN	MAC GUSTY	IRISH-See Footnote
MAC GRAW	See MAC GRATH	MAC HACKETT	CONNACHT TARTAN
MAC GREAD	ULSTER TARTAN	MAC HAFFY	MAC FIE
MAC GREAISH	CONNACHT TARTAN	MAC HAGUE	ULSTER TARTAN
MAC GREAL	MAC NEILL	MAC HAIG	ULSTER TARTAN
MAC GREALLY	See REILLY	MAC HALE	Co. MAYO
MAC GREEDY	See MAC GRADY	MAC HALL	MAC COLL
MAC GREEN(E)	GREENE	MAC HALL	MAC CALL
MAC GREEN(E)	Co. CLARE	MAC HALL	ULSTER TARTAN
MAC GREEVY	CONNACHT TARTAN	MAC HAOL	Co. MAYO
MAC GREEVY	Co. ROSCOMMON	MAC HARG	Co. TYRONE

"IRISH" indicates a choice of a general Irish tartan: "All Ireland", "Tara", "Clodagh", "Irish National", "St. Patrick"

53

TARTANS FOR IRISH NAMES

Mac Haugh   *Mac Kearney*

Anyone with a "County" Tartan may substitute one of the major "District" tartans listed below:

Galway, Leitrim, Mayo, Roscommon, Sligo:	Connacht tartan
Clare, Cork, Kerry, Limmerick, Tipperary, Waterford:	Munster tartan
Armagh, Down, Fermanagh, Louth, Monaghan:	Oriel tartan
Carlow, Dublin, Kildare, Kilkenny, Laois, Longford:	
Meath, Offaly, Westmeath, Wexford, Wicklow:	Leinster tartan
Antrim, Armagh, Cavan, Donegal, Down, Londonderry, Tyrone:	Ulster tartan

SURNAME	TARTAN	SURNAME	TARTAN
MAC HAUGH	Co. CLARE	MAC ILPATRICK	Co. LAOIS
MAC HAUGHEY	ULSTER TARTAN	MAC ILRATH	ULSTER TARTAN
MAC HAUGHNEY	Co. CARLOW	MAC ILREA	ULSTER TARTAN
MAC HEATH	KEITH	MAC ILROY	ULSTER TARTAN
MAC HEATH	ULSTER TARTAN	MAC ILVANY	ULSTER TARTAN
MAC HENRY	HENDERSON	MAC ILVEEN	Co. DOWN
MAC HENRY	ULSTER TARTAN	MAC ILVEIGH	See MAC VEY
MAC HENRY	Co. LIMERICK	MAC ILWAIN(E)	ULSTER TARTAN
MAC HENRY	Co. GALWAY	MAC ILWEE	ULSTER TARTAN
MAC HERBERT	Co. WESTMEATH	MAC ILWRAITH	ULSTER TARTAN
MAC HOOD	O' NEILL	MAC INALLY	Mc INALLY
MAC HOSTY	Co. MAYO	MAC INCH	MAC INNES
MAC HOUL	See MAC COOL	MAC INERNEY	Co. CLARE
MAC HUGH	MAC KAY	MAC INESKER	LEINSTER TARTAN
MAC HUGH	CONNACHT TARTAN	MAC INNES	MAC INNES
MAC HUGH	Co. CAVAN	MAC INNES	ULSTER TARTAN
MAC HUGH	Co. DONEGAL	MAC INOULTY	Co. CLARE
MAC HUGH	Co. LONGFORD	MAC INROE	Co. CAVAN
MAC HUGO	CONNACHT TARTAN	MAC INTEE	ORIEL TARTAN
MAC HULLY	MAC AULAY	MAC INTEER	See MAC INTYRE
MAC HULLY	ULSTER TARTAN	MAC INTOR	See MAC INTYRE
MAC HUTTON	ULSTER TARTAN	MAC INTYRE	MAC INTYRE
MAC HUTTON	Co. ANTRIM	MAC INTYRE	ULSTER TARTAN
MAC HUTTON	Co. LONDONDERRY	MAC INTYRE	Co. TYRONE
MAC ILCAR(R)	Co. DONEGAL	MAC INULTY	Co. CLARE
MAC ILCONN	Co. DOWN	MAC IREAVY	Co. ANTRIM
MAC ILDOON	ORIEL TARTAN	MAC ISOCK	Co. CLARE
MAC ILDOWNEY	Co. LONDONDERRY	MAC IVER	MAC IVER
MAC ILDUFF	MAC FIE	MAC IVOR	MAC IVER
MAC ILDUFF	CONNACHT TARTAN	MAC IVOR	ULSTER TARTAN
MAC ILDUFF	Co. CAVAN	MAC IVOR	Co. TYRONE
MAC ILDUFF	Co. GALWAY	MAC JIMPSEY	Co. DOWN
MAC ILEE	ULSTER TARTAN	MAC KAIG	ULSTER TARTAN
MAC ILGORHAM	ULSTER TARTAN	MAC KAIN	See MAC KEAN
MAC ILGORM	ULSTER TARTAN	MAC KANE	See MAC KEAN
MAC ILHAIR	ULSTER TARTAN	MAC KANGLEY	Co. CAVAN
MAC ILHAIR	Co. DONEGAL	MAC KARLEY	ORIEL TARTAN
MAC ILHARGY	ULSTER TARTAN	MAC KAVANAH	Co. ANTRIM
MAC ILHARGY	Co. ANTRIM	MAC KAY	MAC KAY
MAC ILHARRGA	Co. LONDONDERRY	MAC KAY	MAC DONALD
MAC ILHATTON	ULSTER TARTAN	MAC KAY	ULSTER TARTAN
MAC ILHATTON	Co. ANTRIM	MAC KEADIAN	Co. ROSCOMMON
MAC ILHATTON	Co. LONDONDERRY	MAC KEADY	Co. LAOIS
MAC ILHENNY	ULSTER TARTAN	MAC KEAG	ULSTER TARTAN
MAC ILHERON	ULSTER TARTAN	MAC KEAGNEY	ORIEL TARTAN
MAC ILHOLM	Co. FERMANAGH	MAC KEAGHRY	ULSTER TARTAN
MAC ILHOME	Co. TYRONE	MAC KEAGUE	ULSTER TARTAN
MAC ILHOYLE	ULSTER TARTAN	MAC KEAHAN	CONNACHT TARTAN
MAC ILHOYLE	Co. FERMANAGH	MAC KEAHERY	ULSTER TARTAN
MAC ILHOYLE	Co. LONDONDERRY	MAC KEALAGHAN	Co. WESTMEATH
MAC ILLESHER	CO. FERMANAGH	MAC KEAN(E)	MAC KEAN
MAC ILLESHER	GREENE	MAC KEAN(E)	MAC DONALD
MAC ILMEEL	ORIEL TARTAN	MAC KEAN(E)	ULSTER TARTAN
MAC ILMOYLE	ORIEL TARTAN	MAC KEAN(E)	M'DON,ARDNAMURCHAN
MAC ILMURRAY	Co. FERMANAGH	MAC KEARNEY	Co. MEATH

"IRISH" indicates a choice of a general Irish tartan: "All Ireland", "Tara", "Clodagh", "Irish National", "St. Patrick"

TARTANS FOR IRISH NAMES

Anyone with a "County" Tartan may substitute one of the major "District" tartans listed below:.

Galway, Leitrim, Mayo, Roscommon, Sligo:	Connacht tartan
Clare, Cork, Kerry, Limmerick, Tipperary, Waterford:	Munster tartan
Armagh, Down, Fermanagh, Louth, Monaghan:	Oriel tartan
Carlow, Dublin, Kildare, Kilkenny, Laois, Longford:	
Meath, Offaly, Westmeath, Wexford, Wicklow:	Leinster tartan
Antrim, Armagh, Cavan, Donegal, Londonderry, Tyrone:	Ulster tartan

SURNAME	TARTAN	SURNAME	TARTAN
MAC KEARNEY	ULSTER TARTAN	MAC KERVIN	Co. DOWN
MAC KEARY	Co. MONAGHAN	MAC KETRICK	See MAC KITTRICK
MAC KEATING	Co. TIPPERARY	MAC KETTIRICK	See MAC KITTRICK
MAC KECHNIE	MAC DONALD	MAC KEVANY	CONNACHT TARTAN
MAC KEDIAN	Co. ROSCOMMON	MAC KEVENY	CONNACHT TARTAN
MAC KEE	MAC KAY	MAC KEVIN(S)	ULSTER TARTAN
MAC KEE	ULSTER TARTAN	MAC KEVIN(S)	Co. DONEGAL
MAC KEE	Co. ANTRIM	MAC KEVITT	ORIEL TARTAN
MAC KEEFRY	Co. TYRONE	MAC KEW	MAC KAY
MAC KEEHAN	CONNACHT TARTAN	MAC KEW	ULSTER TARTAN
MAC KEEMAN	MAC KINNON	MAC KEY	MAC KAY
MAC KEEMAN	ULSTER TARTAN	MAC KEY	ULSTER TARTAN
MAC KEEVEEN	CONNACHT TARTAN	MAC KIBBIN(S)	ULSTER TARTAN
MAC KEEVER(S)	MAC KEEVER	MAC KIERAN	Co. DONEGAL
MAC KEEVER(S)	MAC IVER	MAC KIERNAN	CONNACHT TARTAN
MAC KEEVER(S)	ORIEL TARTAN	MAC KIGGAN(S)	CONNACHT TARTAN
MAC KEEVER(S)	ULSTER TARTAN	MAC KIGO	Co. CORK
MAC KEGNEY	ORIEL TARTAN	MAC KILBANE	CONNACHT TARTAN
MAC KEHILLY	Co. CORK	MAC KILBOY	Co. DONEGAL
MAC KEHOE	KEOGH	MAC KILBRIDE	CONNACHT TARTAN
MAC KEHOE	Co. WICKLOW	MAC KILCARR	Co. DONEGAL
MAC KEIGHRY	Co. GALWAY	MAC KILCASH	Co. SLIGO
MAC KEIGUE	Co. GALWAY	MAC KILCAWLEY	Co. SLIGO
MAC KEITH	KEITH	MAC KILCHRIST	See GILCHRIST
MAC KELL	ULSTER TARTAN	MAC KILCOMMON(S)	Co. GALWAY
MAC KELLAN	MAC LELLEN	MAC KILCOOLEY	Co. CLARE
MAC KELLAN	ORIEL TARTAN	MAC KILCOURSE	Co. MAYO
MAC KELLOCH	ULSTER TARTAN	MAC KILCOYLE	ULSTER TARTAN
MAC KELLY	See KELLY	MAC KILCOYNE	CONNACHT TARTAN
MAC KELVY	Co. DONEGAL	MAC KILCULLEN	Co. SLIGO
MAC KEMISH	See JAMES	MAC KILDEA	CONNACHT TARTAN
MAC KEMMIN(S)	See KIMMONS	MAC KILDERRY	Co. CLARE
MAC KENDRY	See MAC HENRY	MAC KILDUFF	MAC FIE
MAC KENERY	Co. OFFALY	MAC KILDUFF	CONNACHT TARTAN
MAC KENNA	ULSTER TARTAN	MAC KILDUFF	Co. GALWAY
MAC KENNA	Co. KERRY	MAC KILDUNN	Co. SLIGO
MAC KENNA	Co. MONAGHAN	MAC KILEENY	Co. LAOIS
MAC KENNAGH	See MAC KENNA	MAC KILELINE	Co. ROSCOMMON
MAC KENNAN	ORIEL TARTAN	MAC KILFEATHER	CONNACHT TARTAN
MAC KENNIFF	Co. CAVAN	MAC KILFEDDER	Co. SLIGO
MAC KENTY	See MAC KINTY	MAC KILGALLEN	Co. MAYO
MAC KEOGH	KEOGH	MAC KILGAR	See KILGORE
MAC KEOGH	CLAN CIAN/O'CARROLL	MAC KILGORE	See KILGORE
MAC KEOGH	Co. ROSCOMMON	MAC KILGREW	CONNACHT TARTAN
MAC KEOGHANE	Co. CORK	MAC KILGUNN	GUNN
MAC KEON	CONNACHT TARTAN	MAC KILGUNN	ULSTER TARTAN
MAC KEON	Co. ANTRIM	MAC KILKY	Co. LONDONDERRY
MAC KEON	Co. LEITRIM	MAC KILLACKY	Co. OFFALY
MAC KEONEEN	CONNACHT TARTAN	MAC KILLAHY	Co. OFFALY
MAC KEOWN	CONNACHT TARTAN	MAC KILLEGAR	ULSTER TARTAN
MAC KERMODE	MAC DERMAID	MAC KILLEN	MAC KILLEN
MAC KERMODY	MAC DERMAID	MAC KILLEN	ORIEL TARTAN
MAC KERNAN	ORIEL TARTAN	MAC KILLERAN	Co. ROSCOMMON
MAC KERRISK	Co. KERRY	MAC KILLERLEAN	Co. SLIGO
MAC KERVEY	Co. FERMANAGH	MAC KILLILEA	Co. GALWAY

"IRISH" indicates a choice of a general Irish tartan: "All Ireland", "Tara", "Clodagh", "Irish National", "St. Patrick"

TARTANS FOR IRISH NAMES

Mac Killop   *Mac Lornan*

Anyone with a "County" Tartan may substitute one of the major "District" tartans listed below:

Galway, Leitrim, Mayo, Roscommon, Sligo:	**Connacht tartan**
Clare, Cork, Kerry, Limmerick, Tipperary, Waterford:	**Munster tartan**
Armagh, Down, Fermanagh, Louth, Monaghan:	**Oriel tartan**
Carlow, Dublin, Kildare, Kilkenny, Laois, Longford:	
Meath, Offaly, Westmeath, Wexford, Wicklow:	**Leinster tartan**
Antrim, Armagh, Cavan, Donegal, Down, Londonderry, Tyrone:	**Ulster tartan**

SURNAME	TARTAN	SURNAME	TARTAN
MAC KILLOP	MAC KILLOP	MAC KRANN	See MAC CRANN
MAC KILLOP	STEWART OF APPIN	MAC KRANN	Co. LEITRIM
MAC KILLOP	ULSTER TARTAN	MAC KURDY	See MAC KIRDY
MAC KILLORAN	Co. SLIGO	MAC KUSKER	Co. TYRONE
MAC KILLOUGHREY	Co. CLARE	MAC LAFFERTY	ULSTER TARTAN
MAC KILMARTIN	CONNACHT TARTAN	MAC LAIN(E)	MAC LAINE
MAC KILMARY	Co. LONDONDERRY	MAC LAIN(E)	ULSTER TARTAN
MAC KILMET	Co. WESTMEATH	MAC LANDRISH	ULSTER TARTAN
MAC KILMORE	Co. SLIGO	MAC LANDRISH	MAC DONALD
MAC KILMURRAY	Co. LONDONDERRY	MAC LANE	See MAC LEAN
MAC KILPATRICK	ULSTER TARTAN	MAC LARDY	MAC DONALD
MAC KILRAIN	Co. ROSCOMMON	MAC LARDY	ULSTER TARTAN
MAC KILROE	Co. ROSCOMMON	MAC LARNEY	ORIEL TARTAN
MAC KILROY	Co. ROSCOMMON	MAC LARNON	MAC LENNAN
MAC KILVANT	Co. WESTMEATH	MAC LARNON	ULSTER TARTAN
MAC KILVEA	Co. SLIGO	MAC LARY	ULSTER TARTAN
MAC KILVEEN	ULSTER TARTAN	MAC LAUGHLIN,-AN	MAC LACHLAN
MAC KILVEEN	Co. DOWN	MAC LAUGHLIN,-AN	ULSTER TARTAN
MAC KIM(M)	FRASER	MAC LAUGHLIN,-AN	Co. LONDONDERRY
MAC KIM(M)	ULSTER TARTAN	MAC LAUGHLIN,-AN	Co. ARMAGH
MAC KIMMONS	See KIMMONS	MAC LAVE	Co. ROSCOMMON
MAC KINIRY	Co. LIMMERICK	MAC LAVERTY	ULSTER TARTAN
MAC KINLAY,-LEY	MAC KINLAY	MAC LAVIN	Co. WESTMEATH
MAC KNLAY,-LEY	ULSTER TARTAN	MAC LAVY	Co. LONGFORD
MAC KINLAY,-LEY	Co. ANTRIM	MAC LAY	MAC LAY
MAC KINLAY,-LEY	Co. DONEGAL	MAC LAY	ULSTER TARTAN
MAC KINN	ULSTER TARTAN	MAC LEA	See MAC LAY
MAC KINNARNEY	Co. OFFALY	MAC LEACH	LEACH
MAC KINNAWE	CONNACHT TARTAN	MAC LEACH	Co. DONEGAL
MAC KINNEAVY	CONNACHT TARTAN	MAC LEAR	Co. TYRONE
MAC KINNEEN	CONNACHT TARTAN	MAC LEARY	ULSTER TARTAN
MAC KINNEN	MAC KINNON	MAC LEE(S)	ULSTER TARTAN
MAC KINNEN	CONNACHT TARTAN	MAC LEE(S)	Co. LONDONDERRY
MAC KINNEY	ULSTER TARTAN	MAC LEHERAN,-ON	ULSTER TARTAN
MAC KINSTRY	ULSTER TARTAN	MAC LELAND	See MAC LELLEN
MAC KINTY	MAC KENZIE	MAC LELLEN,-AN	MAC LELLEN
MAC KINTY	ULSTER TARTAN	MAC LELLEN.-AN	ULSTER TARTAN
MAC KIRDY	MAC KIRDY	MAC LENIGAN	Co. KILKENNY
MAC KIRDY	STUART of BUTE	MAC LENIGAN	ULSTER TARTAN
MAC KIRDY	ULSTER TARTAN	MAC LENNAN,-ON	MAC LENNAN
MAC KISSACK	MAC KUSSACK	MAC LENNAN,-ON	ULSTER TARTAN
MAC KISSACK	ULSTER TARTAN	MAC LENNEN,-IN	See MAC LENNAN
MAC KISSACK	CUSSACK	MAC LERNAN	Co. DOWN
MAC KISSOCK	See MAC KUSSACK	MAC LERNEY	ORIEL TARTAN
MAC KITTERICK	See MAC KITTRICK	MAC LERNON	See MAC LARNON
MAC KITTRICK	DOUGLAS	MAC LEROY	Co. DOWN
MAC KITTRICK	ORIEL TARTAN	MAC LESTER	MAC ALISTER
MAC KITTRICK	ULSTER TARTAN	MAC LEVY	Co. LONGFORD
MAC KIVERKIN	Co. DOWN	MAC LIAMMOIR	Co. TYRONE
MAC KNIFF	See MAC NIFF	MAC LICE	Co. LONDONDERRY
MAC KNIGHT	MAC NACHTEN	MAC LINDON	ULSTER TARTAN
MAC KNIGHT	ULSTER TARTAN	MAC LISE	Co. LONDONDERRY
MAC KONE	Co. LOUTH	MAC LOON(E)	ULSTER TARTAN
MAC KONE	Co. MONAGHAN	MAC LOON(E)	Co. ANTRIM
MAC KOWGE	Co. GALWAY	MAC LORNAN	See MAC LARNON

"IRISH" indicates a choice of a general Irish tartan: "All Ireland", "Tara", "Clodagh", "Irish National", "St. Patrick"

TARTANS FOR IRISH NAMES

Mac Loughlin

Mac Neish

Anyone with a "County" Tartan may substitute one of the major "District" tartans listed below:

Galway, Leitrim, Mayo, Roscommon, Sligo:	Connacht tartan
Clare, Cork, Kerry, Limmerick, Tipperary, Waterford:	Munster tartan
Armagh, Down, Fermanagh, Louth, Monaghan:	Oriel tartan
Carlow, Dublin, Kildare, Kilkenny, Laois, Longford:	
Meath, Offaly, Westmeath, Wexford, Wicklow:	Leinster tartan
Antrim, Armagh, Cavan, Donegal, Down, Londonderry, Tyrone:	Ulster tartan

SURNAME	TARTAN	SURNAME	TARTAN
		MAC MUNIGAL	ULSTER TARTAN
MAC LOUGHLIN,-AN	MAC LACHLAN	MAC MUNN	ULSTER TARTAN
MAC LOUGHLIN,-AN	Co. DONEGAL	MAC MURDY	Co. CAVAN
MAC LYCHOK	CLAN CIAN/O'CARROLL	MAC MURLAND	Co. DOWN
MAC LYNCH(Y)	See LYNCH	MAC MURPHY	See MURPHY
MAC LYNCHEHAN	See LYNCH	MAC MURRAN	CONNACHT TARTAN
MAC LYSAGHT	O' BRIEN	MAC MURRAY	See MURRAY
MAC LYSAGHT	Co. CLARE	MAC MURROUGH	Co. WEXFORD
MAC MACKEN,-IN	ORIEL TARTAN	MAC MURTRY	IRISH-See Footnote
MAC MAGH	MATHESON	MAC MURTY	ULSTER TARTAN
MAC MAHAN	See MAC MAHON	MAC MURTY	Co. ANTRIM
MAC MAHEN	See MAC MAHON	MAC MYLER	Co. WEXFORD
MAC MAHON	ORIEL TARTAN	MAC MYLOYD	Co. MAYO
MAC MAHON	MUNSTER TARTAN	MAC NAB(B)	MAC NAB
MAC MAHON	O' BRIEN	MAC NAB(B)	ULSTER TARTAN
MAC MAHON	Co. CLARE	MAC NABNEY	ULSTER TARTAN
MAC MAHON	Co. MONAGHAN	MAC NABNEY	Co. DOWN
MAC MANAMON	Co. MAYO	MAC NABOE	Co. CAVAN
MAC MANAMY	Co. ROSCOMMON	MAC NABOOLA	Co. SLIGO
MAC MANUS	ULSTER TARTAN	MAC NABOOLA	CONNACHT TARTAN
MAC MANUS	Co. FERMANAGH	MAC NACHTEN	MAC NACHTEN
MAC MANUS	Co. ROSCOMMON	MAC NACHTEN	ULSTER TARTAN
MAC MARTIN	See MARTIN	MAC NACHTEN	Co. LONDONDERRY
MAC MASTER	MAC MASTER	MAC NACHTEN	Co. CLARE
MAC MASTER	ULSTER TARTAN	MAC NACHTEN	Co. GALWAY
MAC MASTER	Co. LONGFORD	MAC NALLY	Mc INALLY
MAC MATH	MATHESON	MAC NALLY	ORIEL TARTAN
MAC MAUGH	MATHESON	MAC NALLY	Co. ANTRIM
MAC MAWE	MATHESON	MAC NALLY	Co. MAYO
MAC MAYO	Co. MAYO	MAC NALLY	Co. MONAGHAN
MAC MEANY	Co. MONAGHAN	MAC NALLY	ULSTER TARTAN
MAC MEARTY	ULSTER TARTAN	MAC NALTY	See MAC NULTY
MAC MEARTY	Co. DONEGAL	MAC NAMARA	MAC NAMARA
MAC MECHAN	MAC MICHAEL	MAC NAMARA	CLAN CIAN/O'CARROLL
MAC MEEKAN	MAC MICHAEL	MAC NAMEE	ULSTER TARTAN
MAC MEEKINS	MAC MICHAEL	MAC NAMEE	Co. ANTRIM
MAC MEEL	MAC MICHAEL	MAC NAMEE	Co. LONDONDERRY
MAC MEEL	ORIEL TARTAN	MAC NAMIRE	MAC NAMARA
MAC MEILER	Co. WEXFORD	MAC NAMIRE	CLAN CIAN/O'CARROLL
MAC MENAMIN	ULSTER TARTAN	MAC NANA	CONNACHT TARTAN
MAC MENAMIN	Co. DONEGAL	MAC NANANY	Co. ROSCOMMON
MAC MENAMIN	Co. TYRONE	MAC NASTY	ULSTER TARTAN
MAC MERTY	Co. DONEGAL	MAC NAUGHER	O' CONNOR
MAC MICHAEL	MAC MICHAEL	MAC NAUGHT	See MAC NACHTEN
MAC MILLAN	MAC MILLAN	MAC NAUGHTON	See MAC NACHTEN
MAC MILLAN	ULSTER TARTAN	MAC NAUL	ULSTER TARTAN
MAC MILLEN	See MAC MILLAN	MAC NAULTY	See MAC NULTY
MAC MISGAR	CLAN CIAN/O'CARROLL	MAC NAVIN	See MAC NIVEN
MAC MORDY	ULSTER TARTAN	MAC NAY	MAC GREGOR
MAC MORELAND	Co. DOWN	MAC NEA	MAC GREGOR
MAC MORROW	Co. LETRIM	MAC NEILL	MAC NEILL
MAC MUIRIS	Co. KERRY	MAC NEILL	ULSTER TARTAN
MAC MULDROW	ULSTER TARTAN	MAC NEILLY	See MAC NEILL
MAC MULKIN	ULSTER TARTAN	MAC NEISH	MAC NEISH
MAC MULLAN,-EN	See MAC MILLAN	MAC NEISH	MAC GREGOR
		MAC NEISH	ULSTER TARTAN

"IRISH" indicates a choice of a general Irish tartan: "All Ireland", "Tara", "Clodagh", "Irish National", "St. Patrick"

Anyone with a "County" Tartan may substitute one of the major "District" tartans listed below:

Galway, Leitrim, Mayo, Roscommon, Sligo:	**Connacht tartan**
Clare, Cork, Kerry, Limmerick, Tipperary, Waterford:	**Munster tartan**
Armagh, Down, Fermanagh, Louth, Monaghan:	**Oriel tartan**
Carlow, Dublin, Kildare, Kilkenny, Laois, Longford:	
Meath, Offaly, Westmeath, Wexford, Wicklow:	**Leinster tartan**
Antrim, Armagh, Cavan, Donegal, Down, Londonderry, Tyrone:	**Ulster tartan**

SURNAME	TARTAN	SURNAME	TARTAN
MAC NEISH	ULSTER TARTAN	MAC PHILLIPS	Co. MAYO
MAC NEIVE	Co. ROSCOMMON	MAC POLIN(N)	ORIEL TARTAN
MAC NEL(L)IS	Co. DONEGAL	MAC PURTLAN(D)	Co. ARMAGH
MAC NELICE	Co. DONEGAL	MAC QUADE	MUNSTER TARTAN
MAC NELLO	Co. LONGFORD	MAC QUADE	Co. MONAGHAN
MAC NERLN	Co. SLIGO	MAC QUAID	See MAC QUADE
MAC NESTOR	Co. CLARE	MAC QUAIL	See QUAIL
MAC NESTRY	ULSTER TARTAN	MAC QUALEY	See QUALLY
MAC NEVEN	See MAC NIVEN	MAC QUALLY	See QUALLY
MAC NEVIN	See MAC NIVEN	MAC QUALYE	See QUAIL
MAC NEVINS	CLAN CIAN/O'CARROLL	MAC QUAY	MAC KAY
MAC NICHOL(L)	MAC NICHOL	MAC QUEALLY	See QUALLY
MAC NICHOLAS	MAC NICHOL	MAC QUEEN	MAC QUEEN
MAC NICKLE	MAC NICHOL	MAC QUEEN	ULSTER TARTAN
MAC NICLE	MAC NICHOL	MAC QUEENY	Co. ROSCOMMON
MAC NIEVE	Co. ROSCOMMON	MAC QUEY	MAC KAY
MAC NIFF	MAC GREGOR	MAC QUIGGAN,-IN	ULSTER TARTAN
MAC NIFF	CONNACHT TARTAN	MAC QUILKIN	ULSTER TARTAN
MAC NIFF	Co. LEITRIM	MAC QUILLAN	ULSTER TARTAN
MAC NINCH	MAC INNES	MAC QUILLAN	Co. ANTRIM
MAC NIVEN	MAC NIVEN	MAC QUILLIAM(S)	See MAC WILLIAM
MAC NIVEN	ULSTER TARTAN	MAC QUILLY	ORIEL TARTAN
MAC NIX	Co. CAVAN	MAC QUILLY	Co. ROSCOMMON
MAC NOLLAG	Co. LONGFORD	MAC QUINN	QUINN
MAC NORGAN	Co. CARLOW	MAC QUINN	Co. KERRY
MAC NORMOYLE	CO. CLARE	MAC QUINNELLY	Co. CORK
MAC NOWD	MAC NACHTEN	MAC QUINNEY	Co. TYRONE
MAC NULLA	ULSTER TARTAN	MAC QUINNIFFE	CONNACHT TARTAN
MAC NULLY	ULSTER TARTAN	MAC QUINTER	MAC WHORTER
MAC NULTY	ULSTER TARTAN	MAC QUISTON	MAC DONALD
MAC NULTY	Co. CAVAN	MAC QUISTON	ULSTER TARTAN
MAC NULTY	Co. DONEGAL	MAC QUITTY	MAC KENZIE
MAC OLIVE	Co.CORK	MAC QUOID	MAC KAY
MAC ONION	ORIEL TARTAN	MAC QUOID	ULSTER TARTAN
MAC OSCAR	ULSTER TARTAN	MAC RAITH	See MAC RATH
MAC OSTRICH	Co. CORK	MAC RANN	Co. LEITRIM
MAC OWENS	ULSTER TARTAN	MAC RANNEL	M'DON CLANRANALD
MAC PADDEN	MAC FADYEN	MAC RANNEL	Co. LEITRIM
MAC PADDEN	CONNACHT TARTAN	MAC RAT(T)IGAN	Co. ROSCOMMON
MAC PADINE	See MAC PADDEN	MAC RATH	MAC GRATH
MAC PARLON(S)	MAC FARLANE	MAC RATH	ULSTER TARTAN
MAC PARLON(S)	Co. WEXFORD	MAC REARY	MAC CREARY
MAC PARRLAN(D)	MAC FARLANE	MAC REAVY	CONNACHT TARTAN
MAC PARTLAN	ULSTER TARTAN	MAC REDMOND	CONNACHT TARTAN
MAC PATRICK	LAMONT	MAC REDMOND	Co. OFFALY
MAC PEAK(E)	ULSTER TARTAN	MAC REEDY	Co. KILKENNY
MAC PHAIL	MAC PHAIL	MAC RICHEY	See RITCHIE
MAC PHAIL	ULSTER TARTAN	MAC RICKARD	IRISH-See Footnote
MAC PHARLON	MAC FARLANE	MAC RIFFERTY	Co. FERMANAGH
MAC PHARLON	ULSTER TARTAN	MAC RINN	Co. LEITRIM
MAC PHELEMY	Co. TYRONE	MAC RITCHIE	See RITCHIE
MAC PHELIM	Co. TYRONE	MAC RIVERTY	Co. FERMANAGH
MAC PHILBIN	CONNACHT TARTAN	MAC ROARKE	Co. DONEGAL
MAC PHILLIPS	MAC KILLOP	MAC ROARTY	Co. DONEGAL
MAC PHILLIPS	M' DON of KEPPOCH	MAC ROBB	See ROBB

"IRISH" indicates a choice of a general Irish tartan: "All Ireland", "Tara", "Clodagh", "Irish National", "St. Patrick"

TARTANS FOR IRISH NAMES

Mac Robbin   *Mac Vann*

Anyone with a "County" Tartan may substitute one of the major "District" tartans listed below:.

Galway, Leitrim, Mayo, Roscommon, Sligo:	**Connacht tartan**
Clare, Cork, Kerry, Limmerick, Tipperary, Waterford:	**Munster tartan**
Armagh, Down, Fermanagh, Louth, Monaghan:	**Oriel tartan**
Carlow, Dublin, Kildare, Kilkenny, Laois, Longford:	
Meath, Offaly, Westmeath, Wexford, Wicklow:	**Leinster tartan**
Antrim, Armagh, Cavan, Donegal, Down, Londonderry, Tyrone:	**Ulster tartan**

SURNAME	TARTAN	SURNAME	TARTAN
MAC ROBBIN	See ROBB	MAC SPORRAN	ULSTER TARTAN
MAC ROBERTS	See ROBERTSON	MAC STAY	Co. DOWN
MAC ROBIN	See ROBB	MAC STEPHENS	See STEPHENSON
MAC RORY	MAC RORY	MAC STEVENS	See STEVENSON
MAC RORY	Co. LONDONDERRY	MAC STOCKER	ULSTER TARTAN
MAC RUDDERERY	Co. WESTMEATH	MAC STRAVICK	ULSTER TARTAN
MAC RUM(M)	ULSTER TARTAN	MAC STRAVICK	Co. TYRONE
MAC RYNNE	CONNACHT TARTAN	MAC SWEENY	Co. CORK
MAC SALLY	ORIEL TARTAN	MAC SWIGGAN	Co. TYRONE
MAC SANAGHY	CONNACHT TARTAN	MAC SWINE	ULSTER TARTAN
MAC SCAHILL	Co. GALWAY	MAC SWINE	Co. DONEGAL
MAC SCALLY	See SCALLY	MAC TAGALIN	MAC DONALD
MAC SCANLAN	Co. LOUTH	MAC TAGALIN	ULSTER TARTAN
MAC SCOLLARD	CO. MONAGHAN	MAC TAGGART	MAC TAGGART
MAC SCOLLOG,-OIG	Co. MONAGHAN	MAC TAGGART	ULSTER TARTAN
MAC SHADY	Co. CLARE	MAC TAGGART	Co. TYRONE
MAC SHAFFRAY	ULSTER TARTAN	MAC TAGHLIN	Co. DONEGAL
MAC SHAFFREY	Co. LONGFORD	MAC TAGHLIN	ULSTER TARTAN
MAC SHANE	MAC SHANE	MAC TAGUE	ULSTER TARTAN
MAC SHANE	O' FARRELL	MAC TAGUE	Co. DONEGAL
MAC SHANE	O' NEILL	MAC TALDRIDGE	ULSTER TARTAN
MAC SHANE	ULSTER TARTAN	MAC TAMINY	See TAMMINAY
MAC SHANE	Co. TYRONE	MAC TANSY,-SAY,-SEY	Co. SLIGO
MAC SHANLEY	Co. LEITRIM	MAC TARSNEY	ULSTER TARTAN
MAC SHARRY	Co. ARMAGH	MAC TAVISH	MAC TAVISH
MAC SHARRY	Co. CAVAN	MAC TAVISH	ULSTER TARTAN
MAC SHEARHOUR	Co. KERRY	MAC TEAGUE	ULSTER TARTAN
MAC SHEEDY	CLAN CIAN/O'CARROLL	MAC TEER	See MAC INTYRE
MAC SHEERA	CLAN CIAN/O'CARROLL	MAC TEIGE	Co. MAYO
MAC SHEERA	Co. LAOIS	MAC TEIGE	ULSTER TARTAN
MAC SHEEY	MAC DONALD	MAC TEIGE	Co. DONEGAL
MAC SHEEY	Co. ARMAGH	MAC TEIGH	Co. DONEGAL
MAC SHEEY	Co. LIMMERICK	MAC TEIGUE	Co. LEITRIM
MAC SHERA	CLAN CIAN/O'CARROLL	MAC TIERNAN	CONNACHT TARTAN
MAC SHERA	Co. LAOIS	MAC TIERNAN	Co. FERMANAGH
MAC SHERRY	ULSTER TARTAN	MAC TIGH(E)	Co. DONEGAL
MAC SKEEHAN	CONNACHT TARTAN	MAC TIGH(E)	Co. MAYO
MAC SKEHAN	CONNACHT TARTAN	MAC TIGUE	Co. DONEGAL
MAC SKIMMINS	ULSTER TARTAN	MAC TIGUE	Co. MAYO
MAC SLAIN(E0	Co. CORK	MAC TIMPANY	ULSTER TARTAN
MAC SLAYNE	Co. CORK	MAC TIMPANY	Co. DOWN
MAC SLINEY	Co. CORK	MAC TORLEY	ULSTER TARTAN
MAC SLYNE	Co. CORK	MAC TULLY	ULSTER TARTAN
MAC SOLL(E)Y	ORIEL TARTAN	MAC TULLY	Co. CAVAN
MAC SORLEY	MAC DONALD	MAC TUMELTY	ORIEL TARTAN
MAC SORLEY	ULSTER TARTAN	MAC TURLEY	ULSTER TARTAN
MAC SPADDEN,-IN	MAC DONALD	MAC TURLOUGH	ULSTER TARTAN
MAC SPADDEN,-IN	ULSTER TARTAN	MAC USKER	ULSTER TARTAN
MAC SPADDEN,-IN	Co. DOWN	MAC USKER	Co. TYRONE
MAC SPARRAN,-EN	See MAC SPORRAN	MAC VADDOCK	Co. WEXFORD
MAC SPEDDIN(G)	See MAC SPADDEN	MAC VALLELLY	ORIEL TARTAN
MAC SPILLANE	See SPILLANE	MAC VALLEY	ORIEL TARTAN
MAC SPORRAN	MAC SPORRAN	MAC VANAMY	CONNACHT TARTAN
MAC SPORRAN	MAC DONALD	MAC VANN	CONNACHT TARTAN
		MAC VANN	ULSTER TARTAN

"IRISH" indicates a choice of a general Irish tartan: "All Ireland", "Tara", "Clodagh", "Irish National", "St. Patrick"

TARTANS FOR IRISH NAMES

Mac Vanny   *Maginver*

Anyone with a "County" Tartan may substitute one of the major "District" tartans listed below:

Galway, Leitrim, Mayo, Roscommon, Sligo:	Connacht tartan
Clare, Cork, Kerry, Limmerick, Tipperary, Waterford:	Munster tartan
Armagh, Down, Fermanagh, Louth, Monaghan:	Oriel tartan
Carlow, Dublin, Kildare, Kilkenny, Laois, Longford, Meath, Offaly, Westmeath, Wexford, Wicklow:	Leinster tartan
Antrim, Armagh, Cavan, Donegal, Down, Londonderry, Tyrone:	Ulster tartan

SURNAME	TARTAN	SURNAME	TARTAN
MAC VANNY	Co. MAYO		
MAC VARILY	CONNACHT TARTAN		
MAC VARLEY	CONNACHT TARTAN		**M**
MAC VARRELLY	CONNACHT TARTAN		
MAC VARRY	ULSTER TARTAN		
MAC VAUGH	Co. LEITRIM		
MAC VAY	See MAC VEIGH		
MAC VEAN	CONNACHT TARTAN	MACK	MACK
MAC VEAN	ULSTER TARTAN	MACKEEN	CO. CLARE
MAC VEIGH	MAC LEAN of DUART	MACKEN	Co. DOWN
MAC VEIGH	ULSTER TARTAN	MACKEN	Co. MAYO
MAC VEIGH	Co. ARMAGH	MACKEY, -IE	MAC KAY
MAC VERLY	CONNACHT TARTAN	MACKEY, -IE	Co. LIMMERICK
MAC VERRY	ULSTER TARTAN	MACKEY, -IE	Co. TIPPERARY
MAC VEY	See MAC VEIGH	MACKIN	Co. MAYO
MAC VICAR	CAMPBELL	MACKLEHATTON	ULSTER TARTAN
MAC VICAR	ULSTER TARTAN	MACKLEHATTON	Co. ANTRIM
MAC VICKER	See MAC VICAR	MACKLEHATTON	Co. LONDONDERRY
MAC VIRLY	CONNACHT TARTAN	MACLEMOYLE	See MAC IMOYLE
MAC VITTY	Co. ANTRIM	MACPARRLAN(D)	See MAC FARLANE
MAC VITTY	ULSTER TARTAN	MADDED	Co. GALWAY
MAC WALTA(H)	WALTERS	MADDED	Co. TIPPERARY
MAC WALTA(H)	CONNACHT TARTAN	MADDEN	Co. GALWAY
MAC WARD	Co. DONEGAL	MADDEN	Co. MAYO
MAC WARD	ULSTER TARTAN	MADDOCK	Co. WEXFORD
MAC WAY	See MAC VEIGH	MADDOX	Co. WEXFORD
MAC WAYNE	CLAN CIAN	MADEEN	CONNACHT TARTAN
MAC WEEN	See MAC QUEEN	MADELL	ORIEL TARTAN
MAC WEEN	CLAN CIAN/O'CARROLL	MADIGAN	Co. LIMMERICK
MAC WEENY	MAC QUEEN	MADILL	ORIEL TARTAN
MAC WEENY	Co. LEITRIM	MAFFET(T)	MOFFET
MAC WEENY	Co. ROSCOMMON	MAGAGHAN	ORIEL TARTAN
MAC WEY	See MAC VEIGH	MAGAN(N)	CLAN CIAN/O'CARROLL
MAC WHANNON	CONNACHT TARTAN	MAGANNON	Co. MAYO
MAC WHINNEY	MAC KENZIE	MAGARR	ULSTER TARTAN
MAC WHINNEY	ULSTER TARTAN	MAGAURAN	Co. CAVAN
MAC WHINNEY	Co. ANTRIM	MAGAW	See MAC GAW
MAC WHIRTER	MAC WHORTER	MAGEE	See MAC GEE
MAC WHIRTER	ULSTER TARTAN	MAGEEAN	ULSTER TARTAN
MAC WHISTON	See MAC QUISTON	MAGEEVER	See MAC KEEVER
MAC WHITE	ULSTER TARTAN	MAGENNESS	See MAGENNIS
MAC WIGGIN(S)	ULSTER TARTAN	MAGENNIS	MAC INNES
MAC WIGGIN(S0	Co. FERMANAGH	MAGENNIS	ULSTER TARTAN
MAC WILLIAM(S)	MAC WILLIAM	MAGEOWN	See MAC GOWAN
MAC WILLIAM(S)	ORIEL TARTAN	MAGETTY	HAY
MAC WILLIAM(S)	ULSTER TARTAN	MAGETTY	ULSTER TARTAN
MAC WILLIAM(S)	Co. LONDONDERRY	MAGHERY	Co. LIMERICK
MAC WORTH	Co. CORK	MAGILL	MAC GILL
		MAGILL	ULSTER TARTAN
		MAGILMARTIN	O' NEILL
		MAGINA	Co. KERRY
		MAGINN	ULSTER TARTAN
		MAGINN	Co. ANTRIM
		MAGINNAW	Co. KERRY
		MAGINTY	ULSTER TARTAN
		MAGINVER	Co. LONGFORD

"IRISH" indicates a general Irish tartan: "All Ireland:, "Tara", "Clodagh", Irish National", "St. Patrick"

60

TARTANS FOR IRISH NAMES

Anyone with a "County" Tartan may substitute one of the major "District" tartans listed below:

Galway, Leitrim, Mayo, Roscommon, Sligo:	Connacht tartan
Clare, Cork, Kerry, Limmerick, Tipperary, Waterford:	Munster tartan
Armagh, Down, Fermanagh, Louth, Monaghan:	Oriel tartan
Carlow, Dublin, Kildare, Kilkenny, Laois, Longford:	
Meath, Offaly, Westmeath, Wexford, Wicklow:	Leinster tartan
Antrim, Armagh, Cavan, Donegal, Down, Londonderry, Tyrone:	Ulster tartan

SURNAME	TARTAN	SURNAME	TARTAN
MAGLAMERY	MONTGOMERY	MALONEY	Co. CLARE
MAGLAMERY	Co. DOWN	MALOON	Co. CLARE
MAGLIN	CLAN CIAN/O'CARROLL	MALOUGHNEY	Co. TIPPERARY
MAGNEL(L)	Co. CORK	MALSEED	Co. DON.
MAGONAGLE	ULSTER TARTAN	MANAHAN	Co. CORK
MAGONAGLE	Co. DONEGAL	MANASAS	Co. TYRONE
MAGONE	Co. DOWN	MANASSES	Co. TYRONE
MAGOURNAHAN	GORDON	MANDEVILLE	Co. DOWN
MAGOWAN	See MAC GOWAN	MANEELY	MAC NEIL
MAGRANE	Co. LOUTH	MANEELY	ULSTER TARTAN
MAGRATH	See MAC GRATH	MANELLIS	See MAC NELIS
MAGREECE	ORIEL TARTAN	MANGAN	ULSTER TARTAN
MAGRILLAN	MAC NEILL	MANGAN	Co. LIMMERICK
MAGUIRE	MAC GUIRE	MANGAN	Co. TYRONE
MAGUIRE	MAGUIRE	MANIHAN	Co. CORK
MAGULLION	Co. LONGFORD	MANKETTRICK	IRISH-See Footnote
MAHADA(Y)	Co. LONGFORD	MANN	MANN
MAHAFFY	MAC FIE	MANN	ULSTER TARTAN
MAHAFFY	Co. DONEGAL	MANNERING	ULSTER TARTAN
MAHANNY	Co. CORK	MANNICE	MENZIES
MAHARG	Co. TYRONE	MANNICE	ULSTER TARTAN
MAHER	CLAN CIAN/O'CARROLL	MANNIN	Co. GALWAY
MAHEW	MAYHEW	MANNING	Co. DUBLIN
MAHEW	Co. MAYO	MANNING	Co. GALWAY
MAHON	Co. DOWN	MANNION	Co. GALWAY
MAHONY	Co. CORK	MANNIS	MENZIES
MAHOOD	LEINSTER TARTAN	MANNIS	ULSTER TARTAN
MAHOOD	O' NEILL	MANNIX	Co. CLARE
MAIILREA	ULSTER TARTAN	MANNY	Co. WESTMEATH
MAINEY	Co. OFFALY	MANOGUE	Co. LIMMERICK
MAINWARING	IRISH-See Footnote	MANRON	ULSTER TARTAN
MAIR(S)	ULSTER TARTAN	MANSELL	Co. LIMMERICK
MAJOR	ULSTER TARTAN	MANSERGH	Co TIPPERARY
MAKEEN	See MAC KEAN	MANSFIELD	DRUMMOND of PERTH
MAKES(S)Y	Co. LIMMERICK	MANSFIELD	Co. WATERFORD
MALADY	Co. WESTMEATH	MANTAN	Co. GALWAY
MALANIFFE	Co. TIPPERARY	MANTON	Co. WATERFORD
MALBROUGH	Co. CLARE	MANYUN	Co. GALWAY
MALBURY	Co. LONDONDERRY	MAPTHER	Co. ROSCOMMON
MALCOLM	MALCOLM	MARA	Co. TIPPERARY
MALCOLM	ULSTER TARTAN	MAREE	CONNACHT TARTAN
MALCOLMSON	See MALCOLM	MARK	ULSTER TARTAN
MALET	Co. CORK	MARKES	Co. LAOIS
MALIFFE	Co. GALWAY	MARKEY	ORIEL TARTAN
MALINN	Co. MONAGHAN	MARKLE	ORIEL TARTAN
MALLAGH	MAC GREGOR	MARLBOURGH	Co. CLARE
MALLAGH	ULSTER TARTAN	MARLEY	ORIEL TARTAN
MALLAHAN	ULSTER TARTAN	MARMELL	Co. KILKENNY
MALLANE	Co. CORK	MARMION	Co. DUBLIN
MALLEY	Co. MAYO	MARNAME	ULSTER TARTAN
MALLON	ULSTER TARTAN	MARNEY	ULSTER TARTAN
MALMORE	MOSS	MARRIAM	ULSTER TARTAN
MALMORE	ULSTER TARTAN	MARRILLY	ORIEL TARTAN
MALONE	Co. OFFALY	MARRINAN	ULSTER TARTAN
MALONE	Co. WESTMEATH	MARRON	ULSTER TARTAN

"IRISH" indicates a choice of a general Irish tartan: "All Ireland", "Tara", "Clodagh", "Irish National", "St. Patrick"

61

Anyone with a "County" Tartan may substitute one of the major "District" tartans listed below:

Galway, Leitrim, Mayo, Roscommon, Sligo:	Connacht tartan
Clare, Cork, Kerry, Limmerick, Tipperary, Waterford:	Munster tartan
Armagh, Down, Fermanagh, Louth, Monaghan:	Oriel tartan
Carlow, Dublin, Kildare, Kilkenny, Laois, Longford:	
Meath, Offaly, Westmeath, Wexford, Wicklow:	Leinster tartan
Antrim, Armagh, Cavan, Donegal, Down, Londonderry, Tyrone:	Ulster tartan

SURNAME	TARTAN	SURNAME	TARTAN
MARRON	CONNACHT TARTAN	MEACLE	CONNEMARA TARTAN
MARRY	Co. LOUTH	MEADE	Co. MEATH
MARSH	ULSTER TARTAN	MEAGHER	CLAN
MARSHALL	KEITH		CIAN/O'CARROLL
MARSHALL	ULSTER TARTAN	MEALIFFE	Co. GALWAY
MARTELL	ULSTER TARTAN	MEALLY	CONNACHT TARTAN
MARTIN	MARTIN	MEANY	Co. CLARE
MARTIN	O' NEILL	MEANY	Co. KILKENNY
MARTIN	CONNACHT TARTAN	MEANY	Co. OFFALY
MARTINSON	See MARIN	MEARA	Co. TIPPERARY
MARUM	Co. KILKENNY	MEARES	Co. DUBLIN
MASON	IRISH-See Footnote	MEARN(S)	ORIEL TARTAN
MASON	ULSTER TARTAN	MEATH	MATHESON
MASSEY	MATHESON	MEE	Co. ROSCOMMON
MASSEY	Co. LIMMERICK	MEEGAN	Co. MONAGHAN
MASTERSON	See MAC MASTER	MEEHAN	CONNACHT TARTAN
MASTERSON	Co. WEXFORD	MEEHAN	Co. LOUTH
MATEER	See MAC INTYRE	MEEKIAN	See MAC KEEN
MATHER	ULSTER TARTAN	MEEKIN	See MAC MICHAEL
MATHESON	MATHESON	MEEL	ORIEL TARTAN
MATHESON	ULSTER TARTAN	MEENAGH	Co. TYRONE
MATHEWS	ULSTER TARTAN	MEENAGHAN	Co. MAYO
MATTHEWS	ULSTER TARTAN	MEENAN	ULSTER TARTAN
MATTIMORE	Co. ROSCOMMON	MEENAN	Co. DONEGAL
MATURIN	IRISH-See Footnote	MEENAUGH	Co. TYRONE
MAUDE	Co. KILKENNY	MEENY	Co. SLIGO
MAUGAREN	See MAC GOVERN	MEERE	CO. CLARE
MAUGHAN	CONNACHT TARTAN	MEGARRY	ULSTER TARTAN
MAUME	Co. MAYO	MEGAW(E)	See MAC GAW
MAUNSEL	Co. LIMMERICK	MEGRATH	See MAC GRATH
MAUNSHENAN	Co. TYRONE	MEGUIGAN	See MAC GUIGAN
MAWAHAON	ULSTER TARTAN	MEHAFFY	MAC FIE
MAWE	ORIEL TARTAN	MEHARG	ORIEL TARTAN
MAWHANON	BUCHANAN	MEHARRY	IRISH-See Footnote
MAWHINNY	See MAC WHINNY	MEHEGAN	Co. CORK
MAWHITTEY	See MAC WHITTY	MEHLODY	Co. LOUTH
MAWN	Co. MAYO	MEIGHAN	Co. LOUTH
MAXEY	Co. LIMMERICK	MEILER	Co. WEXFORD
MAXWELL	MAXWELL	MELAMBY	Co. TIPPERARY
MAXWELL	ULSTER TARTAN	MELAY	CONNACHT TARTAN
MAY	Co. WESTMEATH	MELDON	ULSTER TARTAN
MAYBERRY	Co. KERRY	MELDON	Co. FERMANAGH
MAYBURY	Co. KERRY	MELLON,-AN	ULSTER TARTAN
MAYDELL	ORIEL TARTAN	MELLON,-AN	Co. GALWAY
MAYFIELD	IRISH-See Footnote	MELLON,-AN	Co. LONDONDERRY
MAYHEW	MAYHEW	MELLOT	CONNACHT TARTAN
MAYHEW	Co. MAYO	MELLY	CONNACHT TARTAN
MAYNARD	DE MAYNARD	MELODY	Co. CLARE
MAYNE	ULSTER TARTAN	MELVILLE	MELVILLE
MAYO	CONNACHT TARTAN	MELVILLE	Co. GALWAY
MAYO	Co. MAYO	MELVIN	Co. GALWAY
MAYPOWER	Co. ROSCOMMON	MENAGHT	See MAC NAUGHTON
MAZIERE	Co. CORK	MENARRY	ORIEL TARTAN
MEA	Co. MAYO	MENEELY	SeeMAC NEIL
MEA	Co. WESTMEATH	MERCER	MERCER

"IRISH" indicates a choice of a general Irish tartan: "All Ireland", "Tara", "Clodagh", "Irish National", "St. Patrick"

TARTANS FOR IRISH NAMES

Mercer   *Mulbrandon*

Anyone with a "County" Tartan may substitute one of the major "District" tartans listed below:

Galway, Leitrim, Mayo, Roscommon, Sligo:	Connacht tartan
Clare, Cork, Kerry, Limmerick, Tipperary, Waterford:	Munster tartan
Armagh, Down, Fermanagh, Louth, Monaghan:	Oriel tartan
Carlow, Dublin, Kildare, Kilkenny, Laois, Longford:	
Meath, Offaly, Westmeath, Wexford, Wicklow:	Leinster tartan
Antrim, Armagh, Cavan, Donegal, Down, Londonderry, Tyrone:	Ulster tartan

SURNAME	TARTAN	SURNAME	TARTAN
MERCER	ULSTER TARTAN	MOLON(E)Y	Co. CLARE
MERRY	Co. WATERFORD	MOLONEY	CLAN CIAN/O'CARROLL
MICK	IRISH-See Footnote	MOLONY	CLAN CIAN/O'CARROLL
MIDDLETON	MIDDLETON	MONAHAN	See MONAGHAN
MIDDLETON	Co. KERRY	MONAGHAN	ORIEL TARTAN
MIDLETON	See MIDDLETON	MONAGHAN	Co. FERANAGH
MIHAN	ULSTER TARTAN	MONAGHAN	LEINSTER TARTAN
MIHILL	Co. LOUTH	MONAGHAN	CONNACHT TARTAN
MILAY	CONNACHT TARTAN	MONDAY	Co. DONEGAL
MILEA	Co. KILKENNY	MONK(S)	See MONAGHAN
MILES	CONNACHT TARTAN	MONTAGUE	ULSTER TARTAN
MILFORD	Co. MAYO	MONNELLY	Co. MAYO
MILIFFE(Y)	CONNACHT TARTAN	MONTGOMERY	MONTGOMERY
MILLANE	Co. CLARE	MONTGOMERY	ULSTER TARTAN
MILLAR	See MILLER	MOONEY	LEINSTER TARTAN
MILLER	MILLER	MOONEY	Co. SLIGO
MILLER	ULSTER TARTAN	MOORE	ULSTER TARTAN
MILLET	CONNACHT TARTAN	MOORE	Co. ANTRIM
MILLICAN	See MILLIGAN	MOORE	Co. DOWN
MILLIFFE(Y)	Co. GALWAY	MOORE	Co. KERRY
MILLIGAN	MILLIGAN	MOORE	Co. LAOIS
MILLIGAN	ULSTER TARTAN	MORAN	CONNACHT TARTAN
MILLIGAN	Co. DONEGAL	MORAN	Co. DOWN
MILLIKEN	See MILLIGAN	MORAN	Co. GALWAY
MILLS	ULSTER TARTAN	MORAN	Co. KERRY
MILNE	MILNE	MORAN	Co. MAYO
MILYNN	CO. MONAGHAN	MORAN	Co. SLIGO
MIMNAGH	Co. TYRONE	MORGAN	ULSTER TARTAN
MINCH	Co. KILDARE	MORGAN	Co. ARMAGH
MINCHEN	Co. OFFALY	MORGAN	Co. DOWN
MINEELY	ULSTER TARTAN	MORGAN	Co. ANTRIM
MINIGANE	Co. KERRY	MORIARTY	Co. KERRY
MINIHANCE	Co. CORK	MORRIS	MORRIS
MINIHANS	Co. CORK	MORRIS	LEINSTER TARTAN
MINNAGH	Co. TYRONE	MORRIS	CLAN CIAN/O'CARROLL
MINNAUGH	Co. TYRONE	MORRISON	MORRISON
MINNIS	MENZIES	MORRISON	ULSTER TARTAN
MINNIS	ULSTER TARTAN	MORRISON	Co. ANTRIM
MITCHELL	MITCHELL	MORRISON	Co. DOWN
MITCHELL	ULSTER TARTAN	MORROW	ULSTER TARTAN
MOAN	See MORAN	MORTELL	ULSTER TARTAN
MODOWNY	MODOWNY	MORTON	ULSTER TARTAN
MOFFAT(T)	MOFFAT	MORTON	Co. ANTRIM
MOFFAT(T)	ULSTER TARTAN	MOYLES	Co. MAYO
MOFFAT(T)	Co. SLIGO	MUCKEEN	See MAC KEAN
MOHAN	ORIEL TARTAN	MUCKIAN	See MAC KEAN
MOHAN	Co. MONAGHAN	MUCKL(E)Y	Co. SLIGO
MOHAN	Co. FERMANAGH	MUCKLE	ULSTER TARTAN
MOHERY	Co. CAVAN	MUCKLEBREED	ULSTER TARTAN
MOLDOWNEY	MODOWNY	MUGAN(E)	MAC MUGEN
MOLDOWNEY	CLAN CIAN/O'CARROLL	MUGAN(E)	CONNACHT TARTAN
MOLEDY	Co. WESTMEATH	MUGGANE	See MUGAN
MOLLAHAN	Co. CLARE	MUGGEVAN	Co. CLARE
MOLLOY	LEINSTER TARTAN	MULBERRY	Co. LONDONDERRY
MOLOHAN	Co. LONGFORD	MULBRANDON	Co. CLARE

"IRISH" indicates a choice of a general Irish tartan: "All Ireland", "Tara", "Clodagh", "Irish National", "St. Patrick"

63

TARTANS FOR IRISH NAMES

Anyone with a "County" Tartan may substitute one of the major "District" tartans listed below:

Galway, Leitrim, Mayo, Roscommon, Sligo:	Connacht tartan
Clare, Cork, Kerry, Limmerick, Tipperary, Waterford:	Munster tartan
Armagh, Down, Fermanagh, Louth, Monaghan:	Oriel tartan
Carlow, Dublin, Kildare, Kilkenny, Laois, Longford:	
Meath, Offaly, Westmeath, Wexford, Wicklow:	Leinster tartan
Antrim, Armagh, Cavan, Donegal, Londonderry, Tyrone:	Ulster tartan

SURNAME	TARTAN	SURNAME	TARTAN
MULBREED(Y)	CONNACHT TARTAN	MULLAVIN	Co. WESTMETH
MULBRIDE	CONNACHT TARTAN	MULLEADY	Co. WESTMEATH
MULBURY	Co. LONDONDERRY	MULLED(A)Y	Co. WESTMEATH
MULCAHY	Co. TIPPERARY	MULLEE	CONNACHT TARTAN
MULCAIR	Co. LIMMERICK	MULLEN(S)	MAC MILLAN
MULCHAHY	Co. SLIGO	MULLEN(S)	ULSTER TARTAN
MULCHRONE	Co. MAYO	MULLERICK	CONNACHT TARTAN
MULCLAHY	Co. SLIGO	MULLERY	CONNACHT TARTAN
MULCLARY	Co. SLIGO	MULLETT	Co. WEXFORD
MULCONERY	Co. ROSCOMMON	MULLEY	CONNACHT TARTAN
MULCONRY	Co. ROSCOMMON	MULLHOLAND	See MULHOLLAND
MULCREEVY	ORIEL TARTAN	MULLIGAN	Sww MILLIGAN
MULDERRIG	Co. MAYO	MULLINS	MAC MILLAN
MULDERRY	Co.DONEGAL	MULLINS	Co. CLARE
MULDOON	ULSTER TARTAN	MULLINS	Co. CORK
MULDOON	Co. CLARE	MULLINS	Co. KILKENNY
MULDOWNEY	MODOWNY	MULLOCK	CONNACHT TARTAN
MULDOWNEY	Co. CAVAN	MULLOON	Co. CLARE
MULDROW	ULSTER TARTAN	MULLOVER	Co. MAYO
MULFAIL	Co. DONEGAL	MULLOWNEY	CONNACHT TARTAN
MULGANNAN	Co. CLARE	MULMOHENY	Co. CAVAN
MULGANNON	Co. CLARE	MULMOHER(Y)	Co. CAVAN
MULGEEHY	Co. DONEGAL	MULMONA	MOSS
MULGREEVY	ORIEL TARTAN	MULMONA	ULSTER TARTAN
MULGREW	ULSTER TARTAN	MULMOND	MOSS
MULGREW	Co. TYRONE	MULOCK	CONNACHT TARTAN
MULGRIEVY	ORIEL TARTAN	MULOLOHY	Co. SLIGO
MULHAIR	Co. GALWAY	MULPATRICK	LAMONT
MULHALL	Co. LAOIS	MULPETERS	Co. LAOIS
MULHARE	Co. GALWAY	MULQUEEN(Y)	Co. CLARE
MULHARE	Co. LIMMERICK	MULRAIN(Y)	CONNACHT TARTAN
MULHATTON	Co. TYRONE	MULREADY	Co. DONEGAL
MULHERN	ULSTER TARTAN	MULREADY	Co. ROSCOMMON
MULHOLLAND	MULHOLLAND	MULREAVY	Co. DONEGAL
MULHOLLAND	ULSTER TARTAN	MULRENIN	CONNACHT TARTAN
MULHOOLY	Co. LONGFORD	MULRENIN	Co. MAYO
MULIHAN	Co. CLARE	MULRENIN	Co. ROSCOMMON
MULKEEN	Co. MAYO	MULRENNAN	See MULRENIN
MULKERRILL	Co. ROSCOMMON	MULREVIN	Co. ROSCOMMON
MULKERRIN	Co. ROSCOMMON	MULRINE	CONNACHT TARTAN
MULKERRY	Co. LIMMERICK	MULROE	Co. SLIGO
MULKIERE	Co. GALWAY	MULROON(E)Y	Co. FERMANAGH
MULLALY	Co. GALWAY	MULROON(E)Y	Co. GALWAY
MULLAN	ULSTER TARTAN	MULROY	Co. GALWAY
MULLAN	Co. GALWAY	MULROY	Co. LONGFORD
MULLAN	Co. LONDONDERRY	MULRY	Co. MAYO
MULLANE	Co. CLARE	MULRYAN	Co. TIPPERARY
MULLANE	Co. KERRY	MULSHINNOCK	Co. CORK
MULLANEY	Co. ROSCOMMON	MULTILLY	IRISH-See Footnote
MULLANIFFE	CONNACHT TARTAN	MULVANAUGHTY	Co. LEITRIM
MULLANPHY	Co. TIPPERARY	MULVANY	ORIEL TARTAN
MULLANY	Co. SLIGO	MULVANY	Co. OFFALY
MULLANY	Co. WATERFORD	MULVANY	Co. SLIGO
MULLARKEY	CONNACHT TARTAN	MULVAY	LEINSTER TARTAN
MULLARNEY	ORIEL TARTAN	MULVEIGH	Co. LAOIS

"IRISH" indicates a choice of a general Irish tartan: "All Ireland", "Tara", "Clodagh", "Irish National", "St. Patrick"

TARTANS FOR IRISH NAMES

Anyone with a "County" Tartan may substitute one of the major "District" tartans listed below:

Galway, Leitrim, Mayo, Roscommon, Sligo:	Connacht tartan
Clare, Cork, Kerry, Limmerick, Tipperary, Waterford:	Munster tartan
Armagh, Down, Fermanagh, Louth, Monaghan:	Oriel tartan
Carlow, Dublin, Kildare, Kilkenny, Laois, Longford:	
Meath, Offaly, Westmeath, Wexford, Wicklow:	Leinster tartan
Antrim, Armagh, Cavan, Donegal, Down, Londonderry, Tyrone:	Ulster tartan

SURNAME	TARTAN	SURNAME	TARTAN
MULVENNA	Co. LONDONDERRY	MYLER	Co. WEXFORD
MULVENNA	LEINSTER TARTAN	MYLES	CONNACHT TARTAN
MULVEY	Co. CLARE	MYLNE	MILNE
MULVEY	Co. LEITRIM	MYLNE	MILLER
MULVIHILL	CONNACHT TARTAN	MYLOT(T)	CONNACHT TARTAN
MULVILLE	MELVILLE	MYLOTTE	Co. KERRY
MULVILLE	Co. CLARE	MYNIHAN	Co. KERRY
MULVIN(E)	Co. CLARE	MYTHEN	Co. KERRY
MULVOGUE	CONNACHT TARTAN		
MUNCH	Co. KILDARE		
MUNGEVAN	Co. CLARE		
MUNKETRICK	ORIEL TARTAN		
MUNRO(E)	MUNRO	**N**	
MUNSTER	MUNSTER TARTAN		
MURAY	See MURRAY		
MURCHIE	ULSTER TARTAN	NAGHTEN	See MAC NACHTEN
MURCHIETON	ULSTER TARTAN	NAGHTEN	Co. CLARE
MURCHISON	ULSTER TARTAN	NAGLE	CONNACHT TARTAN
MURDOCH	MURDOCH	NAGLE	MUNSTER TARTAN
MURDOCH	ULSTER TARTAN	NAHANE	Co. CORK
MURDOCK	See MURDOCH	NALLEN	Co. OFFALY
MURHILLA	Co. CORK	NALLY	Mc INALLY
MURHILLY	Co. CORK	NALLY	ORIEL TARTAN
MURHILU	Co. CORK	NALLY	Co. MAYO
MURLEY	Co. CORK	NANANY	Co. ROSCOMMON
MURLY	Co. CORK	NANGLE	MUNSTER TARTAN
MURNAGHAN	ULSTER TARTAN	NANGLE	Co. CORK
MURNANE	Co. CORK	NANGLE	Co. MEATH
MURPHY	MURPHY/TARA	NANNERY	CONNACHT TARTAN
MURPHY	MUNSTER TARTAN	NAPPORT	Co. MEATH
MURPHY	ULSTER TARTAN	NARRY	CONNACHT TARTAN
MURPHY	Co. CORK	NARVIN(E)	Co. MAYO
MURPHY	Co. KERRY	NARY	CONNACHT TARTAN
MURPHY	Co. ROSCOMMON	NASH	Co. KERRY
MURPHY	Co. WEXFORD	NASON	Co. CORK
MURRAN	Co. SLIGO	NATTON	CONNACHT TARTAN
MURRAY	MURRAY of TULLIBARDINE	NAUGHTON	See MAC NACHTEN
MURRAY	ULSTER TARTAN	NAVIN	See MAC NIVEN
MURRAY	Co. DOWN	NAWN	Co. FERMANAGH
MURRAY	Co. LONDONDERRY	NAYLOR	Co. DUBLIN
MURRAY	ULSTER TARTAN	NEALE	O' NEILL
MURRIHY	Co. CLARE	NEALON	CONNACHT TARTAN
MURRIN	Co. OFFALY	NEALY	O' NEILL
MURRIN	Co. SLIGO	NEARY	CONNACHT TARTAN
MURROW	Co. WEXFORD	NEAZER	Co. LIMERICK
MURTAGH	ULSTER TARTAN	NEE	CONNACHT TARTAN
MURTAGH	LEINSTER TARTAN	NEE	Co. GALWAY
MURTAGH	Co. MEATH	NEEDHAM	Co MAYO
MURTELL	Co. DOWN	NEEF	Co. KILKENNY
MURTHA	Co. MEATH	NEELY	O' NEILL
MUSGRAVE	Co. WATERFORD	NEELY	Co. GALWAY
MUST(E)Y	Co. DOWN	NEENEY	CLAN CIAN/O'CARROLL
MUTLOE	Co. WEXFORD	NEESON	See MAC GUINNESS
MYERS	Co. CLARE		
MYHILL	ULSTER TARTAN		

"IRISH" indicates a choice of a general Irish tartan: "All Ireland", "Tara", "Clodagh", "Irish National", "St. Patrick"

65

Anyone with a "County" Tartan may substitute one of the major "District" tartans listed below:

Galway, Leitrim, Mayo, Roscommon, Sligo:	Connacht tartan
Clare, Cork, Kerry, Limmerick, Tipperary, Waterford:	Munster tartan
Armagh, Down, Fermanagh, Louth, Monaghan:	Oriel tartan
Carlow, Dublin, Kildare, Kilkenny, Laois, Longford:	
Meath, Offaly, Westmeath, Wexford, Wicklow:	Leinster tartan
Antrim, Armagh, Cavan, Donegal, Down, Londonderry, Tyrone:	Ulster tartan

SURNAME	TARTAN	SURNAME	TARTAN
NEFF	Co. KILKENNY	NORMAN	Co. DUBLIN
NEGLE	Co. CORK	NORMILE	Co. LIMMERICK
NEILANDS	CONNACHT TARTAN	NORRIS	NORRIS
NEILANDS	Co. CLARE	NORRIS	Co. CORK
NEILL	LEINSTER TARTAN	NORSE	See NORRIS
NEILL	MUNSTER TARTAN	NORTH	Co. WESTMEATH
NEILSON	MAC NEIL	NORTHRIDGE	Co. CORK
NEILSON	ULSTER TARTAN	NORTON	Co. ROSCOMMON
NELIGAN	MUNSTER TARTAN	NOTLY	Co. DUBLIN
NELLIS(S)	ULSTER TARTAN	NOURSE	See NORRIS
NELLIS(S)	Co. DONEGAL	NOWD	Co. KILDARE
NELLY	CONNACHT TARTAN	NOWLAND(S)	Co. CARLOW
NELSON	Co. DUBLIN	NUGENT	LEINSTER TARTAN
NERHENY	CONNACHT TARTAN	NUGENT	Co. MEATH
NERNEY	Co. CLARE	NUGENT	Co. WESTMEATH
NERNEY	CONNACHT TARTAN	NUNAN	Co. CORK
NESBET	See NESBIT	NUNL(E)Y	Co. WEXFORD
NESBIT(T)	NISBIT	NUNN	Co. WEXFORD
NESBIT(T)	Co. DUBLIN	NUNNLY	Co. WEXFORD
NESTOR	Co. CLARE	NURSE	See NORRIS
NESTOR	Co. LIMMERICK	NUTL(E)Y	Co. DUBLIN
NETTERFIELD	Co. MEATH	NUTT	ULSTER TARTAN
NETTERVILLE	Co. MEATH	NYHAN(E0	Co. CORK
NEVILLE	Co. LIMMERICK	NYNANE	Co. CLARE
NEWCOM(B)E	Co. MAYO		
NEWCOMMEN	Co. MAYO		
NEWELL	ULSTER TARTAN		
NEWELL	Co. DOWN		
NEWELL	Co. ANTRM		
NEWELL	Co. KILDARE		
NEWENHAM	Co. CORK		
NEWNAN	Co. CORK		
NEWSOME	Co. CORK		
NEWSON	Co. CORK		
NEYLAN(D)	CONNACHT TARTAN		
NIBLOCK	ULSTER TARTAN		
NIBLOCK	Co. ANTRIM		
NICHOLL	See MAC NICHOL		
NICHOLSON	See MAC NICHOL		
NI(E)LAN(D)	Co. CORK		
NIPE	ORIEL TARTAN		
NIRNEY	CONNACHT TARTAN		
NISH	See MAC NIESH		
NIVEN	See MAC NIVEN		
NIX	Co. LIMMERICK		
NIXON	ULSTER TARTAN		
NOAKLY	CONNACHT TARTAN		
NOBLE	ORIEL TARTAN		
NOBLE	Co. FERMANAGH		
NOCHTIN,-TON	Co. CLARE		
NOHILLY	CONNACHT TARTAN		
NOLAN(D)	Co. CARLOW		
NOONAN	Co. CORK		
NOONE	Co.CLARE		
NORMAN	MUNSTER TARTAN		

O'

O' is from the Irish <u>Ui</u> meaning "of the race of" and is distinct from <u>Mac</u>, "the son of." Many Irish speakers dropped the <u>O'</u> in the move from Irish to English. It has become very common for Irish and descendents of Irish to readopt the O'. If you cannot locate a surname in this list – other than those beginning with a vowel or "Mac"--check the name with or without the prefix O'. See the text before the Name-Tartan List for a more complete explanation.

O' BANNON	Co. OFFALY
O' BANANE	Co. FERMANAGH
O' BANIGAN	ULSTER TARTAN
O' BANIGAN	Co. DONEGAL
O' BEARY	Co. OFFALY
O' BEICE	CLAN CIAN/O'CARROLL

"IRISH" indicates a choice of a general Irish tartan: "All Ireland", "Tara", "Clodagh", "Irish National", "St. Patrick"

Anyone with a "County" Tartan may substitute one of the major "District" tartans listed below:

Galway, Leitrim, Mayo, Roscommon, Sligo:	**Connacht tartan**
Clare, Cork, Kerry, Limmerick, Tipperary, Waterford:	**Munster tartan**
Armagh, Down, Fermanagh, Louth, Monaghan:	**Oriel tartan**
Carlow, Dublin, Kildare, Kilkenny, Laois, Longford:	
Meath, Offaly, Westmeath, Wexford, Wicklow:	**Leinster tartan**
Antrim, Armagh, Cavan, Donegal, Down, Londonderry, Tyrone:	**Ulster tartan**

SURNAME	TARTAN	SURNAME	TARTAN
O' BEIRNE	CONNACHT TARTAN	O' CASEY	MUNSTER TARTAN
O' BERG	Co. OFFALY	O' CASEY	Co. FERMANAGH
O' BERGIN	Co. OFFALY	O' CASEY	Co. KERRY
O' BERRANE	Co. MAYO	O' CASEY	Co. LIMMERICK
O' BIERNE	CONNACHT TARTAN	O' CASTLES	CLAN CIAN/O'CARROLL
O' BIERNE	Co. MAYO	O' CAVANAGH	Co. CARLOW
O' BIERNE	Co. ROSCOMMON	O' CLERY	Co. CAVAN
O' BIGGY	CONNACHT TARTAN	O' CLERY	Co. DONEGAL
O' BIGGY	Co. MAYO	O' COIGLEY	Co. MONAGHAN
O' BLEAHAN	Co. GALWAY	O' COLLINS	CLAN CIAN/O'CARROLL
O' BLEHEEN	Co. GALWAY	O' CONEALY	Co. GALWAY
O' BOGAN	Co. DONEGAL	O' CONELLAN	Co. TYRONE
O' BOGAN	Co. WEXFORD	O' CONLON	Co. LIMMERICK
O' BOHAN	CONNACHT TARTAN	O' CONNELL	Co. KERRY
O' BOLAND	CONNACHT TARTAN	O' CONNELL	Co. LIMMERICK
O' BOLAND	Co. SLIGO	O' CONNELL	Co. LONDONDERRY
O' BOLGER	Co. WEXFORD	O' CONNELLY	Co. MEATH
O' BOYHAN	Co. WESTMEATH	O' CONNER	See O' CONNOR
O' BOYLAN	ORIEL TARTAN	O' CONNOR	O' CONNOR
O' BOYLAN	Co. MONAGHAN	O' CONNOR	Co. KERRY
O' BOYLE	Co. DONEGAL	O' CONNOR	Co. KILDARE
O' BRACKEN	BRACKEN	O' CONNOR	Co. LONDONDERRY
O' BRACKEN	Co. KILDARE	O' CONNOR	Co. OFFALY
O' BRADY	CLAN CIAN/O'CARROLL	O' CONNOR	Co. ROSCOMMON
O' BREEN	Co. OFFALY	O' CONOR	See O' CONNER
O' BRIAN	See O' BRIEN	O' COON(E)Y	CLAN CIAN/O'CARROLL
O' BRIEN	O' BRIEN	O' CORMACAN	CLAN CIAN/O'CARROLL
O' BRIEN	Co. CLARE	O' CORRA	CLAN CIAN/O'CARROLL
O' BRIEN	Co. TIPPERARY	O' CORRY	Co. TYRONE
O' BROCAIN	CLAN CIAN/O'CARROLL	O' CREANE	Co. SLIGO
O' BROGAN	CONNACHT TARTAN	O' CRIGLEY	Co. DONEGAL
O' BROHAN	Co. OFFALY	O' CRONAN(A)	CLAN CIAN/O'CARROLL
O' BRYNE	Co. CORK	O' CUIRNEEN	Co. LEITRIM
O' CAHAN	ULSTER TARTAN	O' CULLEN	CLAN CIAN/O'CARROLL
O' CAHERNY	Co. OFFALY	O' CULLENAN	Co. CLARE
O' CAHON	Co. CLARE	O' CURRAN	Co. DONEGAL
O' CALAHAN	CLAN CIAN/O'CARROLL	O' CURRY	CURRIE
O' CALLAGHAN	Co. CORK	O' CURRY	Co. CAVAN
O' CALLANAN	CONACHT TARTAN	O' CURRY	Co. CORK
O' CALLANAN	Co. GALWAY	O' DALLON	CLAN CIAN/O'CARROLL
O' CALLINAN	See CALLANAN	O' DANIELL	Co. TIPPERARY
O' CANAVAN	See CALLANAN	O' DAY	CLAN CIAN/O'CARROLL
O' CANNY	Co. MAYO	O' DAY	Co. CLARE
O' CAROLAN	Co. LONDONERRY	O' DEA	See O' DAY
O' CAROLAN	Co. MEATH	O' DEEGAN	Co. LAOIS
O' CARRILL	See O' CARROLL	O' DEEHAN	ULSTER TARTAN
O' CARROLL	CLAN CIAN/O'CARROLL	O' DEEHAN	Co. LONDONDERRY
O' CARROLL	Co. KERRY	O' DELL	CLAN CIAN/O'CARROLL
O' CARROLL	Co. KILKENNY	O' DEMPSEY	Co. LAOIS
O' CARROLL	Co. LEITRIM	O' DERRY	ULSTER TARTAN
O' CARROLL	Co. OFFALY	O' DERRY	Co. LONDONDERRY
O' CARRY	CLAN CIAN/O'CARROLL	O' DEVLIN	ULSTER TARTAN
O' CARTHY	CLAN CIAN/O'CARROLL	O' DOLLY	Co. GALWAY
O' CASEY	CASEY	O' DONAGHUE	O' DONOGHUE
		O' DONNELL	CONNACHT TARTAN

"IRISH" indicates a choice of a general Irish tartan: "All Ireland", "Tara", "Clodagh", "Irish National", "St. Patrick"

TARTANS FOR IRISH NAMES

O' Donnell   *O' Malley*

Anyone with a "County" Tartan may substitute one of the major "District" tartans listed below:.

Galway, Leitrim, Mayo, Roscommon, Sligo:	Connacht tartan
Clare, Cork, Kerry, Limmerick, Tipperary, Waterford:	Munster tartan
Armagh, Down, Fermanagh, Louth, Monaghan:	Oriel tartan
Carlow, Dublin, Kildare, Kilkenny, Laois, Longford:	
Meath, Offaly, Westmeath, Wexford, Wicklow:	Leinster tartan
Antrim, Armagh, Cavan, Donegal, Down, Londonderry, Tyrone:	Ulster tartan

SURNAME	TARTAN	SURNAME	TARTAN
O' DONNELL	Co. CLARE	O' GRIFFIN	Co. CLARE
O' DONNELL	Co. DONEGAL	O' GUDA	CLAN CIAN/O'CARROLL
O' DONNELL	Co. GALWAY	O' GUILL	CLAN CIAN/O'CARROLL
O' DONNELL	Co. TIPPERARY	O' GULNEY	Co. KERRY
O' DORAN	CLAN CIAN/O'CARROLL	O' GUNNINA	CLAN CIAN/O'CARROLL
O' DOWD(A)	Co. SLIGO	O' GUNNING	Co. OFFALY
O' DOWNEY	O' SULLIVAN	O' HAFFEY	ULSTER TARTAN
O' DOWNEY	CONNACHT TARTAN	O' HAGAN	See HAGAN
O' DOWNEY	Co.GALWAY	O' HALY	CLAN CIAN/O'CARROLL
O' DOWNEY	Co. KERRY	O' HANLON	ULSTER TARTAN
O' DOYNE	CONNACHT TARTAN	O' HANLON	LEINSTER TARTAN
O' DUIGAN	Co. LAOIS	O' HARA	CONNACHT TARTAN
O' DUNA	CLAN CIAN/O'CARROLL	O' HARA	Co. MAYO
O' DUNLEVY	CONNACHT TARTAN	O' HARA	LEINSTER TARTAN
O' DUNPHY	Co. KILKENNY	O' HARA	ULSTER TARTAN
O' DWYER	Co. TIPPERARY	O' HARE	ORIEL TARTAN
O' EARL	CLAN CIAN/O'CARROLL	O' HARE	Co. LOUTH
O' FAGHENY	Co. ROSCOMMON	O' HARE	Co. CLARE
O' FALLAHER	Co. CLARE	O' HATHCHER	CLAN CIAN/O'CARROLL
O' FALLON	Co. CLARE	O' HAUGHEY	ULSTER TARTAN
O' FALSEY	CO. CLARE	O' HEA	Co. CORK
O' FALVEY	Co. KERRY	O' HEAR	Co. TYRONE
O' FARRELL(Y)	O' FARRELL	O' HEARTY	ORIEL TARTAN
O' FARREN	Co. DONEGAL	O' HEFFERNAN	CLAN CIAN/O'CARROLL
O' FAUGHNAN	CONNACHT TARTAN	O' HEGARTY	CLAN CIAN/O'CARROLL
O' FEDEGAN	ORIEL TARTAN	O' HEHIR	CLAN CIAN/O'CARROLL
O' FELAN	CLAN CIAN/O'CARROLL	O' HENEREY	CLAN CIAN/O'CARROLL
O' FERCINN	CLAN CIAN/O'CARROLL	O' HENRY	See HENRY
O' FERRALL	O' FARRELL	O' HERR	Co. CLARE
O' FERRELL	O' FARRELL	O' HIGGINS	CONNACHT TARTAN
O' FERRON	ORIEL TARTAN	O' HIGGINS	O' NEILL
O' FNNEGAN	FINNEGAN	O' HOLLERAN	Co. GALWAY
O' FINNEGAN	ORIEL TARTAN	O' HOOD	O' NEILL
O' FLANAGAN	CLAN CIAN/O'CARROLL	O' HOOLAGHAN	Co. CORK
O' FLYNN	FLYNN	O' HORA	CLAN CIAN/O'CARROLL
O' FLYNN	CONNACHT TARTAN	O' HOWLEY	CONNACHT TARTAN
O' FRIEL	ULSTER TARTAN	O' HURLEY	CLAN CIAN/O'CARROLL
O' FRIEL	Co. MAYO	O' HURLEY	Co. CORK
O' GALLAGHER	Co.DONEGAL	O' KEAL(L)Y	Co. MEATH
O' GARA	CLAN CIAN/O'CARROLL	O' KEEFE	O' KEEFE
O' GARA	Co. SLIGO	O' KEEFE	CLAN CIAN/O'CARROLL
O' GARRIGA	ORIEL TARTAN	O' KEERAN	Co. SLIGO
O' GARVAN	Co. KERRY	O' KELLAHER	CLAN CIAN/O'CARROLL
O' GARVEY	ULSTER TARTAN	O' LARKINS	Co. CLARE
O' GEARY	Co. ROSCOMMON	O' LEARY	CLAN CIAN/O'CARROLL
O' GLAVIN	Co. CORK	O' LEARY	Co. CORK
O' GOONERY	Co. MEATH	O' LEE	LEE
O' GORMAN	Co. CLARE	O' LEE	CONNACHT TARTAN
O' GORMLY	CONNACHT TARTAN	O' LENEHAN	CLAN CIAN/O'CARROLL
O' GOWAN	ORIEL TARTAN	O' LOAN(E)	ORIEL TARTAN
O' GRAD(D)Y	See GRADY	O' LOUGHNAN	CLAN CIAN/O'CARROLL
O' GRAD(D)Y	Co. CLARE	O' LYNCH	LYNCH
O' GREEFA	Co. CLARE	O' LYNCH	Co. CAVAN
O' GREENAN	CONNACHT TARTAN	O' MAHANY	IRISH-See Footnote
O' GRIBBEN	ULSTER TARTAN	O MALLEY	Co. MAYO

"IRISH" indicates a choice of a general Irish tartan: "All Ireland", "Tara", "Clodagh", "Irish National", "St. Patrick"

TARTANS FOR IRISH NAMES

O' Meagher   *Pay*

"County" Tartan may substitute one of the major "District" tartans listed below:

Galway, Leitrim, Mayo, Roscommon, Sligo:	Connacht tartan
Clare, Cork, Kerry, Limmerick, Tipperary, Waterford:	Munster tartan
Armagh, Down, Fermanagh, Louth, Monaghan:	Oriel tartan
Carlow, Dublin, Kildare, Kilkenny, Laois, Longford:	
Meath, Offaly, Westmeath, Wexford, Wicklow:	Leinster tartan
Antrim, Armagh, Cavan, Donegal, Down, Londonderry, Tyrone:	Ulster tartan

SURNAME	TARTAN	SURNAME	TARTAN
O' MEAGHER	CLAN CIAN/O'CARROLL		
O' MEEHAN	IRISH-See Footnote	**P**	
O' MORONY	Co. CLARE		
O' MORONY	Co. CLARE		
O' NEILL	O' NEILL		
O' NEILL	ULSTER TARTAN		
O' NEILL	Co. ANTRIM	PADINE	MAC FADYEN
O' NEILL	Co. ARMAGH	PAGE	ULSTER TARTAN
O' NOONAN	CLAN CIAN/O'CARROLL	PAGE	Co. GALWAY
O' QUINN	QUINN	PAGNAM	Co. LEITRIM
O' QUINN	CLAN CIAN/O'CARROLL	PAINE	Co. DUBLIN
O' RORY	Co. MEATH	PAISLEY	PAISLEY
O' SEASNAIN	CLAN CIAN/O'CARROLL	PAISLEY	ULSTER TARTAN
O' SLATTERY	CLAN CIAN/O'CARROLL	PALLAS	ORIEL TARTAN
O' SPEALAIN	CLAN CIAN/O'CARROLL	PALLIN	Co. DUBLIN
O' SULLIVAN	See SULLIVAN	PALMER	IRISH-See Footnote
O' TOOLE	Co. GALWAY	PANNEEN	Co. LIMMERICK
O' TRASEY	CLAN CIAN/O'CARROLL	PANTURE	LEINSTER TARTAN
		PARILL	Co. WEXFORD
		PARIS	CONNACHT TARTAN
O		PARISH	Co. CORK
		PARK(E)(S)	M'DON CLANRANALD
		PARK(E)(S)	ULSTER TARTAN
		PARKENHAM	Co. WESTMEATH
OAKES	ULSTER TARTAN	PARKER	ULSTER TARTAN
OAKES	Co. ANTRIM	PARKINSON	ULSTER TARTAN
OATES	Co. TIPPERARY	PARLAN(D)	ORIEL TARTAN
OBBINS	ULSTER TARTAN	PARLE	Co. WEXFORD
OBBYNS	ULSTER TARTAN	PARLONS	Co. WEXFORD
OBINS	ULSTER TARTAN	PARNELL	Co. DUBLIN
ODELL	CLAN CIAN/O'CARROLL	PARNELL	Co. LONGFORD
OGAN	CLAN CIAN/O'CARROLL	PAROGAN	See PARRICAN
ORCHARD	ULSTER TARTAN	PARRICAN	FITZPATRICK
ORGAN	Co. TIPPERARY	PARRICAN	Co. DUBLIN
ORMOND(E)	Co. WATERFORD	PARRIS	Co CORK
ORMSBY	CONNACHT TARTAN	PARSONS	MAC PHERSON
ORPEN	Co. KERRY	PARSONS	ULSTER TARTAN
ORR	ULSTER TARTAN	PARTLAN(D)	ORIEL TARTAN
OSBORN	Co. WATERFORD	PATCHY	FITZPATRICK
OSBOURN(E)	Co. WATERFORD	PATCHY	Co. DUBLIN
OSWELL	ULSTER TARTAN	PATERSON	See PATTERSON
OWENS	ULSTER TARTAN	PATON	PATON
OWENS	CONNACHT TARTAN	PATON	Co. DONEGAL
OWENS	LEINSTER TARTAN	PATRICAN	FITZPATRICK
OWENS	CLAN CIAN/O'CARROLL	PATRICAN	Co. DUBLIN
OWENSON	ULSTER TARTAN	PATRICK	FITZPATRICK
		PATRICK	LAMONT
		PATRIDGE	IRISH-See Footnote
		PATTAN,-EN	See PATON
		PATTERSON	PATTERSON
		PATTERSON	MAC LAREN
		PATTERSON	ULSTER TARTAN
		PATTISON	See PATTERSON
		PATTON	See PATON
		PAY	Co. KILKENNY

"IRISH indicates a choice of a general Irish tartan: "All Ireland", "Tara", "Clodagh", "Irish National", "St. Patrick"

69

Anyone with a "County" Tartan may substitute one of the major "District" tartans listed below:

Galway, Leitrim, Mayo, Roscommon, Sligo:	**Connacht tartan**
Clare, Cork, Kerry, Limmerick, Tipperary, Waterford:	**Munster tartan**
Armagh, Down, Fermanagh, Louth, Monaghan:	**Oriel tartan**
Carlow, Dublin, Kildare, Kilkenny, Laois, Longford:	
Meath, Offaly, Westmeath, Wexford, Wicklow:	**Leinster tartan**
Antrim, Armagh, Cavan, Donegal, Down, Londonderry, Tyrone:	**Ulster tartan**

SURNAME	TARTAN	SURNAME	TARTAN
PAYNE	PAYNE	PHILLIPS	ORIEL TARTAN
PAYNE	Co. DUBLIN	PHILLIPS	CONNACHT TARTAN
PAYTON	See PATON	PHILLIPS	LEINSTER TARTAN
PEACOCK	PEACOCK	PHYLAN	Co. OFFALY
PEACOCK	Co. MEATH	PHYLAND	Co. WESTMEATH
PEARCE	See PEARSE	PICKENS	Co. WESTMEATH
PEARD	Co. CORK	PIDGEON	ORIEL TARTAN
PEARSE	PEARSE	PIDGEON	Co. MONAGHAN
PEARSE	LEINSTER TARTAN	PIERCE	See PEARSE
PEARSON	PEARSON	PIG(G)OT	IRISH-See Footnote
PEARSON	MAC PHERSON	PIKE	PIKE
PEART	Co. KILKENNY	PILKINGTON	Co. LOUTH
PEDLOW	ULSTER TARTAN	PILON	Co. OFFALY
PEEBLES	ULSTER TARTAN	PIM	Co. LAOIS
PEERY	ULSTER TARTAN	PINDAR	Co. TIPPERARY
PEGNAM	Co. FERMANAGH	PIPER	ULSTER TARTAN
PELLY	Co. GALWAY	PIRRIE	ULSTER TARTAN
PEMBROKE	Co. KERRY	PLANT	Co. LONGFORD
PENDER	Co. TIPPERARY	PLOVER	Co. MAYO
PENDERGAST	Co. MAYO	PLUM(M)ER	PLUMMER
PENDERGRAST	Co. MAYO	PLUM(M)ER	Co. LIMMERICK
PENDEVLLE	Co. KERRY	PLUNKET(T)	CLAN CIAN/O'CARROLL
PENDY	Co. TIPPERARY	PLUNKET(T)	Co. LIMMERICK
PEN(N)EFEATHER	CLAN CIAN/O'CARROLL	PLUNKET(T)	Co. DUBLIN
PEN(N)EFEATHER	LEINSTER TARTAN	PLUNKET(T)	Co. MEATH
PENNY	Co. TIPPERARY	POAK	See POLLOCK
PENNYFEATHER	LEINSTER TARTAN	POCKRICH	Co. MONAGHAN
PENROSE	Co. WATERFORD	POE	ULSTER TARTAN
PENTHENY	Co. MEATH	POE	Co. TYRONE
PENTONY	Co. MEATH	POGUE	See POLLOCK
PEOPLES	ULSTER TARTAN	POKE	See POLLOCK
PEOPLES	Co. DONEGAL	POLAN(D)	Co. WESTMEATH
PEPPARD	Co. LOUTH	POLIN	ORIEL TARTAN
PEPPER	Co. LOUTH	POLK	See POLLOCK
PERDUE	Co. CORK	POLLARD	Co. WESTMEATH
PERELL	Co. WEXFORD	POLLOCK	POLLOCK
PERKINS	CLAN CIAN/O'CARROLL	POLLOCK	MAXWELL
PERROT	Co. CORK	POLLOCK	ULSTER TARTAN
PERRY	ULSTER TARTAN	PONSONBY	Co. KILKENNY
PERSSE	See PEARSE	POPE	Co. DUBLIN
PETERS	ULSTER TARTAN	PORTAS	Co. LAOIS
PETERSON	See PATTERSON	PORTEOUS	PORTEOUS
PETERSON	ULSTER TARTAN	PORTEOUS	ULSTER TARTAN
PETIT(E)	Co. MAYO	PORTEOUS	Co. KILKENNY
PETIT(E)	Co. MEATH	PORTER	ULSTER TARTAN
PEY	Co. KILKENNY	PORTER	Co. DUBLIN
PHAIR	See FAIR	PORTESSE	Co. LAOIS
PHELAN,-EN	Co. KILKENNY	POWDERLY	Co. MEATH
PHELAN,-EN	Co. WATERFORD	POWELL	CLAN CIAN/O'CARROLL
PHIBBS	Co. SLIGO	POWER(S)	CLAN CIAN/O'CARROLL
PHILAN(D)	Co. OFFALY	POWER(S)	Co. WATERFORD
PHILAN(D)	Co. WATERFORD	PRATT	GRANT
PHILBIN	CONNACHT TARTAN	PRATT	Co. CORK
PHILBIN	Co. MAYO	PRAY	Co. DOWN
PHILLIPS	PHILLIPS	PRENDERGAST	Co. MAYO

"IRISH" indicates a choice of a general Irish tartan: "All Ireland", "Tara", "Clodagh", "Irish National", "St. Patrick"

TARTANS FOR IRISH NAMES

Anyone with a "County" Tartan may substitute one of the major "District" tartans listed below:

Galway, Leitrim, Mayo, Roscommon, Sligo:	Connacht tartan
Clare, Cork, Kerry, Limmerick, Tipperary, Waterford:	Munster tartan
Armagh, Down, Fermanagh, Louth, Monaghan:	Oriel tartan
Carlow, Dublin, Kildare, Kilkenny, Laois, Longford:	
Meath, Offaly, Westmeath, Wexford, Wicklow:	Leinster tartan
Antrim, Armagh, Cavan, Donegal, Down, Londonderry, Tyrone:	Ulster tartan

SURNAME	TARTAN	SURNAME	TARTAN
PRENDERGRAST	Co. MAYO	QUANEY	Co. ROSCOMMON
PRENDERGRAST	Co. MEATH	QUARRIE	MAC QUARRIE
PRENTY	See PRONTY	QUARRIE	Co. WATERFORD
PRESCOTT	Co. MEATH	QUATTERS	ULSTER TARTAN
PRESTON	Co. DUBLIN	QUAYLE	See QUAIL
PRESTON	Co. MEATH	QUEALLY	See QUALLY
PREY	Co. DOWN	QUEE	MAC KAY
PRIALL	Co. TIPPERARY	QUEELTY	Co. LIMMERICK
PRICE	IRISH-See Footnote	QUEEN	MAC QUEEN
PRINGLE	PRINGLE	QUEEN	ORIEL TARTAN
PRINGLE	ULSTER TARTAN	QUEENAN	Co. SLIGO
PRIOT	Co. CAVAN	QUENTIN	ORIEL TARTAN
PRIOT	Co. LEITRIM	QUHA	MAC KAY
PRITCHARD	PRITCHARD	QUICK	Co. CORK
PRITCHARD	ULSTER TARTAN	QUICK	Co. DOWN
PROCTOR	ULSTER TARTAN	QUIGG	Co. LONDONDERRY
PRONTY	BRONTE	QUIGL(E)Y	ULSTER TARTAN
PRONTY	ULSTER TARTAN	QUIGL(E)Y	Co. LONDONDERRY
PROUDFOOT	Co. MEATH	QUIGNEY	Co. CLARE
PROUT	Co. KILKENNY	QUILKIN	CONNACHT TARTAN
PRUNTY	See PRONTY	QUILL	CLAN CIAN/O'CARROLL
PRYELL	Co. TIPPERARY	QUILL	Co. KERRY
PUNCH	Co. KILDARE	QUILLENANE	Co. ROSCOMMON
PURCELL	CLAN CIAN/O'CARROLL	QUILLIGAN	Co. CLARE
PURCELL	Co. KILKENNY	QUILLY	ORIEL TARTAN
PURCELL	Co. TIPPERARY	QUILTY	Co. LIMMERICK
PURDON	Co. CLARE	QUINANE	Co. TIPPERARY
PURDUE	Co. CORK	QUINLAN	O' NEILL
PUVENS	Co. FERMANAGH	QUINLAN	Co. KERRY
PYKE	PIKE	QUINLAN	Co. TIPPERARY
PYNET	Co. CORK	QUINLEVAN	CLAN CIAN/O'CARROLL
PYPER	See PIPER	QUINN	QUINN
		QUINN	ULSTER TARTAN
		QUINN	Co. ANTRIM
		QUINN	Co. CLARE
		QUINN	Co. DONEGAL
		QUINN	Co. LIMMERICK
		QUINN	Co. LONDONDERRY
		QUINN	Co. LONGFORD
		QUINN	Co. TYRONE
Q		QUINN(E)Y	Co. TYRONE
		QUINNELL	MUNSTER TARTAN
		QUINNELL	Co. CORK
		QUINNELL	Co. TIPPERARY
QUA	MAC KAY	QUINTON	ORIEL TARTAN
QUA	ULSTER TARTAN	QUIRK	CLAN CIAN/O'CARROLL
QUA	Co. ARMAGH	QUISH	Co. TIPPERARY
QUADE	Co. LIMMERICK	QUITTER	Co. KERRY
QUAID(E)	Co. LIMMERICK	QUOID	MAC KAY
QUAIL	ULSTER TARTAN	QUOID	ULSTER TARTAN
QUAIL	CLAN CIAN/O'CARROLL		
QUAIL	Co. LOUTH		
QUAIN	CLAN CIAN/O'CARROLL		
QUAIN	Co. WATERFORD		
QUALEY	See QUALLY		
QUALLY	LEINSTER TARTAN		
QUALLY	Co. KILKENNY		
QUALTER(S)	WALTERS		
QUANE	Co. WATERFORD		

"IRISH" indicates a choice of a general Irish tartan: "All Ireland", "Tara", "Clodagh", "Irish National", "St. Patrick"

TARTANS FOR IRISH NAMES

Rabbit   *Reiny*

Anyone with a "County" Tartan may substitute one of the major "District" tartans listed below:

Galway, Leitrim, Mayo, Roscommon, Sligo:	**Connacht tartan**
Clare, Cork, Kerry, Limmerick, Tipperary, Waterford:	**Munster tartan**
Armagh, Down, Fermanagh, Louth, Monaghan:	**Oriel tartan**
Carlow, Dublin, Kildare, Kilkenny, Laois, Longford:	
Meath, Offaly, Westmeath, Wexford, Wicklow:	**Leinster tartan**
Antrim, Armagh, Cavan, Donegal, Down, Londonderry, Tyrone:	**Ulster tartan**

SURNAME	TARTAN	SURNAME	TARTAN
R		RAUGHTON	Co. KILKENNY
		RAVEY	Co. DOWN
		RAWE	ULSTER TARTAN
		RAWE	Co. ANTRIM
		RAWL	Co. CAVAN
		RAWLEY	Co. LIMMERICK
RABBIT(T)	Co. OFFALY	RAY	MAC RAE
RACKARD	Co. WEXFORD	RAY	REA
RACTIGAN	Co. ROSCOMMON	RADGEWAY	ULSTER TARTAN
RADCLIFF(E)	Co. DUBLIN	REA	REA
RADFORD	Co. WEXFORD	REA	ULSTER TARTAN
RADWELL	Co. WEXFORD	REA	Co. ANTRIM
RAECROFT	Co. CORK	READ(E)	See REID
RAFE	Co. MAYO	READY	Co. KERRY
RAFERTY	See RAFFERTY	REAGAN	REAGAN
RAFFERTY	ULSTER TARTAN	REAGAN	CLAN CIAN/O'CARROLL
RAFFERTY	ORIEL TARTAN	REAGAN	Co. CLARE
RAFFERTY	Co. LOUTH	REAGAN	Co. CORK
RAFFERTY	Co. SLIGO	REAGAN	Co. LAOIS
RAFFERTY	Co. DONEGAL	REAGAN	Co. MEATH
RAFTER	Co. KILKENNY	REAGH	ORIEL TARTAN
RAFTISS	Co. KILKENNY	REAHILL	Co. CAVAN
RAGGERT	Co. KILKENNY	REAL	Co. KERRY
RAGGET	Co. KILKENNY	REAN	Co. CORK
RAGHTEEN	Co. GALWAY	REANY	Co. WESTMEATH
RAGHTIGAN	Co. ROSCOMMON	REAP(Y)	Co. MAYO
RAGHTNEEN	Co. ROSCOMMON	REARDEN	See REARDON
RAHER	Co. WATERFORD	REARDON	Co. CORK
RAHILL	Co. CAVAN	REAVY	CONNACHT TARTAN
RAHILLY	See REILLY	REAVY	Co. DOWN
RAIN	Co. OFFALY	RECIDE	Co. FERMANAGH
RAINEY	ULSTER TARTAN	RECRAFT	Co. CORK
RALIEGH	Co. LIMMERICK	REDAHAN	Co. MAYO
RALL	Co. CAVAN	REDDEN	O' BRIEN
RALPH	LEINSTER TARTAN	REDDER	Co. CLARE
RALSTON	RALSTON	REDDINGTON	Co. MAYO
RALSTON	ULSTER TARTAN	REDDY	Co. CORK
RAMSAY	RAMSAY	REDDY	Co. KILKENNY
RAMSAY	ULSTER TARTAN	REDICAN	Co. CLARE
RAMSEY	See RAMSAY	REDMOND	Co. WEXFORD
RANAGHAN	ORIEL TARTAN	REEHILL	Co. CAVAN
RANDLES	M'DON CLANRANALD	REEN	Co. CORK
RANKIN(E)	RANKIN	REENAN	ORIEL TARTAN
RANKIN(E)	ULSTER TARTAN	REEVES	Co. DOWN
RANKING	RANKING	REGAN	REGAN
RANSEY	See RAMSAY	REGAN	REAGAN
RAPENTERY	Co. MEATH	REGAN	CLAN CIAN/O'CARROLL
RATCHFORD	Co. WEXFORD	REHAN	Co. TYRONE
RATH	Co. LOUTH	REID	"Green" REID
RATHBONE	Co. SLIGO	REID	ULSTER TARTAN
RATIGAN	Co. ROSCOMMON	REIDY	Co. TIPPERARY
RATTICAN	Co. ROSCOMMON	REIGHILL	Co. FERMANAGH
RATTIGAN	Co. SLIGO	REILLY	ORIEL TARTAN
RATTY	Co. DUBLIN	REILLY	Co. CAVAN
		REINY	Co. CORK

"IRISH" indicates a choice of a general Irish tartan: "All Ireland", "Tara", "Clodagh", "Irish National", "St. Patrick"

Anyone with a "County" Tartan may substitute one of the major "District" tartans listed below:

Galway, Leitrim, Mayo, Roscommon, Sligo:	Connacht tartan
Clare, Cork, Kerry, Limmerick, Tipperary, Waterford:	Munster tartan
Armagh, Down, Fermanagh, Louth, Monaghan:	Oriel tartan
Carlow, Dublin, Kildare, Kilkenny, Laois, Longford:	
Meath, Offaly, Westmeath, Wexford, Wicklow:	Leinster tartan
Antrim, Armagh, Cavan, Donegal, Down, Londonderry, Tyrone:	Ulster tartan

SURNAME	TARTAN	SURNAME	TARTAN
RELEHAN	Co. CORK	ROBERTSON	ULSTER TARTAN
RELIS	Co. WEXFORD	ROBINSON	ROBBINS/ROBINSON
RENAN	Co. DONEGAL	ROBINSON	ULSTER TARTAN
RENAN	ULSTER TARTAN	ROBSON	See ROBERTSON
RENEHAN	Co. CORK	ROCHE	Co. CORK
RENNICK	See RENWICK	ROCHE	Co. LIMMERICK
RENNIE	RENNIE	ROCHE	Co. WEXFORD
RENNIE	ULSTER TARTAN	ROCHFORD	Co. MEATH
RENNIX	See RENWICK	ROCK	LEINSTER TARTAN
RENTOUL	IRISH-See Footnote	ROCKET(E)	Co. WATERFORD
RENWICK	RENWICK	RODAHAN	Co. LONGFORD
RENWICK	Co. MEATH	RODAUGHAN	Co. LONGFORD
RENWICK	Co. MONAGHAN	RODDEN, -IN	ULSTER TARTAN
REVILLE	Co. WEXFORD	RODDEN, -IN	Co. DONEGAL
REYNEY	Co. WESTMEATH	RODDY	Co. DONEGAL
REYNOLDS	CONNACHT TARTAN	RODDY	Co. LEITRIM
REYNOLDS	LEINSTER TARTAN	RODEHAN	Co. FERMANAGH
REYNOLDS	Co. LETRIM	RODGERS	ULSTER TARTAN
RHALL	Co. CAVAN	ROE	LEINSTER TARTAN
RHATIGAN	Co. ROSCOMMON	ROE	Co. CAVAN
RHEA	See REA	ROE	Co. WATERFORD
RHYS	Co. CORK	ROGAN	ORIEL TARTAN
RIALL	Co. KERRY	ROGAN	Co. DOWN
RIBBON	CONNACHT TARTAN	ROGAN	Co. LEITRIM
RICE	ORIEL TARTAN	ROHAN	ROWAN
RICHARD	Co. WEXFORD	ROHAN	MUNSTER TARTAN
RICHARDSON	RICHARDSON	ROHAN	Co. CORK
RICHARDSON	Co. WEXFORD	ROHAN	Co. KERRY
RICHEY	See RITCHIE	ROLAN(D)	Co. MAYO
RIDDELL	ULSTER TARTAN	ROLFE	Co. LIMMERICK
RIDDELL	Co. DOWN	ROLLY	Co. LIMMERICK
RIDDLE	See RIDDELL	ROLSTON	RALSTON
RIDGE	CONNACHT TARTAN	ROLSTON	ULSTER TARTAN
RIELLEY	See REILLY	RONAGHAN	ORIEL TARTAN
RIELLY	See REILLY	RONAHAN	ORIEL TARTAN
RILEY	See REILLY	RONAN	Co. CORK
RINEY	Co. KERRY	RONAN	Co. DUBLIN
RING	CLAN CIAN/O'CARROLL	RONAN	Co. LONGFORD
RING	Co. CORK	RONAN	Co. MAYO
RINGROSE	Co. CLARE	RONAYNE	Co. CORK
RINN	Co. CORK	RONEY	Co. DOWN
RINN	Co. LEITRIM	RONOO	Co. GALWAY
RIORDAN	See REARDON	ROOHAN	MUNSTER TARTAN
RIPLEY	Co. MAYO	ROOHAN	Co. CORK
RITCHIE	RITCHIE	ROOHAN	Co. KERRY
RITCHIE	ULSTER TARTAN	ROOK(E)	Co. LEITRIM
RITCHY	See RITCHIE	ROONEEN	Co. SLIGO
ROAN	ROWAN	ROONEY	CONNACHT TARTAN
ROANTREE	See ROWANTREE	ROONEY	Co. DOWN
ROARK(E)	Co. LEITRIM	ROONIAN	Co. SLIGO
ROARTY	Co. DONEGAL	RORKE	Co. LEITRIM
ROBB	ROBB	RORY	MAC RORY
ROBB	ULSTER TARTAN	RORY	Co. MEATH
ROBERTS	ROBERTSON	ROSBOROUGH	IRISH-See Footnote
ROBERTSON	ROBERTSON	ROSE	ROSE

"IRISH" indicates a choice of a general Irish tartan: "All Ireland", "Tara", "Clodagh", "Irish National", "St. Patrick"

TARTANS FOR IRISH NAMES

Anyone with a "County" Tartan may substitute one of the major "District" tartans listed below:

Galway, Leitrim, Mayo, Roscommon, Sligo:	**Connacht tartan**
Clare, Cork, Kerry, Limmerick, Tipperary, Waterford:	**Munster tartan**
Armagh, Down, Fermanagh, Louth, Monaghan:	**Oriel tartan**
Carlow, Dublin, Kildare, Kilkenny, Laois, Longford:	
Meath, Offaly, Westmeath, Wexford, Wicklow:	**Leinster tartan**
Antrim, Armagh, Cavan, Donegal, Down, Londonderry, Tyrone:	**Ulster tartan**

SURNAME	TARTAN	SURNAME	TARTAN
ROSE	Co. LIMMERICK		
ROSEMAN	Co. CAVAN	RUTLEDGE	RUTLEDGE
ROSEMOND	Co. CAVAN	RUTLEDGE	ORIEL TARTAN
ROSS	ROSS	RUTTLE	Co. LIMMERICK
ROSS	ULSTER TARTAN	RYALL	Co. KERRY
ROTHE	Co. CLARE	RYAN	Co. CARLOW
ROTHE	Co. KILKENNY	RYDER	CONNACHT TARTAN
ROUGHAN	CLAN CIAN/O'CARROLL	RYDER	ORIEL TARTAN
ROUGHAN	Co. CLARE	RYLAND	Co. CARLOW
ROUGHNEEN	Co. MAYO	RYLE	Co. KERRY
ROUGHTNEEN	Co. MAYO	RYNNE	CONNACHT TARTAN
ROUINE	CONNACHT TARTAN	RYNNE	Co. CLARE
ROULSTON	RALSTON	RYNNE	Co. CORK
ROULSTON	ULSTER TARTAN	RYVES	Co. DOWN
ROUNDTREE	See ROWANTREE		
ROURKE	LEINSTER TARTAN		
ROURKE	CONNACHT TARTAN		
ROURKE	Co. LEITRIM		
ROUTH(E)	Co. KILKENNY		
ROVERTY	ORIEL TARTAN		
ROWAN	ROWAN		**S**
ROWANTREE	ROWAN		
ROWANTREE	ORIEL TARTAN	SADDLER	See SADLIER
ROWHAN	CLAN CIAN/O'CARROLL	SADLIER	LEINSTER TARTAN
ROWINE	ROWAN	SADLEIR	Co. CORK
ROWINE	CONNACHT TARTAN	SADLIER	Co. DUBLIN
ROWLAN(D)	Co. MAYO	SAGE	Co. DOWN
ROWLAY,-EY	ULSTER TARTAN	SALKELD	Co. WICKLOW
ROWNEY	Co. DOWN	SALL	Co. WATERFORD
ROY	Co. FERMANAGH	SALLENGER	Co. KILKENNY
ROYAN	Co. GALWAY	SALLY	ORIEL TARTAN
ROYCE	Co. LIMMERICK	SALMON	LEINSTER TARTAN
ROYCROFT	Co. CORK	SALMON	CONNACHT TARTAN
ROYNANE	Co. KERRY	SAMMON	Co. CLARE
ROYSE	Co. LIMMERICK	SAMPSON	Co. LIMMERICK
RUANE	Co. GALWAY	SANAGHY	CONNACHT TARTAN
RUBY	Co. CORK	SANDES	Co. KERRY
RUCKLE	Co. LIMMERICK	SANDS	ULSTER TARTAN
RUDD	Co. WEXFORD	SANDYS	Co. KERRY
RUDDELL	Co. ARMAGH	SANFEY	LEINSTER TARTAN
RUDDER	O' BRIEN	SANKEY	MUNSTER TARTAN
RUDDER	Co. CLARE	SANSFIELD	Co. DUBLIN
RUDDLE	Co. ARMAGH	SANTY	Co. CORK
RUDICAN	Co. LONGFORD	SARAHAN	ORIEL TARTAN
RUFE	IRISH-See Footnote	SARGE(A)NT	ULSTER TARTAN
RULE	Co. DONEGAL	SARSFIELD	Co. LIMMERICK
RUMLEY	IRISH-See Footnote	SAUL	SAUL
RUSH	Co. MAYO	SAUL	Co. TIPPERARY
RUSSELL	RUSSELL	SAUNDERS	M'DON GLENGARRY
RUSSELL	ULSTER TARTAN	SAUNDERS	ULSTER TARTAN
RUSSELL	Co. DOWN	SAUNDERSON	See SAUNDERS
RUSSELL	Co. ANTRIM	SAURIN	ORIEL TARTAN
RUSSELL	Co. LIMMERICK	SAVAGE	ULSTER TARTAN
RUTH	Co. KILKENNY	SAVAGE	Co. DOWN
RUTHERFORD	ULSTER TARTAN	SAVIN	Co. CLARE
RUTHWELL	Co. WEXFORD	SAYERS	Co. KERRY

"IRISH" indicates a choice of a general Irish tartan: "All Ireland", "Tara", "Clodagh", "Irish National", "St. Patrick"

TARTANS FOR IRISH NAMES

Anyone with a "County" Tartan may substitute one of the major "District" tartans listed below:

Galway, Leitrim, Mayo, Roscommon, Sligo: Co cht tartan
Clare, Cork, Kerry, Limmerick, Tipperary, Waterford: Mu   tartan
Armagh, Down, Fermanagh, Louth, Monaghan: Oriel tartan
Carlow, Dublin, Kildare, Kilkenny, Laois, Longford:
Meath, Offaly, Westmeath, Wexford, Wicklow: Leinster tartan
Antrim, Armagh, Cavan, Donegal, Down, Londonderry, Tyrone: Ulster tartan

SURNAME	TARTAN	SURNAME	TARTAN
SAYERS	ULSTER TARTAN	SHACKLETON	Co. KILDARE
SCADDEN	Co. TIPPERARY	SHADY	Co. CLARE
SCADDING	Co. TIPPERARY	SHAFFEREY	Co. LONGFORD
SCAHILL	CONNACHT TARTAN	SHALLOW	Co. CORK
SCAHILL	Co. GALWAY	SHALLY	Co. CORK
SCAHILL	Co. MAYO	SHALOO	Co. CORK
SCALES	Co. CLARE	SHALVEY	Co. CORK
SCANLAN,-LIN	See SCANLON	SHAMROCK	Co. WATERFORD
SCANLON	CLAN CIAN/O'CARROLL	SHANAHAN	Co. ROSCOMMON
SCANLON	Co. FERMANAGH	SHANAHAN	Co. TIPPERARY
SCANLON	Co. LIMMERICK	SHANAHER	Co. ROSCOMMON
SCANLON	Co. LOUTH	SHANAHY	Co. OFFALY
SCANNELL	Co. CORK	SHANDON	SHANDON
SCARRY	Co. WATERFORD	SHANE	See MAC SHANE
SCHAILL	Co. MAYO	SHANESSY	Co. LIMMERICK
SCHIRRA	Co. LAOIS	SHANKS	ULSTER TARTAN
SCHOFIELD	Co. GALWAY	SHANLEY	CONNACHT TARTAN
SCHOULES	ULSTER TARTAN	SHANLEY	Co. LEITRIM
SCOLLAN(D)	LEINSTER TARTAN	SHANNON	ULSTER TARTAN
SCOLLARD	Co. KERRY	SHANNON	Co. ANTRIM
SCOLLIN(G)	LEINSTER TARTAN	SHANNY	Co. ROSCOMMON
SCOTT	SCOTT	SHANUGHER	Co. ROSCOMMON
SCOTT	ULSTER TARTAN	SHARKETT(E)	Co. ROSCOMMON
SCRIVEN	Co. CORK	SHARKEY	ORIEL TARTAN
SCRIVEN	Co. DUBLIN	SHARKEY	ULSTER TARTAN
SCUFFLE	CONNACHT TARTAN	SHARMAN	Co. KILKENNY
SCULLANE	ULSTER TARTAN	SHARP(E)	Co. DONEGAL
SCULLIN	ULSTER TARTAN	SHARRIG	Co. CORK
SCULLION	ULSTER TARTAN	SHARRY	Co. LEITRIM
SCULLY	CLAN CIAN/O'CARROLL	SHARRY	ULSTER TARTAN
SCULLY	Co. GALWAY	SHARVIN(E)	Co. ROSCOMMON
SCULLY	Co. TIPPERARY	SHASNAN	Co. LIMMERICK
SCULLY	Co. WESTMEATH	SHAUGHNESSY	SHAUGHNESSY
SCURLOCK	See SHERLOCK	SHAUGHNESSSY	Co. GALWAY
SCURRY	Co. KILKENNY	SHAW	MAC DONALD
SCYTHES	Co. KILKENNY	SHAW	SHAW. of TORRDARROCH
SEAGRAVE(S)	Co. DUBLIN	SHAW	ULSTER TARTAN
SEALE(Y)	LEINSTER TARTAN	SHEA	Co. KERRY
SEALY	Co. CORK	SHEA	Co. KILKENNY
SEALY	Co.KERRY	SHEAHAN	See SHEEHAN
SEARS	Co. KERRY	SHEALY	Co. CLARE
SEARSON	Co. KERRY	SHEANE	See MAC SHANE
SEAVER	ORIEL TARTAN	SHEARES	Co. CORK
SEERY	Co. WESRMEATH	SHEARHOUR	Co. KERRY
SEGRAVE(S)	Co. DUBLIN	SHEARMAN	Co. KILKENNY
SEGRUE	Co. KERRY	SHEE	See SHEA
SEIX	KILKENNY	SHEEDY	CLAN CIAN/O'CARROLL
SEMPLE	SEMPLE	SHEEDY	Co. CLARE
SEMPLE	ULSTER TARTAN	SHEEHAN	Co. CORK
SEWALL	ULSTER TARTAN	SHEEHAN	Co. GALWAY
SEWARD	Co. CORK	SHEEHAN	Co. KERRY
SEWELL	ULSTER TARTAN	SHEEHAN	Co. LIMMERICK
SEXTON	Co. LIMMERICK	SHEEHY	See MAC SHEEHY
SEXTON	Co. TIPPERARY	SHEEKEY	ORIEL TARTAN
SEYMOUR	Co. CORK	SHEENAN	Co. TYRONE

"IRISH" indicates a choice of a general Irish tartan: "All Ireland", "Tara", "Clodagh", "Irish National", "St. Patrick"

TARTANS FOR IRISH NAMES

Anyone with a "County" Tartan may substitute one of the major "District" tartans listed below:

Galway, Leitrim, Mayo, Roscommon, Sligo:	**Connacht tartan**
Clare, Cork, Kerry, Limmerick, Tipperary, Waterford:	**Munster tartan**
Armagh, Down, Fermanagh, Louth, Monaghan:	**Oriel tartan**
Carlow, Dublin, Kildare, Kilkenny, Laois, Longford:	
Meath, Offaly, Westmeath, Wexford, Wicklow:	**Leinster tartan**
Antrim, Armagh, Cavan, Donegal, Down, Londonderry, Tyrone:	**Ulster tartan**

SURNAME	TARTAN	SURNAME	TARTAN
SHEERA	Co. LAOIS	SHOVELIN	Co. MONAGHAN
SHEERAN	Co. DONEGAL	SHOYE	Co. GALWAY
SHEHAN	See SHEEHAN	SHRYHANE	Co. DONEGAL
SHEILDS	See SHIELDS	SHUGRUE	Co. KERRY
SHELDON	ULSTER TARTAN	SHUNAGH	CONNACHT TARTAN
SHELLEY	Co. CORK	SHUNNY	CONNACHT TARTAN
SHELLOE	Co. CORK	SIBBERY	Co. LEITRIM
SHELLY	Co. CORK	SIDES	Co. DUBLIN
SHEPHERD	Co. DUBLIN	SIDNEY	CLANCIAN/O'CARROLL
SHEPHERD	Co. KILDARE	SIGERSON	Co. KERRY
SHEPPARD	See SHEPHERD	SIGGINS	Co. WEXFORD
SHERA	Co. LAOIS	SILKE	CLAN CIAN/O'CARROLL
SHERIDAN	LEINSTER TARTAN	SILKE	Co. GALWAY
SHERIDAN	Co. LAOIS	SIMMINGTON	ULSTER TARTAN
SHERIDAN	Co. LONGFORD	SIMMS	See SIMPSON
SHERKIN	Co. CORK	SIMPSON	FRASER
SHERLOCK	LEINSTER TARTAN	SIMPSON	ULSTER TARTAN
SHERLOCK	Co. MEATH	SINCLAIR	SINCLAIR
SHERLOCK	Co. WATERFORD	SINCLAIR	ULSTER TARTAN
SHERLOCK	Co. WESTMEATH	SINEY	Co. MEATH
SHERRARD	Co. LONDONDERRY	SINGEN	Co. TIPPERARY
SHERRY	ULSTER TARTAN	SINGLETON	ORIEL TARTAN
SHERWIN(E)	ULSTER TARTAN	SINNOT	Co. WEXFORD
SHERWOOD	Co. DUBLIN	SINON	Co. CORK
SHEVLIN	ORIEL TARTAN	SISK	Co. CORK
SHIEL	See SHIELDS	SITLINGTON	Co. DUBLIN
SHIELDS	ULSTER TARTAN	SKEFFINGTON	Co. DUBLIN
SHIELDS	Co. ANTRIM	SKEHAN	CONNACHT TARTAN
SHIELDS	Co. DONEGAL	SKELLY	CONNACHT TARTAN
SHIER	Co. LIMMERICK	SKELTON	ULSTER TARTAN
SHINAGH	CONNACHT TARTAN	SKELTON	Co. DUBLIN
SHINANE	Co. CLARE	SKERETT	Co. GALWAY
SHINANE	Co. TYRONE	SKERRELL	Co. GALWAY
SHINE	MUNSTER TARTAN	SKERRET	CONNACHT TARTAN
SHINE	Co. CORK	SKERRY	Co. WATERFORD
SHINE	Co. KERRY	SKIDDY	Co. CORK
SHINKWIN	Co. CORK	SKILLEN	Co. DOWN
SHINNAGH	CONNACHT TARTAN	SKILLING	Co. DOWN
SHINNICK,-NOCK	Co. CORK	SKIMMONS	ULSTER TARTAN
SHINNORS	Co. LIMMERICK	SKINNION	Co. ROSCOMMON
SHIPSEY	Co. CORK	SKOOLIN	ULSTER TARTAN
SHIRA	Co. LAOIS	SKUSE	Co. CORK
SHIRE	Co. LIMMERICK	SLACK(E)	IRISH-See Footnote
SHIRLEY	IRISH-See Footnote	SLAMON	Co. OFFALY
SHIVERS	ULSTER TARTAN	SLANE(Y)	IRISH-See Footnote
SHIVERS	Co. TYRONE	SLATER, SLATOR	Co. DUBLIN
SHIVERS	Co. WEXFORD	SLATTER	Co. DUBLIN
SHIVNAN	CONNACHT TARTAN	SLATTERY	CLAN CIAN/O'CARROLL
SHOLDS	ULSTER TARTAN	SLATTERY	Co. CLARE
SHOLEDICE	ULSTER TARTAN	SLATTERY	Co. TIPPERARY
SHORT(T)	ULSTER TARTAN	SLAVIN(E)	ULSTER TARTAN
SHORT(T)	Co. DUBLIN	SLAYNE	Co. CORK
SHORTALL	Co. KILKENNY	SLEATORS	Co. DUBLIN
SHORTEN	Co. WEXFORD	SLEETH	ULSTER TARTAN
SHOULDICE	ULSTER TARTAN	SLEVIN(E)	Co. LONGFORD

"IRISH" indicates a choice of a general Irish tartan: "All Ireland", "Tara", "Clodagh", "Irish National", "St. Patrick"

TARTANS FOR IRISH NAMES

Slevine   *Steel(e)*

"County" Tartan may substitute one of the major "District" tartans listed below:

Galway, Leitrim, Mayo, Roscommon, Sligo:	Connacht tartan
Clare, Cork, Kerry, Limmerick, Tipperary, Waterford:	Munster tartan
Armagh, Down, Fermanagh, Louth, Monaghan:	Oriel tartan
Carlow, Dublin, Kildare, Kilkenny, Laois, Longford:	
Meath, Offaly, Westmeath, Wexford, Wicklow:	Leinster tartan
Antrim, Armagh, Cavan, Donegal, Down, Londonderry, Tyrone:	Ulster tartan

SURNAME	TARTAN	SURNAME	TARTAN
SLEVIN(E)	ULSTER TARTAN	SPELLAINE	See SPILLANE
SLEVIN(E)	Co. OFFALY	SPELLANE	See SPILLANE
SLINEY	Co. CORK	SPEL(L)MAN	Co. SLIGO
SLOAN(E)	ULSTER TARTAN	SPELON	Co. OFFALY
SLOYAN	Co. MAYO	SPENCE	SPENS
SLYNE	Co. CORK	SPENCE	ULSTER TARTAN
SMALL	M'RY of TULLIBARDINE	SPENS	SPENS
SMALL	ULSTER TARTAN	SPIERS	ULSTER TARTAN
SMALL	Co. GALWAY	SPILLANE	CLAN CIAN/O'CARROLL
SMALLEN	ORIEL TARTAN	SPILLANE	Co. OFFALY
SMIDDY	See SMITH	SPILLANE	Co. TIPPERARY
SMIDDY	Co. CORK	SPILLMAN	CLAN CIAN/O'CARROLL
SMILLEY	ULSTER TARTAN	SPLAINE	Co. TIPPERARY
SMITH	SMITH	SPOLLANE	See SPILLANE
SMITH	Co. CAVAN	SPOLLEN,-IN	See SPILLANE
SMITHWICK	Co. CARLOW	SPOTSWOOD	IRISH-See Footnote
SMOLLEN	ORIEL TARTAN	SPRATT	IRISH-See Fotnote
SMULLEN	ORIEL TARTAN	SPRING	Co. KERRY
SMYLIE	ULSTER TARTAN	SPROOL	ULSTER TARTAN
SMYTH	SMITH	SPROTT	IRISH-See Footnote
SMYTH	Co. DOWN	SPROUL(E0	ULSTER TARTAN
SMYTH	Co. CAVAN	SPUHAN	Co. KILKENNY
SNEE	Co. MAYO	SREENAN	Co. MONAGHAN
SNODDIE	ULSTER TARTAN	SRUFFAN,-EN	Co. WATERFORD
SNODDY	ULSTER TARTAN	ST. CLAIR	SINCLAIR
SODAN	ORIEL TARTAN	ST. CLAIR	ULSTER TARTAN
SOD(D)EN	ORIEL TARTAN	ST. JOHN	Co. TIPPERARY
SODEN	Co. SLIGO	ST. LAWRENCE	Co. CLARE
SOLAN, SOLEN, SOLIN	Co. MAYO	ST. LAWRENCE	Co. DUBLIN
SOLLY	ORIEL TARTAN	ST. LEGER	Co. KILKENNY
SOMALGAN	Co. SLIGO	STACEY	Co. WICKLOW
SOMERVILLE	SOMERVILLE	STACK	Co. KERRY
SOMERVILLE	ULSTER TARTAN	STAC(K)POOL	Co. CLARE
SOMMERS	LEINSTER TARTAN	STACPOOLE	Co. KILKENNY
SOMMERVILLE	See SOMERVILLE	STACY	Co. WICKLOW
SOOLIVAN	See SULLIVAN	STAENSON	See STEVENSON
SORAHAN	ORIEL TARTAN	STAFFORD	Co. WEXFORD
SORAN	ORIEL TARTAN	STAMERS	IRISH-See Footnote
SOTHERN	Co. MEATH	STANFORD	Co. CAVAN
SOTTOR	ULSTER TARTAN	STANKARD	CONNACHT TARTAN
SOUGHLEY	ULSTER TARTAN	STANLEY	LEINSTER TARTAN
SOUTAR	ULSTER TARTAN	STANTON	CONNACHT TARTAN
SOUTHERN	Co. MEATH	STAPLETON	Co. KILKENNY
SOUTHWELL	IRISH-See Footnote	STARKEY	Co. DUBLIN
SOWNEY	Co. CORK	STARR	STARR
SPAIGHT	Co. LIMMERICK	STARR	ULSTER TARTAN
SPAIN	IRISH-See Footnote	STARR	Co. TIPPERARY
SPALLANE	Co. OFFALY	STARRETT	ULSTER TARTAN
SPARLING	Co. LIMMERICK	STARRS	See STARR
SPARROW	Co. WEXFORD	STAUNTON	CONNACHT TARTAN
SPEARD	IRISH-See Footnote	STAUNTON	Co. DOWN
SPEARS	ULSTER TARTAN	STAVES	STAVES
SPEED	Co. MAYO	STAWELL	IRISH-See Footnote
SPEERS	ULSTER TARTAN	STEACY	Co. WICKLOW
SPEIRS	ULSTER TARTAN	STEEL(E)	ULSTER TARTAN

"IRISH indicates a choice of a general Irish tartan: "All Ireland", "Tara", "Clodagh", "Irish National", "St. Patrick"

TARTANS FOR IRISH NAMES

Steen   *Tallent*

"County" Tartan may substitute one of the major "District" tartans listed below:.

Galway, Leitrim, Mayo, Roscommon, Sligo:	**Connacht tartan**
Clare, Cork, Kerry, Limmerick, Tipperary, Waterford:	**Munster tartan**
Armagh, Down, Fermanagh, Louth, Monaghan:	**Oriel tartan**
Carlow, Dublin, Kildare, Kilkenny, Laois, Longford:	
Meath, Offaly, Westmeath, Wexford, Wicklow:	**Leinster tartan**
Antrim, Armagh, Cavan, Donegal, Down, Londonderry, Tyrone:	**Ulster tartan**

SURNAME	TARTAN	SURNAME	TARTAN
STEEN	See STEVENSON	SUNDERLAND	Co. WEXFORD
STEENSON	See STEVENSON	SUPPLEE	Co. LIMMERICK
STENSON	CONNACHT TARTAN	SURGENOR	ULSTER TARTAN
STENSON	Co. SLIGO	SURTILL	Co. KILKENNY
STEPHENS	Co. DUBLIN	SUTOR	ULSTER TARTAN
STEPHENS	See STEPHENSON	SUTTON	LEINSTER TARTAN
STEPHENSON	STEPHENSON	SUTTON	Co. KILDARE
STEPHENSON	Co. LIMMERICK	SUTTON	Co. WEXFORD
STERLING	STIRLING FAMILY	SWAN	SWAN
STERRITT	ULSTER TARTAN	SWAN	ULSTER TARTAN
STEVENSON	STEVENSON	SWANTON	Co. CORK
STEVENSON	ULSTER TARTAN	SWAYNE	ORIEL TARTAN
STEWART	OLD STEWART	SWEENY	ULSTER TARTAN
STEWART	ULSTER TARTAN	SWEENY	Co. DONEGAL
STEWART	Co. ANTRIM	SWEENY	LEINSTER TARTAN
STINSON	STINSON	SWEENY	MUNSTER TARTAN
STINSON	ULSTER TARTAN	SWEETMAN	Co. KILKENNY
STIRLING	STIRLING FAMILY	SWEETNAM	Co. CORK
STIRLING	ULSTER TARTAN	SWIFT	ORIEL TARTAN
STOKES	IRISH-See Footnote	SWIFT	Co. MAYO
STONE	CLAN CIAN/O'CARROLL	SWINEY	ULSTER TARTAN
STONE(Y)	Co. SLIGO	SWINEY	Co. DONEGAL
STORAN	CONNACHT TARTAN	SWITZER	IRISH-See Footnote
STOREEN	Co. LIMMERICK	SWORDS	Co. DUBLIN
STOUT	IRISH-See Footnote	SYDES	Co. KILKENNY
STRACHAN	STRACHAN	SYMONS	Co. WESTMEATH
STRACHAN	ULSTER TARTAN	SYNAN	Co. CORK
STRAHAN	Co. DONEGAL	SYNAN	Co. TYRONE
STRAHAN	See STRACHAN	SYNEY	Co. MEATH
STRAIN	STRACHAN	SYNGE	IRISH-See Footnote
STRAIN	ULSTER TARTAN	SYNNOTT	Co. WEXFORD
STRAIN	Co. DOWN	SYNON	Co. CORK
STRAIN	Co. LONDONDERRY	SYRON	Co. MAYO
STRANAHAN	Co. DOWN	SYTHES	Co. KILKENNY
STRAWN	See STRACHAN		
STRAWN	Co. DONEGAL		
STRICH	Co. LIMMERICK	**T**	
STRONG	IRISH-See Footnote		
STUART	STUART of BUTE		
STUART	ULSTER TARTAN		
STUDDART	Co. CLARE	TAAFE(E)	CONNACHT TARTAN
STYLES	Co. WEXFORD	TAAFE(E)	Co. SLIGO
SUCKLEY	ULSTER TARTAN	TACKABERRY	Co. WICKLOW
SUGRUE	Co. KERRY	TACKNEY	Co. CLARE
SULLADHAN	ORIEL TARTAN	TAGAN	Co. LAOIS
SULLADHAN	See SULLIVAN	TAGGART	ULSTER TARTAN
SULLIVAN	SULLIVAN	TAGNEY	Co. KERRY
SULLIVAN	SULLIVAN, Sept of BEARE	TAHENY	Co. ROSCOMMON
SULLIVAN	MUNSTER TARTAN	TAIT	TAIT
SULLIVAN	Co. CORK	TAIT	ULSTER TARTAN
SULLIVAN	Co. KERRY	TALBOT(T)	Co. DUBLIN
SULLIVAN	Co. TIPPERARY	TALBOT(T)	Co. WICKLOW
SUMMERIL(L)	See SOMERVILLE	TALLANT	Co. CARLOW
SUMMERLY	CONNACHT TARTAN	TALLENT	Co. CARLOW
SUMMERS	LEINSTER TARTAN		
SUMMERVILLE	See SOMERVILLE		

"IRISH" indicates a choice of a general Irish tartan: "All Ireland", "Tara", "Clodagh", "Irish National", "St. Patrick"

78

TARTANS FOR IRISH NAMES

Tallon   *Tormay*

"County" Tartan may substitute one of the major "District" tartans listed below:

Galway, Leitrim, Mayo, Roscommon, Sligo:	Connacht tartan
Clare, Cork, Kerry, Limmerick, Tipperary, Waterford:	Munster tartan
Armagh, Down, Fermanagh, Louth, Monaghan:	Oriel tartan
Carlow, Dublin, Kildare, Kilkenny, Laois, Longford:	
Meath, Offaly, Westmeath, Wexford, Wicklow:	Leinster tartan
Antrim, Armagh, Cavan, Donegal, Down, Londonderry, Tyrone:	Ulster tartan

SURNAME	TARTAN	SURNAME	TARTAN
TALLON	LEINSTER TARTAN	TERRY	Co CORK
TALLY	Co. FERMANAGH	TESKY	Co. LIMMERICK
TALLY	Co. WICKLOW	TEVLIN	Co. CAVAN
TALTY	Co. CLARE	TEVNAN	IRISH-See Footnote
TAMINY	See TAMMINAY	TEW	Co. WATERFORD
TAMMANY,-ENY	See TAMMINAY	THACKABERRY	Co. WICKLOW
TAMMINAY	ULSTER TARTAN	THOMAS	MAC THOMAS
TAMMINAY	Co. LONDONDERRY	THOMAS	ULSTER TARTAN
TAMMINAY	Co. DOWN	THOMPSON	Dress MAC TAVISH/THOMPSON
TAMMINAY	CLAN CIAN/O'CARROLL	THOMPSON	ULSTER TARTAN
TANCRED	LEINSTER TARTAN	THOMSON	See THOMPSON
TANGLEY	Co. KERRY	THORAN	BROOKE
TANGNEY	Co. KERRY	THORNE	Co. LIMMERICK
TANNER	ULSTER TARTAN	THORNHILL	MUNSTER TARTAN
TANNIAN	Co. GALWAY	THORNHILL	Co. CORK
TANSAY,-SEY	Co. SLIGO	THORNHILL	Co. LIMMERICK
TAOFFE	Co. LOUTH	THORNTON	CONNACHT TARTAN
TARLETON	Co. OFFALY	THULIS(H)	ULSTER TARTAN
TARMEY	Co. LONGFORD	THUNDER	Co. LOUTH
TARPAY	CONNACHT TARTAN	THYNNE	Co. CLARE
TARPEY	Co. SLIGO	TIDINGS	ULSTER TARTAN
TARRANT	Co. CORK	TIERNAN	CONNACHT TARTAN
TARRY	Co. CORK	TIERNAN	Co. FERMANAGH
TARSNANE	Co. CLARE	TIERNEY	CLAN CIAN/O'CARROLL
TARSNEY	ULSTER TARTAN	TIERNEY	Co. MAYO
TATE	See TAIT	TIGER	ULSTER TARTAN
TAUGHER	Co. MAYO	TIGH(E)	Co. MAYO
TAULTY	Co. CLARE	TIGH(E)	Co. TYRONE
TAVEY	ORIEL TARTAN	TIGH(E)	Co. WICKLOW
TAVEY	Co. MONAGHAN	TIMMONS	Co. MAYO
TAVISH	MAC TAVISH	TIMPANY	ULSTER TARTAN
TAVNEY	CLAN CIAN/O'CARROLL	TIMPANY	Co. DOWN
TAYLOR	TAYLOR	TINNALLY	IRISH-See Footnote
TAYLOR	CAMERON	TINNENN	IRISH-See Footnote
TAYLOR	ULSTER TARTAN	TINNEY	ULSTER TARTAN
TAYLOR	Co. DUBLIN	TINNEY	Co. DONEGAL
TEAGUE	ULSTER TARTAN	TIRNEY	See TIERNEY
TEAHAM	Co. KERRYP	TOB(B)IN	Co. TIPPERARY
TEEFY	Co. TIPPERARY	TODD	TODD
TEEGAN	Co. LAOIS	TODD	ULSTER TARTAN
TEEHAN	Co. LAOIS	TOLAN	ULSTER TARTAN
TEEVAN	ORIEL TARTAN	TOLAND	Co. MAYO
TEGAN	Co. LAOIS	TOL(L)ER	Co. WESTMEATH
TEHAN	Co. TIPPERARY	TOLLERAN	Co. MAYO
TELFORD	IRISH-See Footnote	TOMALTY	Co. TYRONE
TEMPANY	Co. DOWN	TONER	ULSTER TARTAN
TEMPAST	ULSTER TARTAN	TONER	Co. DONEGAL
TEMPAY	ULSTER TARTAN	TOOFY	Co. MAYO
TENNENY	IRISH-See Footnote	TOOKE	LEINSTER TARTAN
TENPENNY	ULSTER TARTAN	TOOKER	ULSTER TARTAN
TENPENNY	Co. DOWN	TOOLEN	ULSTER TARTAN
TERENCE	See TERRENCE	TOOLIS	ULSTER TARTAN
TERRENCE	BROOKE	TOOMAY	Co. LIMMERICK
TERRENCE	ULSTER TARTAN	TOORISH	ULSTER TARTAN
TERRY	TERRY	TORLEY	ULSTER TARTAN
TERRY	ULSTER TARTAN	TORMAY	Co. LONGFORD

"IRISH" indicates a choice of a general Irish tartan: "All Ireland", "Tara". "Clodagh", "Irish National", "St. Patrick"

TARTANS FOR IRISH NAMES

"County" Tartan may substitute one of the major "District" tartans listed below:

Galway, Leitrim, Mayo, Roscommon, Sligo:	Connacht tartan
Clare, Cork, Kerry, Limmerick, Tipperary, Waterford:	Munster tartan
Armagh, Down, Fermanagh, Louth, Monaghan:	Oriel tartan
Carlow, Dublin, Kildare, Kilkenny, Laois, Longford:	
Meath, Offaly, Westmeath, Wexford, Wicklow:	Leinster tartan
Antrim, Armagh, Cavan, Donegal, Down, Londonderry, Tyrone:	Ulster tartan

SURNAME	TARTAN	SURNAME	TARTAN
TORMEY	Co. GALWAY	TUNRY	ULSTER TARTAN
TORNEY	ULSTER TARTAN	TUOHY	Co. CORK
TORPEY	Co. CORK	TUOHY	Co. GALWAY
TORRENCE	See TERRENCE	TUORNEY	Co. CORK
TORRENS	See TERRENCE	TURINGTON	ULSTER TARTAN
TORSNEY	ULSTER TARTAN	TURINGTON	Co. ARMAGH
TOUGHER	ULSTER TARTAN	TURK(E)	ULSTER TARTAN
TOUHILL	Co. CORK	TURK(E)	Co. ARMAGH
TOUHY	Co. GALWAY	TURLEY	ULSTER TARTAN
TOURISH	WALTERS	TURNER	TURNER
TOWELL	Co. WATERFORD	TURNER	ULSTER TARTAN
TOWEY	CONNACHT TARTAN	TURNER	LEINSTER TARTAN
TOWNL(E)Y	Co. LOUTH	TURNER	Co. DUBLIN
TOWNSEND	Co. CORK	TURNER	MUNSTER TARTAN
TOWNSHEND	Co. CORK	TURNER	Co. CORK
TOWNSLEY	ULSTER TARTAN	TURRIDY	Co. CLARE
TOY(E)	CONNACHT TARTAN	TURTLE	IRISH-See Footnote
TRAC(E)Y	CONNACHT TARTAN	TUTTON	See SUTTON
TRAC(E)Y	CLAN CIAN/O'CARROLL	TUTTY	Co. GALWAY
TRAC(E)Y	Co. GALWAY	TWAMLEY	Co. WICKLOW
TRADDEN	CONNACHT TARTAN	TWEEDY	FRASER
TRAHY	Co. CLARE	TWEEDY	ULSTER TARTAN
TRAINER	See TRAYNOR	TWIGG	ULSTER TARTAN
TRANT	Co. KERRY	TWIGLEY	ULSTER TARTAN
TRAVERS	Co. LEITRIM	TWISS	Co. KERRY
TRAYNOR	TRAYNOR	TWOHIG	Co. CORK
TRAYNOR	CONNACHT TARTAN	TWOHILL	Co. CORK
TRAYNOR	Co. MEATH	TWOMEY	See TOOMEY
TREACY	Co. LAOIS	TYDINGS	ULSTER TARTAN
TREANOR	See TRAYNOR	TYE	Co. MAYO
TREHY	Co. CLARE	TYMM	Co. MAYO
TRENCH	Co. LAOIS	TYNAN	Co. LAOIS
TRENT	Co. KERRY	TYNE	Co. CLARE
TREVOR	Co. LEITRIM	TYNEY	ULSTER TARTAN
TRIMBLE	TURNBULL	TYQUIN	Co. OFFALY
TRIMBLE	ULSTER TARTAN	TYRELL	Co. DUBLIN
TRODDEN	CONNACHT TARTAN	TYRRELL	Co. WESTMEATH
TROLAN(D)	Co. LONDONDERRY		
TROWER	Co. LEITRIM		
TROWLAND	Co. LONDONDERRY		
TROY	MUNSTER TARTAN		
TROY	Co. LIMMERICK	**U**	
TROY	Co. TIPPERARY		
TRUELL	Co. WICKLOW		
TUBRID(E)	Co. CLARE	ULTAGH	ULSTER TARTAN
TUBRIT	Co. CLARE	UNCHAN	Co. CARLOW
TUCKER	ULSTER TARTAN	UNIACKE	Co. CORK
TUFFY	Co. MAYO	UPRICHARD	See PRITCHARD
TUITE	Co. WESTMEATH	UPRITCHARD	See PRITCHARD
TUKE	See TOOKE	UPTON	Co. ANTRIM
TULLY	Co. CAVAN	URELL	Co. WESTMEATH
TULLY	Co. FERMANAGH	URIEL(L)	Co. WESTMEATH
TUMANY	ULSTER TARTAN	USHER, USSHER	IRISH-See Footnote
TUMELTY	ORIEL TARTAN	USSER	IRISH-See Footnote
TUMPANE	Co. TIPPERARY	UTAGH	Co. WESTMEATH
TUNNEY	Co. MAYO		

"IRISH" indicates a choice of a general Irish tartan: "All Ireland", "Tara", "Clodagh", "Irish National", "St. Patrick"

TARTANS FOR IRISH NAMES

Vaddock   *Wauchope*

"County" Tartan may substitute one of the major "District" tartans listed below:

Galway, Leitrim, Mayo, Roscommon, Sligo:	Connacht tartan
Clare, Cork, Kerry, Limmerick, Tipperary, Waterford:	Munster tartan
Armagh, Down, Fermanagh, Louth, Monaghan:	Oriel tartan
Carlow, Dublin, Kildare, Kilkenny, Laois, Longford:	
Meath, Offaly, Westmeath, Wexford, Wicklow:	Leinster tartan
Antrim, Armagh, Cavan, Donegal, Down, Londonderry, Tyrone:	Ulster tartan

SURNAME	TARTAN	SURNAME	TARTAN
V		**W**	
VADDOCK	Co. WEXFORD	WADDELL	ULSTER TARTAN
VADY	Co. MAYO	WADDING	Co. WATERFORD
VAHY	CONNACHT TARTAN	WADDING	Co. WEXFORD
VAIL	ULSTER TARTAN	WADDOCH,-DOCK	Co. WEXFORD
VALE	ULSTER TARTAN	WADE	ORIEL TARTAN
VALENTINE	Co. WICKLOW	WAFER	Co. WEXFORD
VALLELLY	ORIEL TARTAN	WAGH	ULSTER TARTAN
VALL(E)Y	ORIEL TARTAN	WALDAM	CONNACHT TARTAN
VANCE	VANS	WALDRON	ULSTER TARTAN
VANCE	ULSTER TARTAN	WALE	Co. LIMMERICK
VANDELEUR	Co. CLARE	WALKER	WALKER
VANSE	See VANCE	WALKER	ULSTER TARTAN
VARGUS	CONNACHT TARTAN	WALL	Co. LIMMERICK
VARIAN	Co. CORK	WALL	Co. WATERFORD
VARILY	CONNACHT TARTAN	WALLACE	WALLACE
VARLEY	CONNACHT TARTAN	WALLACE	ULSTER TARTAN
VARRELLY	CONNACHT TARTAN	WALLER	Co. LIMMERICK
VAUGH	Co. LEITRIM	WALLIS	See WALLACE
VAUGHAN	Co. CLARE	WALPOLE	Co. LAOIS
VEAL(E)	ULSTER TARTAN	WALSH	Co. WEXFORD
VEALE	Co. WATERFORD	WALSH	CONNACHT TARTAN
VEIGH	See MAC VEY	WALSH	LEINSTER TARTAN
VEITCH	ORIEL TARTAN	WALSH	MUNSTER TARTAN
VELDON	Co. DUBLIN	WALTA	WALTERS
VELDON	CO. FERMANAGH	WALTERS	WALTERS
VERDON	Co. LOUTH	WALTON	ULSTER TARTAN
VEREKER	Co. LIMERICK	WANDESFORD	IRISH-See Footnote
VERGUS	CONNACHT TARTAN	WARBURTON	Co. OFFALY
VERLING	CO. CORK	WARD	CONNACHT TARTAN
VESEY	Co. MAYO	WARD	Co. GALWAY
VICAR	See MAC VICAR	WARD	ULSTER TARTAN
VICARS	Co. LAOIS	WARD	Co. DONEGAL
VICKER(S)	See MAC VICKER	WARE	Co. DUBLIN
VICKERY	Co. CORK	WARING	Co. DOWN
VICTORY	Co. LONGFORD	WARKE	ULSTER TARTAN
VIGORS	Co. CARLOW	WARNER	Co. CORK
VILLERS	Co. LAOIS	WARNOCK	Co. DOWN
VILLIERS	Co. LAOIS	WARREN	Co. DUBLIN
VINCENT	VINCENT	WARREN	Co. OFFALY
VINCENT	Co. DUBLIN	WARRING	Co. DOWN
VINITER	Co. CORK	WATERS	LEINSTER TARTAN
VOGAN	ORIEL TARTAN	WATERS	MUNSTER TARTAN
		WATERSON	Co. CAVAN
		WATKINS	CONNACHT TARTAN
		WATSON	WATSON
		WATSON	ULSTER TARTAN
		WATT	ULSTER TARTAN
		WATTERS	ULSTER TARTAN
		WAUCHOPE	ULSTER TARTAN

"IRISH" indicates a choice of a general Irish tartan: "All Ireland", "Tara", "Clodagh", "Irish National", "St. Patrick"

TARTANS FOR IRISH NAMES

Waugh   *Wrafter*

"County" Tartan may substitute one of the major "District" tartans listed below:

Galway, Leitrim, Mayo, Roscommon, Sligo:	Connacht tartan
Clare, Cork, Kerry, Limmerick, Tipperary, Waterford:	Munster tartan
Armagh, Down, Fermanagh, Louth, Monaghan:	Oriel tartan
Carlow, Dublin, Kildare, Kilkenny, Laois, Longford:	
Meath, Offaly, Westmeath, Wexford, Wicklow:	Leinster tartan
Antrim, Armagh, Cavan, Donegal, Down, Londonderry, Tyrone:	Ulster tartan

SURNAME	TARTAN	SURNAME	TARTAN
WAUGH	ULSTER TARTAN	WHORISKEY	Co. DONEGAL
WEAFER	Co. WEXFORD	WHYTE	See WHITE
WEBB	WEBB	WICKHAM	CONNACHT TARTAN
WEBB	ULSTER TARTAN	WICKHAM	Co. WEXFORD
WEBB	Co. DUBLIN	WICKSTEAD	Co. OFFALY
WEBSTER	WEBSTER	WIGAN(S)	ULSTER TARTAN
WEBSTER	ULSTER TARTAN	WIGAN(S)	Co. FERMANAGH
WEER	See WEIR	WIGGINS	ULSTER TARTAN
WEIR	WEIR	WIGGINS	Co. FERMANAGH
WEIR	ULSTER TARTAN	WILDE	Co. MAYO
WELBY	Co. GALWAY	WILEY	See WYLIE
WELDON	Co. DUBLIN	WILHAIR	ULSTER TARTAN
WELDON	CO. FERMANAGH	WILHAIR	Co. DONEGAL
WELDON	CO. FERMANAGH	WILHARE	See WILHAIR
WELLESLEY	Co. MEATH	WILKINSON	ULSTER TARTAN
WELLS	WELLS	WILLIAMS	See MAC WILLIAM
WELLS	ULSTER TARTAN	WILLIAMSON	See MAC WILLIAM
WELSH	ULSTER TARTAN	WILLIS	IRISH-See Footnote
WESLEY	Co. KILDARE	WILLS	IRISH-See Footnote
WESTON	WESTON	WILMORE	Co. TYRONE
WESTON	ULSTER TARTAN	WILMOT(E)	Co. KERRY
WESTROPP	MUNSTER TARTAN	WILSON	ULSTER TARTAN
WESTROPP	Co. CLARE	WILSON	WILSON
WESTROPP	Co. LIMMERICK	WIMS	See WEYMSS
WEYMES	See WEMYSS	WINDLE	IRISH-See Footnote
WEYMS	See WEMYSS	WINGFIELD	ULSTER TARTAN
WEYMSS	WEYMSS	WINKLE	Co. GALWAY
WEYMSS	CONNACHT TARTAN	WINSTON	Co. WATERFORD
WHARTON	Co. KERRY	WINTERS	ULSTER TARTAN
WHEARTY	Co. LOUTH	WINTERS	Co. TYRONE
WHEELER	Co. KILKENNY	WINTHROP	IRISH-See Footnote
WHELAN	Co. TIPPERARY	WISDOM	Co. LOUTH
WHINISKEY	WALTERS	WISE	Co. WATERFORD
WHIRTER	MAC WHORTER	WISEMAN	Co. CORK
WHITAKER	Co. MEATH	WIXSTEAD	Co. OFFALY
WHITE	ULSTER TARTAN	WIXTED	Co. OFFALY
WHITE	Co. DOWN	WOFFINGTON	Co. DUBLIN
WHITE	Co. OFFALY	WOGAN	Co. KILDARE
WHITE	CONNACHT TARTAN	WOLFE	WOLFE
WHITE	Co. SLIGO	WOLFE	CLAN CIAN/O'CARROLL
WHITEHEAD	Co. CAVAN	WOLFE	Co. KILDARE
WHITELOCK	Co. CAVAN	WOLFINGTON	Co. DUBLIN
WHITELOCK	Co. GALWAY	WOL(L)OHAN	Co. WICKLOW
WHITESIDE	IRISH-See Footnote	WOLSEY	ULSTER TARTAN
WHITESTEED	Co. GALWAY	WOOD	ULSTER TARTAN
WHITLA(W)	ULSTER TARTAN	WOODCOCK	Co. DUBLIN
WHITLEY	CONNACHT TARTAN	WOODLOCK	Co. WATERFORD
WHITLOCK	Co. CAVAN	WOODMAN	ULSTER TARTAN
WHITLY	Co. WEXFORD	WOODMAN	Co. LOUTH
WHITMORE	Co. WEXFORD	WOODS	ULSTER TARTAN
WHITNEY	LEINSTER TARTAN	WOOLAHAN	Co. KILKENNY
WHITTEN	ULSTER TARTAN	WOOLEY	Co. KILDARE
WHITTLE	Co. WATERFORD	WOOLSEY	ULSTER TARTAN
WHITTON	ULSTER TARTAN	WORTH	Co. CORK
WHITTY	IRISH-See Footnote	WOULFE	See WOLFE
WHO(O)LEY	Co. CORK	WRAFTER	Co. DUBLIN

"IRISH" indicates a choice of a general Irish tartan: **"All Ireland"**, **"Tara"**, **"Clodagh"**, **"Irish National"**, **"St. Patrick"**

TARTANS FOR IRISH NAMES

Wray   *Zorkin*

"County" Tartan may substitute one of the major "District" tartans listed below:

Galway, Leitrim, Mayo, Roscommon, Sligo:	Connacht tartan
Clare, Cork, Kerry, Limmerick, Tipperary, Waterford:	Munster tartan
Armagh, Down, Fermanagh, Louth, Monaghan:	Oriel tartan
Carlow, Dublin, Kildare, Kilkenny, Laois, Longford:	
Meath, Offaly, Westmeath, Wexford, Wicklow:	Leinster tartan
Antrim, Armagh, Cavan, Donegal, Down, Londonderry, Tyrone:	Ulster tartan

SURNAME	TARTAN	SURNAME	TARTAN
WRAY	ULSTER TARTAN		**ADDITIONAL NAMES & NOTES**
WREN	WREN		
WREN	Co. CORK		
WRIGHT	ULSTER TARTAN		
WRIGHT	Co. FERMANAGH		
WRIGHT	Co. ANTRIM		
WRINNE	See WREN		
WRYNN	See WREN		
WYCOMB	CONNACHT TARTAN		
WYCOMB	Co. WEXFORD		
WYER	See WEIR		
WYETH	WYETH		
WYLIE	WYLIE		
WYLIE	ULSTER TARTAN		
WYMBS	See WEYMSS		
WYMS	See WEYMSS		
WYNDHAM	Co. GALWAY		
WYNNE	Co. WESTMEATH		
WYSE	Co. WATERFORD		

Y

YAGO	Co. ROSCOMMON
YARE(S)	ULSTER TARTAN
YARR(S)	ULSTER TARTAN
YATES	Co. SLIGO
YEATS	Co. SLIGO
YONGE	See YOUNG
YORE	CONNACHT TARTAN
YORE	Co. MEATH
YOUNG	YOUNG
YOUNG	ULSTER TARTAN
YOURELL	Co. WESTMEATH

Z

ZORKIN	Co. SLIGO

"IRISH indicates a choice of a general Irish tartan: "All Ireland", "Tara", "Clodagh", "Irish National", "St. Patrick"

ABOUT THE AUTHOR

Philip D. Smith, Jr. is Professor *Emeritus* of Languages and Linguistics at West Chester University. Dr Smith holds a variety of degrees, a BA in Spanish, an MA in history, and a PhD in applied linguistics. He is a member of the "Guild of Tartan Scholars" (one of nine world-wide) and Past-President of the International Association For Tartan Studies. Including *Tartans For The Irish*, he has written nine books on Celtic names and four on tartans. Currently he serves as a Consultant to the International Tartan Index. Dr. Smith writes an Irish language "Learner's Column" for *The Boston Irish Reporter* under his Irish name Philip Mac An Gabhain.

www.ingramcontent.com/pod-product-compliance
Lightning Source LLC
Chambersburg PA
CBHW081159270326
41930CB00014B/3221